"Lewis and Sharpe have written the best sort of bird book, one that exemplifies the principle: think globally, act locally. Their finely detailed account of San Juan birds is firmly set in the broader context of global environmental processes. This book expands our awareness of the commonplace and familiar in its attention to detail, and will serve as the essential ornithological reference for the islands for years to come."

— Eugene Hunn, author
Birding in Seattle and King County

"*Birding in the San Juan Islands* introduces us to the charm of this Pacific Northwest archipelago and the diversity of its bird life. A readable account of San Juans birds and where to find them, it will enhance the already great appeal of these beautiful islands."

— Dennis Paulson, co-author
A Guide to Bird Finding in Washington

"I'm excited and happy to see a book that so thoroughly covers the bird life of the San Juan Islands. Lewis and Sharpe have provided us with an accurate and useful account of our feathered neighbors. This book can only lead to a greater appreciation of our wildlife community. *Birding in the San Juan Islands* is a valuable addition to my library."

— Dr. Jessica A. Porter, D.V.M.
Wolf Hollow Wildlife Rehabilitation Centre

"As varied and beautiful as the scenery of the San Juan Islands are the birds that inhabit it and who pause here on their migratory flights. Now, happily, there is a guide to this marvelous facet of the islands. *Birding in the San Juan Islands* goes beyond the run-of-the-mill identification guide and gives fascinating insights into the presence of birds in this unique archipelago. The book is written not just for the dedicated birdwatcher, but also for anyone who wants to know more about the vast variety of birds seen in the islands."

— Marge Mueller, author
San Juan Islands, Afoot and Afloat

·BIRDING·
IN THE
San Juan Islands

Mark G. Lewis
&
Fred A. Sharpe

The Mountaineers
Seattle

THE MOUNTAINEERS: Organized 1906
" . . . to explore, study, preserve and enjoy
the natural beauty of the Northwest."

© 1987 by The Mountaineers
All rights reserved

Published by The Mountaineers
306 2nd Avenue West, Seattle, Washington 98119

Published simultaneously in Canada by
Douglas & McIntyre Ltd.
1615 Venables Street
Vancouver, B. C. V5L 2H1

Manufactured in the United States of America

Edited by Barbara Chasan
Cover design by Elizabeth Watson
Book design by Bridget Culligan
Maps and illustrations by Fred Sharpe
Cover photo: Black Oystercatcher by Mark Lewis
Title page illustration: Great Blue Heron
Page 4: Black Turnstone

Library of Congress Cataloging-in-Publication Data

Lewis, Mark G., 1959-
    Birding in the San Juan Islands.

    Bibliography: p.
    Includes index.
    1. Birds--Washington (State)--San Juan Islands.
2. Bird watching--Washington (State)--San Juan Islands.
I. Sharpe, Fred. II. Title.
QL684.W2L48   1987   598'.07'23479774   87-23997
ISBN 0-89886-133-0 (pbk.)

Contents

Foreword

The San Juan Islands invade the senses. Off the southern edges of San Juan the boiling surge of the Strait of Juan de Fuca comes together with the land in a most palatable manner against the backdrop of the Olympic Range and a vaulting sky. At this point I've hiked along Mt. Finlayson in the autumn to follow the raptors spiraling up on geysers of air. I've heard the "zing" of a diving peregrine come in overhead just above the 300-foot shoulders of the mountain. And it's here that I've stepped into the edge of a flock of snow buntings that tore away in the wind like a wild translucent veil.

The San Juan Islands are not of this world. If you stay here you begin to measure time more by the level of the tide than by a watch. Decisions are often made in response to the departure of wood warblers in the fall or the drumming of woodpeckers in the spring. Isolated by a moat of turbulent waters, many of the islands have been spared the insult inflicted on nature by the enterprises of humankind. Species of birds that have disappeared or dramatically diminished in numbers on the mainland can still be found in the archipelago. Here we can look back briefly to some distant primal time. Along the edges of rocky peninsulas black oystercatchers whistle, dance, and bow in spring courtship ritual and by early autumn frenetic flocks of turnstone are striking the gravel and cobblestone beaches. Bald Eagles nest here with a density that is exceeded only in remote Alaskan country.

The San Juan Islands are under-appreciated. That of course may be a mixed blessing as there is that matter of loving something to death. Still, as the millions of people who are within a fifty-mile radius of these Islands make their plans and use the region's resources, we should realize fully the extraordinary value of these jewels placed within the crown of Puget Sound. This book, *Birding in the San Juan Islands,* is a great step toward such realization. Whether we watch birds from a ferry deck, a biking path, or a stroll on a beach trail, we can now direct a sharper focus on the winged spirits of these places. Lewis and Sharpe have provided us with not only an accounting of what we might expect to see, but a formula for understanding where birds call "home" and what they do "for a living." This is not simply a "checklist" scheme for ticking off birds, but a means by which we can quite genuinely discover and better understand the birds we share these islands with. Reading the book, you know that these two naturalists have lived here and gently wandered over the lands and waters and wondered deeply over their subjects. With this book in hand you can do the same.

Tony Angell
Artist-Naturalist

Acknowledgments

We wish to express our sincere gratitude to all who contributed to this work. Special thanks go to Phil Mattocks for his helpful guidance and impeccable editing of the manuscript. Scott Atkinson was also instrumental—he was a prominent figure during the conception of this book and his desire to share his voluminous knowledge on the topic of San Juan birds made him a chief contributor and editor. Walter Harm and Dick Wright, longtime birders and residents of the islands, provided valuable commentary on the manuscript. Other reviewers that we are indebted to include Steve Speich, Terry Wahl, and Gene Hunn. Charlie Nash and Steve Layman contributed much information on San Juan birds of prey. Wenonah Sharpe helped us solve many problems with the initial draft. Stephen Whitney and Margaret Davidson are thanked for their crucial advice concerning the artwork. Athena Speers and Gretchen Junker were supportive companions and field assistants in the early phases of the project.

Many other individuals cheerfully granted us interviews or supplied us with data pertinent to this book, including Tony Angell, Ward and Josie Beecher, Thais Bock, Dave Castor, David Drummond, Charles Eaton, Mark Egger, Walter English, Chuck Flaherty, Jim Fackler, Ken and Suzanne Franklin, Buck Gates, Betty Gilson, Ami Greenberg, Ken Lowe, Barbara Meyer, Matt and Kathy Mattola, Kelly McCallister, John O'Connell, Dennis Paulson, Emily Reid, Michael Sacca, Eric Seabloom, Tony Scruton, Antoni Sobieralski, Eugene Smirnov, Bill Harrington-Tweit, Jim and Karen Vedder, Lori Wilson, Robert Wilson, and the late Dr. Frank Richardson. Additional help was provided by the staff of The Whale Museum of Friday Harbor, King Typesetting, the Friday Harbor Marine Laboratories, and Scott Leopold.

We appreciate the professional assistance provided by Donna DeShazo, Ann Cleeland, Barbara Chasan, Evelyn Peaslee, members of the Editorial Review Committee, and others on the staff of The Mountaineers Books.

Introduction

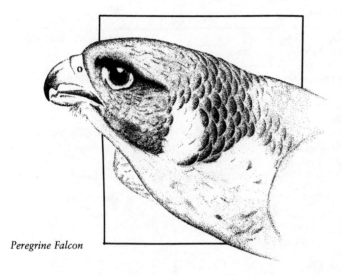

Peregrine Falcon

Recent years have witnessed a meteoric rise in the popularity of bird-watching throughout the world. Birding is now enjoyed by a broad range of people who have elevated the hobby to an art, a science, and a competitive sport. Many birders are discovering that the San Juan Islands of Washington State, one of the most beautiful and fascinating natural areas in North America, are a premier location for the study of birds. Within this archipelago, the rich, productive waters and varied terrestrial habitats promote large and diverse bird communities that are easily accessible to boaters and land-bound observers. Dense seabird nesting colonies, abundant birds of prey, and breeding species not usually found elsewhere west of the Cascade Mountains, all make for an exciting and unique San Juan Islands avifauna. This book is the first comprehensive guide to the area's feathered inhabitants and is intended to encourage and facilitate bird-watching in the islands.

Whether you are a novice, observing for the first time a hummingbird sipping nectar from a flower, or an experienced naturalist, seeking a rare gull among the vast flocks of migrating marine birds, *Birding in the San Juan Islands* is designed to enhance your birding enjoyment and success. The information contained in this volume is organized in three different ways. To best utilize it: 1) study Bird Habitats (page 20) so that you can recognize avian habitats and have an idea what their typical denizens should be; 2) review the Site Guide (page 25) and visit the areas recommended with an eye for mentioned species; 3) read the Species Accounts (page 49) either to obtain help in locating a sought-after bird or to learn more about it during or after observation. Appendix A (page 191) offers a distillation of the information found in Bird Habitats and Species Accounts in graph form with symbolic annotations.

VANCOUVER

British Columbia

Canada
United States

Washington
State

Strait of Georgia

GULF ISLANDS

BELLINGHAM

VANCOUVER
ISLAND

SAN JUAN

ISLANDS

ANACORTES

VICTORIA

Strait of Juan de Fuca

PORT
ANGELES   SEQUIM

PORT
TOWNSEND

Olympic Peninsula

EVERETT

AREA IN RAINSHADOW OF THE OLYMPIC MOUNTAINS (DASHED LINE)

We have included in the text many points on bird identification, particularly for those species whose proper identification poses a specific problem in this region. However, this book is not intended to be a general guide to field identification of birds, as this subject has been well covered in other publications. For a list of recommended bird identification guides see Going Birding (page 17).

Birding in the San Juan Islands is a summary of information gathered over the last several years. The senior author has resided within the study area since 1981 and the junior author has visited the islands during prolonged research forays through the same period. We have combined our own experiences and recorded observations with data gleaned from books, journals, reports, and personal communications with a great number of individuals through 1986. Biologists, wildlife managers, land-use planners, and conservationists should find this volume a helpful reference when faced with issues concerning the avifauna of the San Juan Archipelago.

Although intended specifically for the San Juan Islands, this guide can be used to great benefit in nearby areas that are also situated within the rainshadow of the Olympic Mountains. These include the islands of Whatcom, Skagit, and Island counties, as well as the northeastern corner of the Olympic Peninsula, with Sequim, Dungeness Spit, and Protection Island. Canadian territory within this region encompasses Victoria and the Saanich Peninsula, located on the extreme southeastern end of Vancouver Island, and the Gulf Islands.

Perhaps the most important goal of this book is to make readers aware of the effects human activities have upon the birdlife of the San Juan Islands and to emphasize the fragility of the environment found here. Armed with knowledge concerning the status and distribution of the species that inhabit the archipelago, every concerned individual and organization will be better equipped to detect problems and changes in local populations and to act as their "safety alarm" or "guardian." Avian communities, possessing a high degree of sensitivity to their surroundings, may be used as a barometer of environmental health, thereby warning us of dangers to our own quality of life.

THE SAN JUAN ISLANDS

Located in northwestern Washington State, the San Juan Islands are strategically situated amid a number of important biological areas. These approximately 350 rocks and islands rise from the cold waters of northern Puget Sound to form a series of stepping stones between the mainland river estuaries, southern Vancouver Island, and the Olympic Peninsula. The San Juans' highest peak, Mt. Constitution (2409 feet), towers far above the nearby lowlands of western Washington, but the majority of the land mass averages less than 1000 feet above sea level. The area, often referred to as a submarine mountain range, traverses the Puget Trough in a generally east-west direction.

Beneath the surrounding water's surface a variety of depths can be found, ranging from more than 1000 feet in Haro Strait to the many shallow banks and bays. Nearly all of the numerous straits and channels reach or exceed 300 feet at their deepest points. A huge volume of water continually flushes through the islands—as a result of the tidal exchange between the Strait of Georgia and the Strait of Juan de Fuca. Strong tidal convergences and rips are common throughout the region and create areas of high biological productivity heavily utilized by the local fauna. Parts of the coastline have shelves occupied by luxuriant kelp forests, as do many shallow areas well off shore, referred to as banks and reefs. In areas where the rock-bound coast drops off almost vertically to deep water, or lacks both upwelling currents and extensive kelp growth, the shores appear relatively sterile and unused by animal

AREA COVERED IN THIS BOOK

or plant life. Shallow bays often nurture eelgrass beds and support large numbers of marine birds and animals, as well as important bottom-dwelling prey communities. The many waterways that pass between the islands are highways for myriad life forms, and the 385 miles of shoreline create a vast area of fertile interface between land, sea, and air.

The topography of the San Juan Islands is the result of a very complex geologic past. Of primary importance in this history was a series of glaciations ending only 12,000 years ago. At that time the region was completely covered and scoured by a blanket of ice, which was sometimes a mile thick. The retreat of this last glacier marked the birth of the San Juans as an island group. The present landscape shows a general downward sloping toward the north and steep, glacially plucked escarpments facing to the south. Rising abruptly from the glacial plain that covers most of the Puget Sound lowlands, the asymmetrically domed peaks display large amounts of exposed bedrock. Rock outcrops are usually covered by a thin veneer of glacial deposits, and thicker layers have accumulated along some shorelines and in interior valleys. The soils retain little moisture, as they consist of coarse-textured particles with fragments of clay and rock. Huge boulders are strewn over the surface in many areas and by their granitic composition are known to be glacial erratics, transported by the ice sheets from what is now British Columbia. Prior to the glacial invasions, deposits of sandstones, conglomerates, and other sedimentary materials from an ancient shallow marine area and river delta were uplifted and folded in a narrow belt forming the northern tier of islands. The larger islands to the south are older, more complex, partially metamorphosed formations from deep-water sediments and volcanics.

Strongly influenced by marine surroundings, the San Juan Islands climate is typically cool and humid, rarely experiencing extremes of temperature. Sunny summers and overcast, rainy winters are characteristic, with 70 percent of the precipitation falling between October and April. The rainfall averages 29 inches per year, making the archipelago one of the driest areas along the Pacific coastline north of San Francisco Bay. Most of the moisture-laden winds blowing off the ocean are wrung dry by the Olympic Mountains, leaving the San Juans in the heart of a rainshadow. Plant and animal communities along the southern edge of the island group, closest to the Olympics, subsist on only 19 inches of annual rainfall. A scant 15 miles away, on the summit of Mt. Constitution, an average of 45 inches per year rains down, still dry compared to similar elevations outside of the rainshadow.

Near-drought conditions occur in the San Juans during summer, a result of these climatic, topographic, and geologic factors. Only the larger islands possess standing bodies of water and nearly all of these have been enlarged by human activity. Similarly, farm ponds and reservoirs have been constructed throughout the main islands. Very few streams exist and nearly all are intermittent in nature.

The plant life of the San Juans reflects these harsh conditions with extensive prairies and grassy balds—usually uncommon in the Puget Sound— dominating the arid sites. In slightly moister areas of the islands, open, savannahlike woodlands of Garry Oak and Rocky Mountain Juniper thrive—another uncommon floral community in western Washington. Coniferous trees take over where more water is available, with Western Red-cedar and Western Hemlock subordinate to Douglas-fir in the forest gallery. Many plant species typical of the west side of the Cascades are absent from the archipelago while several varieties from the drier east side flourish. Over 800 kinds of vascular plants have been cataloged in the San Juan Islands—roughly one-third of non-native origin. For an exhaustive treatment of the flora, see *Wild Plants of the San Juan Islands* by Atkinson and Sharpe (The Mountaineers, Seattle, 1985).

HUMAN PRESENCE IN THE ARCHIPELAGO

The San Juan Islands were originally inhabited by a group of Native Americans, the Straits Salish, who made a relatively small impact on the land and its wildlife. In the mid-1800s the area was colonized by Euro-Americans attracted by the logging, fishing, trapping, grazing, and mining opportunities. Nearly all of the land was cleared of timber to produce lumber, agricultural acreage, and charcoal fuel for local lime-processing factories. Native vegetation was further altered by plowing and overgrazing the natural prairies. Several species of wildlife, especially large mammals such as bear, elk, and wolf, were extirpated from the islands in these early days of Euro-American exploitation.

Bird populations have been affected even more by human activities in the San Juan Islands. But, generally speaking, their greater mobility in an island environment, allowed by their powers of flight, have enabled them to respond to the changing conditions more quickly than other animals. Land clearing attracted many species of open-country birds, such as European Starlings, House Finches, and Brown-headed Cowbirds, to the archipelago while simultaneously selecting against forest varieties. After the heyday of logging passed, extensive areas were allowed to regenerate into impressive and mature second-growth woodlands with a corresponding increase in birds associated with this habitat, such as the Cooper's Hawk, Pileated Woodpecker, and Red Crossbill.

Many species of animals have been artificially introduced to the San Juan Islands with varying degrees of impact on the rest of the ecosystem. A number of game birds, including the Chilean Tinamou, Chukar, and Ring-necked Pheasant, were brought to the islands with little permanent success and their effect has been negligible. Other additions, like the California Quail and Wild Turkey, have been quite successful. Of much greater importance are the exotic mammals, the overwhelmingly most influential of these being the European Rabbit. This prolific creature has been a primary source of disturbance by overgrazing and burrowing, causing soil erosion and changes in floral composition. On the positive side, the rabbit population has helped to sustain a very high density of predatory birds, including eagles, hawks, and owls.

As the exploitation of natural resources becomes a decreasingly significant factor in the economy of the San Juan Islands, a more indirect danger threatens the local flora and fauna. Today, not a single habitat is exempt from the pressures of land development and the burgeoning industries of tourism and real estate. Construction of roads and homes destroys or alters habitat, and the most conspicuous victims are birds of prey that require minimal disturbance during their breeding season. Recently, many eagles have abandoned their traditional nesting sites because of man's building activity. Some have suffered even more drastically through illegal nest-tree cutting by developers and landowners.

Other birds highly sensitive to human-caused disturbances are marine species such as loons, grebes, cormorants, gulls, terns, alcids, and shorebirds. The list of activities deleterious to these creatures includes commercial fishing and aquaculture, oil transportation and refining, industrial use of toxic chemicals, shoreline development, and recreational boating. These dangers warrant careful scrutiny in the San Juans, as the area remains one of the most important locations for breeding, migrating, and wintering seabirds in Washington State.

Every summer and fall large numbers of drowned alcids and grebes may be found swirling in tidal eddies or littering the south-facing beaches of San Juan Island, victims of gill nets operated by commercial fishermen. Discarded or lost nets destroy loons, grebes, cormorants, alcids, and many marine mammals while drifting free or washed up on rocks or beaches. Shorebirds also become entangled in them while foraging during low water; then they drown in the next rising tide. Nonbiodegradable plastics, a related problem, are found floating everywhere and litter the beaches. They imperil marine birds and mammals with strangulation and starvation through entanglement. Ingestion of plastics, such as styrofoam particles, has been shown to cause poisoning and digestive tract blockage.

Aquaculture ventures are often destructive to the ecosystem since they are placed in zones of high biological productivity and therefore compete with local wildlife. This forces marine birds and mammals to either leave the area or face a barrage of ultrasonic devices, explosives, electric fences, repulsing chemicals, or guns, intended to discourage predation of the industry's product. Birds are particularly susceptible to entanglement in the defensive nets and fences used in aquaculture. Perhaps the greatest impact of aquaculture, particularly in the case of fish-raising pens, is the continuous release of concentrated amounts of antibiotics, excessive food wastes, and feces into the environment. This has been known to cause blooms of dangerous bacteria and plankton in the vicinity of fish farms by altering nutrient levels and complex food webs, just as untreated human sewage does when disposed in our waters. Similar situations are found near seafood farms, processors, and canneries that dump raw fish offal and by-products into the water, thereby threatening the health of marine ecosystems.

A more obvious threat to marine organisms, and not just those living in the San Juan Islands, is the presence of crude oil transportation, storage, and refinement systems. Petrochemicals released anywhere in the inland waters of Washington State could have terrible consequences for wildlife in a vast area. Drifting layers of these substances may travel long distances when propelled by wind and tidal currents, affecting whole populations of marine birds and mammals. In the San Juan Islands, dense, localized rafts of migrating and wintering seabirds, and crowded breeding colonies of cormorants, gulls, and alcids are particularly at risk from ingestion and physical contact with these and other insidious compounds. Indirectly, marine wildlife may be adversely affected months or years later due to decreased food supplies. Petrochemicals, especially refined products, can cause severe damage to the complex food web that marine birds and mammals depend upon for their survival.

Oil spills in the 1980s have underscored the need to monitor this industry and to develop emergency clean-up plans in the event of another accidental or intentional discharge. Thousands of marine birds died during these episodes through ingesting toxic crude oil and from losing the waterproofing inherent in their feathers. Despite attempts by volunteers to rehabilitate birds affected by oil spills the majority die within 24 hours or develop secondary symptoms of oil contamination in the form of abnormally molting plumage, chemically burned tissues, and aberrant social behavior. A much more effective way of safeguarding these species is to prevent them from entering slicks in the first place. It is possible that, in the event of another spill, boat owners could assist rescuers by driving potential victims from the polluted area before they become contaminated. To report a spill or for information on volunteering time, equipment, or vehicles in the event of a clean-up operation, contact the San Juan County Sheriff Department, the United States Coast Guard, or the San Juan Islands Oil Spill Association (see Appendix B).

Other toxins that enter our marine waters, including polychlorinated biphenyls and pesticides, also threaten wildlife because they concentrate in the food chain and accumulate in body tissues. These long-lived and persistent substances can cause disease, reduced fertility, lower reproductive success, birth defects, and, in very high doses, death. Marine birds and mammals are not the only species affected; humans, birds of prey, and other creatures at the top of the food chain are at risk. Some sources of these pervasive hazards are industrial effluents and agricultural runoff, which, like oil slicks, can strike from afar. Other points of origin for harmful substances entering the ecosystem are marinas and fish-rearing pens. These sites can toxify a localized area with powerful solvents, detergents, antifouling bottom paints, or drugs.

The recent growth in tourism and outdoor recreation in the San Juan Islands has posed another, often unrecognized, problem: that of loving the outdoors and its inhabitants to death. This can be seen when inexperienced or unconcerned commercial operators navigate at excessive speeds or anchor their boatloads of birders, whale watchers, or scuba divers too near breeding colonies, roosting locations, and haul-out sites of marine birds and mammals. The growing boat traffic also includes many unaware yachters and kayakers who, drawn to the beauty and remoteness of these same offshore locations, are tempted to explore them on foot and stay for a picnic despite the distress their presence causes to nesting oystercatchers or denning otters. Sport fishermen are routinely seen maneuvering their vessels a few yards from cormorant, gull, and alcid nests, obviously attracted, like the birds, by the adjacent fishing hot-spots. Sea kayakers, in their sleek crafts, can hardly resist gliding up to tiny islands and exposed reefs that are unapproachable in any other boat. Eager for an intimate wildlife experience, they frequently paddle too closely and end up stampeding the seals and sending the birds into a flapping frenzy. Even educated researchers in the pursuit of scientific data are sometimes guilty of agitating the very species that they are attempting to learn more about. Unfortunately for most wildlife living in the archipelago, the summer tourist season exactly coincides with crucial reproductive activities and greatly increases susceptibility to disturbance and subsequent breeding failure.

The actual damage to seabirds stemming from these recreational activities include trampled eggs and chicks, progeny knocked by their panicked parents from nests onto waves and rocks below, and lethal exposure of vulnerable offspring to sun, rain, and predators. Ultimately, an entire colony may be abandoned if the disturbances continue. New-born seal pups in these situations may be separated from their mothers and crushed by a herd of panicked adults or, through becoming frightened, be forced into the cold, swift water prematurely.

The simple way to avoid peril for marine birds and mammals is to treat them with respect. When boating, never land on or approach any offshore

The long decurved bill of the Whimbrel,
a large sandpiper, enables it to probe
deeply into the tunnels of burrowing
invertebrates.

rock or islet if breeding animals are present. Pilots should refrain from operating their aircraft at low altitudes in the vicinity of nesting seabirds or hauled-out marine mammals. Fortunately, the vast majority of offshore sites used by wildlife have been made a part of the San Juan Islands National Wildlife Refuge (NWR). In recognition of their biological significance and fragility, 82 separate locations are closed to entry by any person, except those who have obtained prior permission from the United States Fish and Wildlife Service (USFW). Two other islands under the jurisdiction of the USFW, Turn and Matia, are managed by the Washington State Parks and Recreation Commission and are currently open to the public.

Sadly, many people remain ignorant of the rules that protect these precious sanctuaries, as trespassers and other violators remain an all too common sight in the archipelago. A strong effort must be made now to educate all types of recreators about this important and pressing issue. Prohibited entry at the National Wildlife Refuges means that there is absolutely *no* landing, hiking, picnicking, photography, camping, hunting, fishing, or bird-watching allowed on the islands. Vessels operating within the 200-yard buffer zone surrounding the refuges must conduct themselves in a manner that prevents any disturbance, harrassment, or endangerment of wildlife. The agencies involved with the enforcement of these laws include not only the USFW, but also the National Marine Fisheries Service, the Washington State Wildlife Department, the United States Coast Guard, and the San Juan County Sheriff Department. Federal penalties for simple trespassing and wildlife harrassment are prison terms of up to six months with fines of $500. If animals sheltered by the Marine Mammal Protection Act or the Endangered Species Act are affected, the prison sentence may be five years with fines up to $10,000 levied.

Since law-enforcement officers will not always be at hand to issue citations or make arrests, it is the obligation of anyone concerned about the welfare of our natural environment to help maintain surveillance of these islands. Obtain the names and addresses of violators or, if this is not possible, record the registration numbers and names of vessels involved. Report the information as soon as possible to one of the above agencies (refer to Appendix B for phone numbers and addresses). Notify the agency that is able to respond in the least amount of time—usually the one with a patrol boat in the immediate area. Contact with more than one law-enforcement organization may be appropriate.

Although the brunt of the tourism and recreation impact is hitting the marine fauna, terrestrial wildlife communities are not unaffected. The use of off-road vehicles, mopeds, and mountain bikes on foot trails, beaches, and back-country areas results in the destruction of native vegetation and soil erosion. Many people allow their dogs to roam the countryside, where they harrass deer and ground-nesting birds. Along the waterfront, some owners allow their dogs to chase resting ducks and foraging shorebirds engaged in long and taxing migratory movements. Boaters have ignorantly loosed their pets on refuge islands occupied by seabird colonies in order that they may relieve themselves and get some exercise. Tame and feral cats take a large number of nesting birds and small mammals, simultaneously vectoring some diseases to our native wildlife. Poachers destroying wildlife outside the parameters of game management plans endanger the status of troubled species such as the Trumpeter Swan, a fully protected bird that has suffered from illegal shootings in the islands. The near-drought conditions characteristic of San Juan summers make fire danger extremely high in the islands. (A large fire generating intense heat is always destructive to some wildlife and property, although the role of fire in maintaining a natural ecosystem is now only beginning to be appreciated.)

The pristine beauty and richness of the San Juan Islands can be protected through great care and effort. Together, our land, water, air, flora, and fauna directly reflect our quality of life, and they are only as safe as we choose to make them. With so many potential disasters and subtle dangers threatening the lives of all organisms, including ourselves, we must maintain a ceaseless vigil. Environmentalism and conservation represent the best interests of all who live, work, or recreate in this area.

Going Birding

Sea fog creeping up Rosario Strait

Regardless of your bird-watching skills, the San Juan Islands have something to offer you. With 291 species of birds recorded in the archipelago and avian events occurring throughout the year, novices and experts alike are kept alert with binoculars ready. Enjoyable birding can be done in a variety of ways to suit each person's level of expertise. From the comfort of your living room, a peaceful and rewarding day may be spent watching the activity of Purple Finches around a feeding station. An aggressive birder may spend the same time scrambling on the steep slopes of Mt. Young hoping to locate a new Purple Martin colony or a species never before recorded in the San Juans.

Finding someone with knowledge of the local avifauna is the fastest and easiest way to gain experience and become indoctrinated into birding. When taken on a stroll by a seasoned birder the averge person is usually surprised at the number and diversity of birds present in a given area, even if it happens to be his own backyard. People who enjoy a challenge may choose to learn about birds on their own, a more time-consuming method, but possibly a more rewarding one as well. Persons who like more social contact or the support of

fellow birders will probably seek out one of the many groups that have out-
ings designed to observe wildlife and study natural history. Probably the best
for the purpose of birding are those sponsored by local chapters of the National Audubon Society.

Whether you go solo or with a gaggle of fellow birders, books and field
guides on the subject are absolutely essential. There have been a staggering
number of books published on the topic of birds, but the three that we recom-
mend most for field identification are (in ascending order of thoroughness and
price): Golden Press's *Birds of North America: A Guide to Field Identification,* National Geographic Society's *Field Guide to the Birds of North America,* and *The Audubon Society Master Guide to Birding.* We consider the
National Geographic Society's book to be the best all-round identification
guide for this continent. Although a bit unwieldy in the field, the Audubon Society's three-volume set contains the most information. Many novice birders
choose the Golden Press's guide as it is perhaps the easiest of the three to use.
Keep in mind that no field identification guide is perfect—you may wish to
have all three because they complement each other very well.

The only other required piece of equipment for birders is a pair of good-
quality, optically bright binoculars, preferably with a wide visual field and
close-focus abilities. Optional items include a spotting scope mounted on a
sturdy tripod, notebooks and pencils, tide table, compact tape recorder with
recorded bird songs and calls, and camera with powerful telephoto lens. Interesting birds have a habit of popping up unexpectedly while one is driving to
work, gardening, or taking a ferry ride. For this reason the wise birder will always keep binoculars, field guide, and now, *Birding in the San Juan Islands,*
handy at all times when in the archipelago. Birding activities elsewhere in the
state will be greatly enhanced by Wahl and Paulson's *A Guide to Bird Finding
in Washington* (Whatcom County Museum, Bellingham, revised 1981).

You will find that most birding trips need some advance planning to
make them successful. Putting your gear to effective use often requires a little
forethought and information on current local conditions, especially when
trying to find a rare species. The time of day is an important aspect of birding
since the majority of birds are most active from dawn to midmorning and
again in the evening. Midday birding often entails a lot of sky-searching, as
this it the time to observe soaring birds of prey and aerial flocks of swifts and
swallows cavorting in rising columns of solar-heated air. Consulting tide
tables is a crucial step before seeking shorebirds, as most are observed on the
exposed intertidal zone of rocks and beaches. Other marine species, including
phalaropes and alcids, will be found concentrating in and around predictable
tidal rips. Nocturnal explorations, such as "owl prowls" and "snipe hunts,"
reveal a completely different cast of feathered creatures. Storms and windy
weather can make small terrestrial birds difficult to observe, at the same time
increasing the liklihood of spotting a rare pelagic bird over open water. Wind
direction is also an important consideration because most rafting flocks will
seek protection in the lee of islands just as land birds find shelter behind hills
and hedgerows.

Be sure to wear the proper outdoor clothing (in drab colors) when on
field trips. Birds, equipped with color vision and acute hearing, have a tendency to be shy and skittish. Move quietly and deliberately and speak only in
hushed tones if you wish to avoid frightening your quarry away. Keep your

eyes peeled for any movement and quickly freeze if a bird comes into view. This is when some previous experience with a pair of binoculars comes in handy. Many beginners have a difficult time quickly locating an object through binoculars and need to practice before going into the field. Study every bird you see carefully and compare it with the plates and descriptions in your field guide. Listen intently for calls and songs and, if you cannot identify the vocalizing bird by these distinctive notes, follow them to their source. Since most birds will respond to imitations of their voices, tape recordings or other artificial sounds can be used to coax them into view. This works exceptionally well for nocturnal birds such as owls, extremely timid species like rails, and treetop "dickey birds" (originating in the British Isles, this expression is used when referring to any small passerine). The call of a Northern Pygmy-Owl, either whistled or played on a tape recorder, may not only attract the target species if present but also hordes of perching birds that wish to scold their enemy. Birders also entice passerines into revealing themselves by making "pishing" noises or tiny squeaks.

Birding etiquette is an important topic as all birds are subject to disturbance by even the most well-intentioned observer, especially during the breeding season. Poking around a bird's nest often leads predators to the site or prevents the parents from taking proper care of their offspring. Particular care must be taken when playing tapes of bird songs during the nesting season as this may disrupt normal courtship and reproductive activities. It is best to keep a discreet distance away and use a spotting scope to observe these aspects of a bird's life. Spotting scopes allow birders to get good views while still long distances away and often prove invaluable for examining tide flats, open bays, seabird rookeries, and raptor eyries. At any time of year, avoid tromping insensitively through a bird's home area. This is very harmful to its well-being and is therefore not proper birding etiquette. Using common sense while bird-watching will not only minimize your impact on sought-after birds but on other organisms in the ecosystem as well. Responsible birders are also concerned with the welfare of fellow humans and their property. Permission must always be obtained before entering posted land and both littering and fire-building are taboo. Always keep your vehicle off the right-of-way when stopped or parked and remain on well-marked roadways when traveling. In essence, always treat other people's property as you would have them treat yours, and act as if all the islands were your home.

There's one way to go bird-watching that doesn't even require leaving your home and yard. This is to establish and maintain bird-feeding stations filled with grain, seeds, and suet. Not only is this a good method to observe birds, but it also helps many species survive through periods of exceptionally bad weather. Vagrant birds that find themselves drastically off course and those individuals that could not undergo their normal migration due to injury or illness may also find life-giving sustenance at feeders. Many important facets of bird behavior have been discovered at feeding stations, as have rare species far from their normal haunts. Providing birdbaths also helps to attract large numbers of feathered neighbors and increase the backyard entertainment, especially during the dry summer months. Other useful and fun birding projects to get involved in are the annual Audubon Society sponsored Christmas Bird Count, "bird-athons," breeding-bird surveys, and wildlife enhancement programs, such as providing nesting boxes for certain declining species of cavity-nesting birds. If you should find an injured or dead bird it may be brought to the Wolf Hollow Wildlife Rehabilitation Centre on San Juan Island (see Appendix B) for medical care or necropsy.

Keeping track of your bird observations and discoveries in a journal can be most rewarding and useful. Books such as this one would not be possible without large amounts of recorded data. Whether a journal is maintained or not, most birders make simple lists of the birds they have seen or heard. This is a favorite pastime of some people and bird lists for yards, counties, and states are commonly maintained. (Appendix A can serve as your San Juan Islands checklist. Every species recorded from the archipelago is listed there with a box next to its name.) Nearly all birders keep a "life list," a compilation of all the species an individual has ever observed in the wild, regardless of political boundaries.

As you become a more experienced naturalist, your chances of finding a rare bird increase. If you feel that you have found something unusual, be sure to report it to the senior author (see Appendix B) or to the San Juan Islands Audubon Society (see Appendix B). When documenting your sighting, be sure to include the species name, exact location, date and time, number present, and a full description of the bird's appearance and behavior. Your name, address, telephone number, as well as those of other observers present will be needed in the report. At the time of discovery, a notebook and camera will be extremely valuable aids toward an accurate description, and, lacking a photograph of the specimen, another witness may be crucial to the acceptance of a highly unusual observation. Remember that rare birds are not the only ones worth reporting. Data is constantly needed on the breeding status of uncommon birds, late departure and early arrival dates of migrants, and unusually high or low counts of individuals. Your bird sighting information will further our understanding of the San Juan Islands' avifauna and may eventually help to preserve the wildlife of this productive and beautiful area.

BIRD HABITATS

Becoming acquainted with the types of habitats in the San Juan Islands can be a tremendous help in locating and identifying birds because most varieties show a marked preference for one or more particular habitats. In addition, many fascinating aspects of a bird's life, such as its behavior, appearance, vocalizations, and distribution can be better understood when contemplated in the context of its chosen habitat. As seasons change, many species will occupy a different part of the same habitat or shift to a new one altogether. For instance, Red-winged Blackbirds spend the autumn and winter carousing farm fields, but with the onset of lengthening days they quickly depart for fresh-water marshes and lakeshores. Some birds, like American Robins and Northern Flickers, exploit a broad range of habitats while others, such as Black Swifts and American Dippers, are specialized and occur in only one. Keep in mind that birds are among the most mobile of all creatures and can occasionally be observed in habitats not normally frequented, a situation that occurs most often during the nonbreeding season.

A bird's preference for a specific habitat can be used as a tool in its identification. As an example, you may see a large, dark goose standing on the edge of a pond in farmland habitat and be quite sure that it is a Canada Goose and not a Brant, a similar species that restricts itself to salt-water situations. Conversely, when searching for a particular kind of bird, knowledge of its preferred habitat may enhance your success by directing you to a likely location. The importance of habitats to some species cannot be overstated; for them their only chance of survival may be in the preservation of their natural home.

The authors recognize 13 avian habitats in the San Juan Islands. Two of them, dry grassland and open woodland, are very distinctive and possibly unique when compared with the surrounding Puget Sound lowlands. For the sake of expediency, each habitat has been given two-letter initials that are used throughout the Site Guide. However, keep in mind that some areas cannot be neatly partitioned and are an intergrade between two different habitat types. In the course of these descriptions, place names enclosed by parentheses are used as examples to typify the habitat.

OPEN SALT WATER (SW): Perhaps no other habitat can offer such a volume and diversity of birds with a single sweep of the binoculars. By the same token, open salt water can be the most devoid of bird life with vast expanses sometimes completely unoccupied. This extensive habitat includes all of the marine waters surrounding the San Juan Islands. Bird concentrations occur near areas of strong tidal convergences (Cattle Pass), kelp reefs (Salmon Bank) and shelves (Lime Kiln State Park), and eelgrass beds (Griffin Bay), which are all used as foraging areas. Sheltered sites, usually found in enclosed bays protected from strong winds and currents, are also widely used by marine birds (Wescott Bay, Friday Harbor). These attract flocks of roosting birds that prefer quiet waters and seek shelter from stormy weather. Inhabitants of open salt water include loons, grebes, tubenoses, cormorants, bay ducks, sea ducks, mergansers, phalaropes, gulls, terns, jaegers, and alcids.

ROCKY SHORELINE (RS): This is another extensive habitat in the San Juan Islands; most of our coast is of this type (Eagle Point). Rocky shoreline supports many prey communities for the marine birds and is used during low tide by herons, gulls, and specialized shorebirds, such as the Black Oystercatcher, Black Turnstone, Wandering Tattler, Surfbird, and Rock Sandpiper. During high tide, open-salt-water species forage over the sections that are inundated with water; most notable among such foragers is the Harlequin Duck. The offshore rocks and islets (San Juan Islands National Wildlife Refuge), free from all mammalian predators except River Otters, are used by nesting Pelagic and Double-crested Cormorants, oystercatchers, Glaucous-winged Gulls, Pigeon Guillemots, Tufted Puffins, and probably Marbled Murrelets. Additionally, these isolated islets (Whale Rocks) are important roosting areas for Brandt's Cormorants as well as for the above nesters. Bald Eagles find these offshore locations virtual smorgasbords and routinely visit them to prey on both adult marine birds and their young. Throughout this habitat, American Crows, eagles, and gulls may be observed scavenging dead animal matter.

SANDY AND GRAVELLY SHORELINE, MUD FLAT, AND SALT MARSH (SS):

Of our marine habitats in the San Juan Islands this is the most limited in extent. Mud flats and other intertidal zones are the most important part of this habitat and are utilized by herons, ducks, shorebirds, gulls, and terns for either foraging or roosting (Fisherman Bay). Many open-salt-water species move in over the shallows (Spencer Spit) to feed at high tide, including loons and grebes. Other birds frequenting the area (False Bay) are hunting Bald Eagles, falcons, and Belted Kingfishers, with scavenging being conducted by crows and several of the above species. Burrows in glacial banks above the intertidal zone are inhabited by nesting kingfishers, guillemots, and Northern Rough-winged Swallows (Swifts Bay).

FRESH-WATER LAKE, MARSH, AND FARM POND (FW):

Totally absent from the smaller islands, this habitat is restricted to the larger land masses. Often it is only temporary, as many of the smaller bodies dry up or recede drastically in the summer months. For this reason, many of the ponds and lakes in the San Juan Islands are artificial or have been enlarged by human activity. Birds that come to forage in this habitat include Ospreys, Northern Harriers, Soras, Virginia Rails, all three swan species, bay and marsh ducks, shorebirds, and all of the swallows (Three Meadows Marsh). Many others, such as Double-crested Cormorants, gulls, and most passerines, come to drink and bathe (Sportsman Lake). Pied-billed Grebes and many of the species listed above nest in this habitat (Killebrew Lake, Frank Richardson Wildfowl Preserve).

FIELD, FARMLAND, AND PASTURE (FL):

This habitat, created and maintained by humans, is quite extensive in the interior portions of the larger islands. When flooded or under plow it attracts large gull flocks composed of many species and at all times draws American Robins, European Starlings, crows, Common Ravens, Brown-headed Cowbirds, and Brewer's and Red-winged Blackbirds (Crow Valley). In autumn, flocks of Water Pipits and Western Meadowlarks forage here, followed in winter by marsh ducks and shorebirds after the lower portions become soggy and flooded (San Juan Valley). Throughout the year, a wide variety of raptors is seen, attracted to the many prey species found in this habitat.

DRY GRASSLAND, GRASSY BALD, AND ROCKY SLOPE (DG):

These open, herb-dominated communities are a characteristic San Juan habitat and, with the presence of several east-slope species of plants and birds, they help to set the islands apart from the rest of Puget Sound country. Historically, fire has been a critical factor in maintaining this treeless habitat, which is now slowly succumbing to an invasion of shrubs and conifers because of modern-day fire suppression. These grassy areas are usually found on ridges and south-facing slopes where exposure to sun and wind during the growing season is intense and soils are gravelly (Little Summit). Only in areas where there has not been a history of overgrazing or plowing are there natural prairies with a high incidence of native plant species (Yellow Island). Rock outcrops and glacially polished benches, covered with dense mats of lichen and moss, often punctuate these slopes, furnishing suitable habitat for cacti and Rock Wrens (Mt. Dallas). Denizens of the grassy habitats include nesting

Savannah Sparrows, Eurasian Skylarks, American Goldfinches, and Vesper Sparrows. Raptors are a constant sight as they ply the air or sit on perches patiently awaiting their next meal.

OPEN WOODLAND AND OAK SAVANNAH (OW): This distinctive San Juan habitat consists of scattered trees in a grassland matrix and is closely allied to the prairies and rocky slopes described above. Open woodlands and savannahs occur where there is a slightly greater amount of available moisture than in the previous habitat and can often be found fringing shorelines (West Sound), meadows, and rocky balds (Mt. Dallas). The indicator trees of this habitat include Garry Oak, Rocky Mountain Juniper, Pacific Madrone, Lodgepole Pine, Bigleaf Maple, and Douglas-fir, an unusual assemblage in western Washington. American Kestrels, Common Nighthawks, Northern Flickers, and Chipping Sparrows are nesting inhabitants of the savannahs, while during migration Townsend's Solitaires and Yellow-rumped Warblers are visitors.

DRY CONIFEROUS FOREST (DC): Although most woodlands in the San Juan Islands are of this type, a full spectrum between wet and dry coniferous forests is displayed and there is no clean dividing line between the two. Closed canopy forests on south-facing slopes are at the dryer end of this moisture gradient and are dominated by Douglas-fir with a sparse understory of shrubby plants (south slope of Mt. Finlayson). Mixed irregularly throughout this habitat are Pacific Madrone, Lodgepole Pine, Grand Fir, Bigleaf Maple, Pacific Yew, and in disturbed sites, Red Alder and Bitter Cherry. Bird species characteristic of this extensive habitat are the Cooper's Hawk, House Wren, and Red Crossbill.

WET CONIFEROUS FOREST (WC): As precipitation and shelter from wind and direct sun increases, the closed coniferous forest becomes a moister habitat. Prime examples of wet coniferous forests may be found on north-facing slopes (Mt. Constitution) and interior flatlands. Dominant plants are Douglas-fir, Western Hemlock, Sword Fern, and Salal, with Western Red-cedar and Grand Fir sometimes taking important roles (north slope of Mt. Finlayson). The wettest areas, gullies and interior valleys, develop Red-cedar/Grand Fir climax communities (Mountain Lake). Few sites harbor old-growth stands as most of these have been logged in the last 100 years. In disturbed areas of this habitat the early successional plants are Red Alder, Bigleaf Maple, and Douglas-fir. Look for Olive-sided Flycatchers, Winter Wrens, and Varied Thrushes nesting in these forests.

RIPARIAN WOODLAND (RW): This habitat is more appropriately called "riparian thicket" in the San Juans and is restricted almost exclusively to the larger islands. Where lakes and marshes lack a rocky substrate, they are often bordered by willows and Pacific Crabapple, the dominant plants of this scarce habitat (Egg, Sportsman, and Killebrew lakes). The few year-round streams that exist in the islands have cut deeply into the bedrock, preventing the development of riparian growth and forming instead deep gullies choked with coniferous species. Typical birds of this habitat include Downy Woodpecker, Willow Flycatcher, Cedar Waxwing, and Yellow Warbler.

SHRUBBY THICKET (ST): A product of human activities such as forest clearing, fire suppression on grasslands, and abandonment of agricultural fields, this habitat is expanding in the San Juan Islands. Shrubby thickets are found distributed throughout farmland, cut-over areas, roadsides, old burns, and other recently disturbed areas (Mt. Dallas). Transitional by nature, they are an early successional phase in the development of woody plant communities and are widely distributed amongst many other habits. Possibly they occur as a more or less permanent vegetational scheme only in shallow depressions of rocky benchland (American Camp). The shrubby thicket assemblage consists of blackberry, Snowberry, Nootka Rose, Oceanspray, Tall Oregon Grape, and others. Its accompanying avifauna includes California Quail, Bushtit, MacGillivray's Warbler, Rufous-sided Towhee, and numerous sparrows and wrens.

TOWN AND GARDEN (TG): Blissfully lacking in urban areas, the San Juan Islands are dotted with many small villages and towns. Friday Harbor, with less than 2000 year-round residents, is the largest of these, yet from the middle of town Bald Eagles and many other birds of prey may be seen. This habitat is a mixture of buildings, native and ornamental plants, lawns, and feeding stations (Eastsound), and provides the diversity needed by many birds. These areas are frequented by American Crows, American Robins, and Orange-crowned Warblers, and many of the species typical here, such as Rock Doves, House Sparrows, and Barn Swallows, prefer to nest on structures built by humans.

AERIAL (AR): Although used at times by just about every bird, especially while migrating long distances, this vast habitat is truly the domain of raptors, swifts, and other high fliers. Consisting of nothing but airspace, the key locations are found where oceanic breezes are deflected upward (Mt. Finlayson) and rising columns of solar-heated air develop (Mt. Constitution). Search the sky for Black and Vaux's Swifts and many types of swallows as they congregate in large flocks during hatches of airborne insects or at the approach of stormy weather. In the evening, listen carefully as the sounds of "winnowing" Common Snipes and nighthawks drift down from above. Common Ravens and birds of prey often steal the show as they soar overhead while migrating, hunting for prey, and performing courtship rituals.

SITE GUIDE

The purpose of this section is to provide birders with several tour routes designed to reveal the diversity of wildlife and habitats in the San Juan Islands. Field trip descriptions have been given for the four largest islands serviced by the Washington State Ferry System, the ferry route through the archipelago, and a private boat tour. The best birding hot-spots and nearly all public lands have been included on the routes. For each location visited on the tours there may be one or more birds and/or habitats listed. **Habitats are given with their two-letter initials as found in the previous chapter.** Remember that most species are quite seasonal in their distribution and a quick glance at Appendix A will clearly illustrate the relative abundance of the bird in question throughout the year. The Bird Habitats and Species Accounts may also be used as cross-references.

When using this chapter, be sure to examine not only the detailed maps shown in this book but also ones provided in Marge Mueller's *The San Juan Islands, Afoot and Afloat* (The Mountaineers, Seattle, 1979). Of course, none of these maps is intended for marine navigation, and boaters should always obtain the proper navigational charts before embarking on a voyage through the San Juans. As previously mentioned, boaters need to be especially careful about disturbing birds, seals, and whales. Captains are encouraged to maintain a respectful distance from the National Wildlife Refuge islands and to avoid creating any impact on these sensitive areas. Land-bound birders should remember to observe all "no trespassing" signs, park vehicles off any right-of-way, and maintain proper birding etiquette at all times.

SAN JUAN ISLANDS FERRY ROUTE: This trip is a great way to introduce new visitors to the excitement of birding in the San Juans. From late summer through spring a staggering number and variety of seabirds may be seen from the ferry as it passes through the heart of the archipelago. Most travelers begin their journey at the Anacortes ferry terminal on Fidalgo Island, a good birding location in its own right. If you happen to arrive there early or your boat is late (an all too common situation during summer weekends and holidays) some "warm-up" bird-watching may be done from the terminal's parking lot. Looking to the west, a tiny lake (FW, RW) can be scanned for nesting Wood Ducks, Hooded Mergansers, Tree Swallows, and other birds typical of fresh-water and riparian habitats in the San Juans. Another place worth checking for a wide variety of species is the Ship Harbor Salt Marsh (SS), bordering the eastern edge of the parking lanes. The ferry dock is home to breeding Cliff and Barn Swallows while the adjacent embankments are pocked with the nesting holes of Northern Rough-winged Swallows and Belted Kingfishers (SS). Many kinds of marine fowl may be observed on nearby pilings or on the surrounding waters (SW).

When the ferry departs, take a position high up on the front of the boat, the best vantage point for birding and sightseeing. Depending upon time of year, loons, grebes, cormorants, waterfowl, phalaropes, gulls, terns, jaegers, and alcids may be seen on a ferry voyage (SW). Seals, sea lions, porpoises, and whales are further possibilities for sharp-eyed observers. Immediately entering the rich waters of the San Juans, the boat first crosses Rosario Strait in an area with several converging channels and strong tidal currents. This strait, a major migrational route through the archipelago for seabirds, is particularly good for watching Pacific Loons, all three cormorant species, Red-necked Phalaropes, Heermann's Gulls, Common Terns, Parasitic Jaegers, Common Murres, Ancient Murrelets, and Rhinoceros Auklets. Many rarities have been seen in Rosario Strait so maintain a vigil for pelagic species such as tubenoses, Red Phalarope, Sabine's Gull, and others that may have been driven into the inland waters by foggy or stormy conditions. On the western side of the strait, just before entering the interior waterways of the archipelago, you will see an islet about a half-mile to the right of the ferry route. This is Pointer Island (NWR), the site of a dense Glaucous-winged Gull nesting colony.

After threading Thatcher Pass, the ferry travels the length of Harney Channel. This area is most exciting in the winter months when concentrations of seabirds gather here, attracted by excellent food resources and relative protection from high winds and waves. Common Loons, Western and Red-necked Grebes, scoters, Red-breasted Mergansers, Bald Eagles, Thayer's and Mew Gulls, and Marbled Murrelets are among the most abundant species that utilize this waterway. Also commonly seen are Red-throated Loons, Horned Grebes, Double-crested Cormorants, Great Blue Herons, Harlequin Ducks, Oldsquaws, and Common Murres. Shortly after exiting Thatcher Pass the boat makes a close pass of tiny Willow Island (NWR), often a summer home to a small colony of breeding Pigeon Guillemots. Viewed from the right side of the ferry, white splashes of guano mark the location of the guillemot's nesting crevices as well as the favorite roosts of Pelagic Cormorants (RS). Another small NWR site, Flower Island, may be seen a little farther on from the left side of the ferry. Although the island is some distance away, breeding Glaucous-winged Gulls may be seen tending to their nest sites, and dozens of Harbor Seals may be observed sunning themselves on the rocks at the north tip of the island and at Leo Reef nearer the ferry. Offshore of Humphrey Head, an immense flock of sea ducks is usually present in the winter, largely dominated by White-winged Scoters. A Bald Eagle nest, located in a high conifer back from shore, is visible at Humphrey Head.

Even while temporarily docked at one of the islands it pays to keep your eyes open. Throughout the year subtle plumage characteristics may be noted on the larger gulls seen perched on the pilings, and stunning close-up views of high-plumaged Pelagic Cormorants are available in the spring months. The Shaw and Orcas ferry docks are excellent places to watch Horned Grebes, Greater Scaups, Buffleheads, Common Goldeneyes, Hooded Mergansers, and Belted Kingfishers. Several pairs of Glaucous-winged Gulls have recently nested atop a piling of the Shaw Island terminal, providing regular ferry riders with the chance to observe at close range the breeding cycle of this species. After leaving the Orcas dock, the ferry occasionally heads due west through narrow Wasp Passage, sometimes affording glimpses of Barrow's Goldeneyes along the shore of Crane Island. Usually the vessel backtracks a short distance and turns southwest into Upright Channel, soon passing close by Flat Point of Lopez Island (SS). Lucky birders may be able to spot a flock of Brant at this time. These sea geese may also be seen by looking beyond Flower Island (NWR) to Spencer Spit on the east side of the island.

Seabird activity increases near San Juan Channel. The strong tiderips that occur in this waterway are usually thronged with frantically feeding seabirds at all times of the year. The climax is reached during the fall migration when thousands of gulls and terns hover over rafts of diving alcids and cormorants. Observant birders will quickly detect swift Parasitic Jaegers piercing the swirling clouds of Bonaparte's Gulls and Common Terns. By sifting through these vast flocks, rarities such as Little Gulls, Arctic Terns, or Long-tailed Jaegers may be espied. Rhinoceros Auklets forage here by the hundreds in the summer and a small flock winters near the entrance of Friday Harbor. Large numbers of Common Murres and Brandt's Cormorants also feed in the turbulent waters here, except in the warmer months.

Friday Harbor, relatively empty of seabirds during summer, is positively swarming with loons, grebes, Double-crested Cormorants, Great Blue Herons, sea ducks, mergansers, gulls, Marbled Murrelets, and Belted King-fishers at other times of year. Fall and early winter are usually the best seasons as hundreds of Common Mergansers join with lesser numbers of Red-breasted Mergansers, Common and Red-throated Loons, cormorants, and several species of gulls to herd and trap schools of herring against the piers. Flocks of terns draw jaegers into the harbor and many other exciting species have been seen here. Some rarities, such as Smew and Kittlitz's Murrelet, have been recorded here and nowhere else in the state.

For those heading on into British Columbia, this is a good time to take a coffee break because the section of San Juan Channel north of Friday Harbor is less frequented by marine birds. Avian activity and Bald Eagle sightings pick up again in fast-flowing Spieden Channel with many of the same species present here as in previously traveled tidal convergences. Haro Strait is rather dull birdwise but watch for porpoises and whales. Just past the international border, Mandarte Island, smeared white with the guano of thousands of nest-ing Double-crested Cormorants and Glaucous-winged Gulls, comes into view on the left side of the ferry. Nearer the Sidney ferry landing, look over Sidney Spit for flocks of Brant, and scan the shallow waters and tide flats along the Vancouver Island shoreline for Eurasian Wigeons feeding among the vastly more numerous American Wigeons (SS). After disembarking in Sidney, open your copy of *A Birders Guide to Vancouver Island* (self-published, 1983) by Keith Taylor, to continue your guided birding exploration.

LOPEZ ISLAND: The third largest of the San Juan Islands, Lopez is the flattest and most heavily farmed in the archipelago. It is an ideal location for a combination bicycle/birding trip, but whatever mode of transportation you choose, be sure to wave at passing residents, as this friendly rural custom is still observed here. Beginning at the ferry dock on the northern tip of the is-land, head south on Ferry Road, keeping alert for Pileated Woodpeckers, Var-ied Thrushes, and other denizens of the wet coniferous forests (WC). At the intersection with Port Stanley Road, turn right into Odlin County Park to hike through the mixed woodlands (DC, WC) and view the surrounding waters (SS, SW) from the public dock. While meandering along the trails here, look and listen for Hairy and Downy Woodpeckers, Western and Olive-sided Flycatchers, American Crows, Chestnut-backed Chickadees, Red-breasted Nuthatches, Brown Creepers, kinglets, Solitary Vireos, Swainson's Thrushes, Orange-crowned, Wilson's, and Townsend's Warblers, and Pine Siskins.

Head south of Ferry Road again and follow the signs to Lopez Village, being sure to scan any flooded farm fields and ponds (FL, FW) for shorebirds

LOPEZ ISLAND AREA

and waterfowl. Arriving in Lopez Village, investigate the shrubby thickets (ST) for California Quails, Bewick's Wrens, Rufous-sided Towhees, and many species of sparrows. Good vistas of marine waters (SW) are found here and also farther south along Fisherman Bay Road. One of the highlights of any birding trip on Lopez Island is Fisherman Spit, accessible from Bayshore Drive, where there are excellent views of San Juan Channel and Fisherman Bay. On the east side of the spit, the bay is home to many birds that enjoy protected waters, tide flats, and salt marsh (SW, SS). Seen here are Horned Grebes, Double-crested Cormorants, Great Blue Herons, all types of ducks, Ospreys, Merlins, Peregrine Falcons, many gulls, roosting terns, foraging plovers, yellowlegs, dowitchers, peeps, and nearly every other species of shorebird that utilizes exposed mud flats. West is San Juan Channel, populated by birds typical of exposed salt-water habitat (SW) and, along the spit itself (SS), may be seen flocks of Brants, Lapland Longspurs, and Snow Buntings.

Back at Fisherman Bay Road, continue southward and carefully follow the signs to Richardson. The bordering expanses of farmland (FL), punctuated by patches of woods and shrubs, provide excellent habitat for birds of prey and other open-country species. Look for Northern Harriers, accipiters, Red-tailed and Rough-legged Hawks, Turkey Vultures, Mourning Doves, Common Barn-owls, Snowy and Short-eared Owls, American Crows, Water Pipits, Northern Shrikes, Brewer's Blackbirds, Brown-headed Cowbirds, and American Goldfinches. Just before Richardson are a few highly productive farm ponds west of the road. Despite being somewhat difficult to view from the right-of-way, they are well worth checking as they have yielded some particularly interesting shorebird records, including American Avocet and Wilson's Phalarope, along with the more typical spectrum of fresh-water inhabitants. From the Richardson dock it is possible to observe marine birds, especially Bald Eagles and Marbled Murrelets, and marine mammals such as River Otters and Harbor Seals.

Drive a short distance back up Richardson Road and take three consecutive right hand turns onto Vista Road, Mud Bay Road, and MacKaye Harbor Road. Eventually, this last road leads to MacKaye Harbor where more marine species may be viewed (SS, SW), especially at the southern end of the bay, which is most protected from wave action and strong winds. On the opposite side of the road are several ponds and sloughs (FW) with many dabbling ducks, possible Ruddy Ducks, and wintering Greater Yellowlegs. Continue a short distance farther and you will arrive at Agate Beach County Park with access to Outer Bay (SW) and more seabirds.

Retrace your path to Aleck Bay Road and take a right, continuing until you reach the first paved road to the left. Take this to Mud Bay Road, turn right, then go left when you reach Sperry Road. This road eventually curves right but, instead, go straight ahead a short distance to the public boat ramp. From here it is possible to scan Mud Bay (SW) with its ample mud flats and extensive salt marsh to the east (SS). Back on Sperry Road, follow the curve down to a sandy, crescent-shaped beach with views of Shoal Bight and Rosario Strait (SW). This entire area has been largely neglected by bird watchers and could be sheltering many interesting species. Look carefully for rare or localized birds such as Yellow-billed Loon, Eared Grebe, geese, and Ruddy Duck. Another inspection of the Mud Bay area may be profitable so return to Mud Bay Road via Sperry Road, turn right, and take another right at Islandale Road. From this intersection follow the road about three quarters of a mile and turn left on a narrow road that descends to the Hunter Bay County boat launch and dock. This side of Lopez Island is a stronghold for Red-throated Loons and other marine birds that prefer shallow waters (SW).

Return to the interior farmland (FL) of the island by turning right at Mud Bay Road and again at Center Road, always watching for bird life appropriate to your surroundings. When you see Hummel Lake, look for the public parking area and boat ramp just south of the intersection with Hummel Lake Road and stop there to observe. This small lake, surrounded by a cattail marsh and riparian ticket (FW, RW), is a great place for Pied-billed Grebes, pond ducks, bay ducks, Buffleheads, Northern Harriers, Soras, Virginia Rails, American Coots, Willow Flycatchers, Marsh Wrens, Yellow Warblers, Common Yellowthroats, Red-winged Blackbirds, and other species typical of these habitats. Turn right on Hummel Lake Road to get more views of the lake and then continue to Port Stanley Road. Take a left and follow this to Baker View Road, which will lead you straight into Spencer Spit State Park. This sandy spit and lagoon (SS) is a good shorebirding location and is also used by hunting falcons, migrating geese, roosting gulls, and foraging Lapland Longspurs and Snow Buntings. Flocks of 50 to 150 Brant are a frequent sight in early spring. The surrounding waters are excellent for open salt-water (SW) species and the woodlands are thronged with the same birds found in Odlin County Park and other forested habitats in the San Juan Islands.

Back at Port Stanley Road, turn right and look for the ponds on the left side of the road just before reaching Swifts Bay. This hot little spot harbors good numbers of teals, Northern Pintails, Northern Shovelers, American Wigeons, plovers, sandpipers, dowitchers, Lesser and Greater Yellowlegs, Common Snipes, and swallows. Swifts Bay (SW) should be checked for seabirds, and the shrubby thickets and backyard feeding stations (ST, PG) in the area may turn up something interesting, especially in winter. A little farther north on Swifts Bay Road you will come to a dirt road on the right side that leads to Humphrey Head. Go a short distance down this until you emerge from the woods and see a small lagoon and Shoal Bay to the left and Swifts Bay on the right. The open salt water (SW) is usually good, but the lagoon (SS) may be limited to Buffleheads, Killdeers, and Greater Yellowlegs. Follow Port Stanley Road to Ferry Road, turn right and you will wind up right where you began this circuit, at the Lopez ferry landing.

SHAW ISLAND: Although dwarfed by the other ferry-served islands and nearly devoid of public access, Shaw Island does offer some pleasant birdwatching and may be easily explored in a day on foot or by bicycle. The main attraction of Shaw is Blind Bay, indenting the northern shore of the island. Views of open water (SW) and large rafts of wintering marine birds are available along Blind Bay Road and Smugglers Bay Road. Pastures around Blind Bay are probably the best areas for raptors, Turkey Vultures, and other open-country birds (FL, ST). The island cover is predominantly coniferous forests (DC, WC) and is good for flock birding in the winter months along the nearly deserted roadsides. Be sure to check any small fens surrounded by willows and other deciduous species (FW, RW), as these are magnets for migrant passerines such as warblers and flycatchers and occasionally host teals or other fresh-water ducks. To get to the only public beach on the island, head south on Squaw Bay Road and turn left on Indian Cove Road, following the signs into Shaw Island County Park. From the boat launch and campground there is access to the sandy shore of Indian Cove and the woodlands of the park (SW, SS, DC). Forest birds are abundant and there are good chances of seeing Ospreys and a variety of shorebirds. A little farther down Squaw Bay Road, where muddy Squaw Bay is visible, it is sometimes possible to observe raccoons foraging on the tidelands in total daylight. Squaw Bay may also be the best shorebird site on Shaw Island and the salt grasses near the beach yield Pectoral Sandpipers and other interesting species. Foot trails extend along both sides of the peninsula that divides Indian cove and Squaw Bay, allowing for some open salt-water scanning and woodland birding. Return to the ferry landing by continuing on Squaw Bay Road, taking a right on Hoffman Cove Road and another on Blind Bay Road.

ORCAS ISLAND: The largest and most sprawling of the San Juans, Orcas is a rambling, hilly island dominated by rocky cliffs and domed mountains. Begin your tour at the ferry dock located at the town of Orcas on the southern shore. Drive north on the Horseshoe Highway until you reach the first major intersection; then turn left, following the signs to West Sound. From the marina and along the road, check the sound for various loons, grebes, cormorants, gulls, and a variety of waterfowl, especially scoters, Oldsquaws, Harlequin Ducks, and Barrow's Goldeneyes (SW, RS). Sometimes Black Turnstones and other rock-loving shorebirds stalk the water's edge at promontories and headlands. Leaving the village of West Sound behind, keep scanning the bay for dense rafts of wintering seabirds, and enjoy the beautiful scenery. Take time to study the oak and juniper belt paralleling the shore as this is an excellent example of a fascinating habitat (OW) and many uncommon or rare birds have been seen here, including Townsend's Solitaire, Northern Pygmy-Owl, Say's Phoebe, and Bohemian Waxwing. Some of the finest wildflower meadows on Orcas Island are found along this road. Keep going ahead on Deer Harbor Road until you reach Sunset Beach Road (this road appears on the right side just before the village of Deer Harbor). Turn right and cross the bridge that divides the harbor from a small lagoon, good for views of a wide spectrum of birds (SW, SS). A short distance farther you may take the driveway that leads to a boat launch with vistas of Deer Harbor or, after climbing the hill and coming to a level area, visit the Deer Harbor Marsh, now known as the Frank Richardson Wildfowl Sanctuary (FW). This superb marsh is one of the most extensive fresh-water habitats in the San Juans and is home to breeding Pied-billed Grebes, Mallards, Blue-winged and Cinnamon Teals, Hooded Mergansers, rails, and American Coots. Usually more than one brood of each of these aquatic species are visible in the spring months, making it one of the most productive wetlands in the archipelago. Ring-necked Ducks have nested here as well. Colonies of Marsh Wrens, Common Yellowthroats, and Red-winged Blackbirds set the marsh vibrating with their songs. Also attracted are many types of birds that hawk insects on the wing, such as Willow Flycatchers, five types of swallows, and Cedar Waxwings (AR).

Retreat all the way back to the intersection with Crow Valley Road (at

ORCAS ISLAND AREA

Rosario Strait

Pt. Lawrence

The Sisters NWR

Clark Is. State Pk.

Barnes Is.

Peapod Rocks NWR

Doe Is. State Park

Matia Is. NWR   Puffin Is. NWR

Mab Is. State Park

Obstruction Is.

Twin Lakes

Mountain Lake

Obstruction Pass

Blakely Is.

ORCAS ISLAND

Summit Lake

Moran Park

Mt. Constitution

Cascade Creek

Cascade Lake

Mountain Lake Rd.

OLGA

Buck Bay

Sucia Islands State Park

Obstruction Pass

Obstruction Pass D.N.R. Campground

ROSARIO

EAST SOUND

Rosario Way

Crescent Beach

Horseshoe Highway

East   Sound

Otters Pt.

North Beach Rd.

Mt. Baker Rd.

North Beach

Dolphin Bay Rd.

Killebrew Lake

Killebrew Lake Rd.

Mt. Woolard

Harney Channel

Patos Is. State Park

North Beach Rd.

Lovers Lane

Fowler's Ponds

Enchanted Forest Rd.

West Beach Rd.

West Beach Rd.

Turtleback Mountain

Crow Valley Rd.

Crow Valley

Horseshoe Hwy.

West Sound

Pt. Doughty

President Channel

Deer Harbor Rd.

Harbor Rd.

WEST SOUND

WEST SOUND

ORCAS VILLAGE

Shaw Is.

Bare Is. NWR

Orcas Knob

Deer Harbor Rd.

DEER HARBOR

Deer Harbor

Skipjack Is. NWR

Waldron Island

Cowlitz Bay

Sandy Pt.

Pt. Disney

Sunset Beach Rd.

Boat Launch

Del.

Wasp Islands

Crane Is.

Wasp Passage

Yellow Is. NWR

Low Is. NWR

White Rk. NWR

Danger Rk. NWR

Jones Is. State Park

Flattop Is. NWR

the first stop sign in West Sound) and turn left to drive along the largest agricultural district on the island (FL). Go left on West Beach Road to the resort
for salt-water access (SW) and then up Enchanted Forest Road to Lover's
Lane. Keep an eye out for Steller's Jays and Black-headed Grosbeaks along
these last two roads as they comprise the best location in the San Juans for
both of these species. Turn left on Lover's Lane, then right on Mt. Baker
Road, and left on North Beach Road. At the end of this road you will find a
public access site with fine views of the northern San Juan Islands and marine
habitats (SS, SW). In the opposite direction down North Beach Road is the
town of Eastsound with typical birds of backyards and gardens (PG). You
may also see some marine species like Horned Grebes, Buffleheads, and Great
Blue Herons from the shore of this village or a bit farther east at Crescent
Beach (SS, SW). Also look for Bald Eagles or an occasional wintering Peregrine Falcon overhead. Just behind Crescent Beach a stand of alders, aspens,
and willows offers a chance of finding Red-eyed Vireos, Black-headed Grosbeaks, Northern Orioles, and other unusual riparian woodland inhabitants
(RW). The marsh here is worth checking for teals, rails, and more (FW).

Continue the tour by heading south on the Horseshoe Highway, paralleling the eastern shore of East Sound until you get to a pond known as Otter's
Lair (FW, RW) located just before the turnoff to Rosario. Check it for the
usual fresh-water and riparian species, such as Pied-billed Grebes, dabbling
ducks, Wood Ducks, American Coots, Yellow Warblers, Red-winged Blackbirds, muskrats, or even Trumpeter Swans. Take Rosario Road to the resort if
you want to examine the waters here for many of the same birds found at
West Sound (SW). Return to the highway and turn right to enter Moran State
Park, a beautiful place full of interesting birds. The first birding area you
come to in the park is Cascade Lake, noteworthy for the Common and
Hooded Mergansers, breeding Ospreys, and occasional Common Loons that
forage in its waters (FW). There is no marsh and very little riparian habitat
except near Rosario Lagoon and the dam (RW). Feeding the lake is Cold
Creek, which should be inspected for American Dippers. This unique bird
possibly nests here or at nearby Cascade Creek and you may want to hike the
latter stream its lengh up to Mountain Lake (also reached via Mountain
Road). Mountain Lake sometimes has nesting Common Mergansers but is
otherwise very similar to Cascade Lake. Over both of these lakes look for
Bald Eagles, Belted Kingfishers, Vaux's Swifts, and several species of swallows (AR).

The road steepens past Mountain Lake, winding through habitats rang-
ing from wet coniferous to open woodlands (WC, DC, OW). A great variety
of birds lives here, including accipiters, Band-tailed Pigeons, Great Horned
Owls, Hairy and Pileated Woodpeckers, Northern Flickers, Varied Thrushes,
Golden-crowned Kinglets, Red-breasted Nuthatches, Brown Creepers, Winter
Wrens, Yellow-rumped and Townsend's Warblers, Dark-eyed Juncos, Purple
Finches, Red Crossbills, and Pine Siskins. Eventually, open balds covered
with grasslands and meadows are encountered (DG) and around their sparsely treed borders Blue Grouse, American Kestrel, and Chipping Sparrow may
be found.

The road levels abruptly at the 2000-foot elevation, revealing a broad
plateaulike area covered with a patchwork of pine stands, hemlock woods,
and sedge fens (FW, DG, DC, WC). From here to the rocky knolls at the sum-

mit of Mt. Constitution you should be alert for alpine and subalpine bird life such as Hammond's Flycatcher, Horned Lark, Gray Jay, Clark's Nutcracker, Water Pipit, White-winged Crossbill, Pine Grosbeak, and Rosy Finch, all of which may ocur in this area from time to time. In general, you may find the plateau rather depauperate in bird life with the exceptions of Townsend's Warbler, Yellow-rumped Warbler, and Varied Thrush, all of which reach their greatest densities in the archipelago at this location. Ascend the stone tower at the peak of the mountain for breath-taking views of the Puget Trough and to scout for Turkey Vultures, raptors, Common Nighthawks, Black and Vaux's Swifts, Common Ravens, and swallows (AR). The trail from the stone tower to Little Summit passes through a forest of dwarf pines and thickets of manzanita (DC). This habitat brings many treetop species, such as the kinglets and wood warblers, to eye level. The manzanita patches along the trail are good places to flush nesting nighthawks. Stop at the top of the cliff to admire the aerial skills of swallows and ravens and listen for a variety of calls and songs drifting up from the forest below. The trail enters mature timber and leads past Summit Lake (FW), worth checking for birds and abundant Rough-skinned Newts.

After descending Mt. Constitution, you may want to turn left on the Horseshoe Highway to bird the areas of Olga and Obstruction Pass. The village of Olga has a dock with views of Buck Bay and its bird life (SW). Just before entering Olga the main road curves to the left (becoming Olga-Point Lawrence Road) and passes close by the beach (SS). These areas are both worth checking for marine species as is the boat launch located near the end of Obstruction Pass Road. To reach the boat ramp, bear right at the fork just beyond Buck Bay and follow the signs to Obstruction Pass. A better spot to observe Marbled Murrelets, Pigeon Guillemots, and other alcids is the Obstruction Point Campground maintained by the Department of Natural Resources. This site is tucked away down a small gravel lane that branches off to the west side of Obstruction Pass Road. Check the small marsh along the gravel lane for nesting rails. The observation point (RS, SW) is reached by hiking a half-mile down the trail from the parking area.

Return to the Horseshoe Highway and drive all the way around the island back to the ferry landing. On the way, take a look at the Mute Swans and other fresh-water birds at Fowler's Pond (FW), located on the west side of the highway just past the intersection with Crow Valley Road. If you have some time to spare before getting in line for the ferry, take a left turn on Dolphin Bay Road to travel through an area of mixed woodlots and farm land (DC, FL, ST). Check the small lake visible from the road, and a short way farther take a right on Killebrew Lake Road. This leads to a similar body of water, Killebrew Lake, with nesting Pied-billed Grebes, Mallards, Wood Ducks, Hooded Mergansers, Virginia Rails, Willow Flycatchers, Yellow Warblers, and other birds of fresh-water and riparian habitats (FW, RW). Ring-necked Ducks have been seen at Killebrew Lake during the breeding season. Continue west on Killebrew Lake Road and you will return to the Orcas ferry dock.

SAN JUAN ISLAND: The premier birding island in the archipelago, San Juan has the greatest variety of habitats and species and deserves more than a single day of birding. Begin the tour by carefully checking Friday Harbor from the town's many docks (SW, PG). Several rare birds have been recorded here among the more common marine inhabitants (see Ferry Route description). Perched on the docks or hunting near shore are Great Blue Herons, Bald Eagles, Rock Doves, Belted Kingfishers, American Crows, and (in winter) Sharp-shinned Hawks and Merlins. In yards and gardens you may encounter Common Barn-owls, Rufous Hummingbirds, Olive-sided and Western Flycatchers, Barn and Violet-green Swallows, Chestnut-backed Chickadees, American Robins, Orange-crowned and Wilson's Warblers, Rufous-sided Towhees, Song and White-crowned Sparrows, Dark-eyed Juncos, House Finches, Pine Siskins, House Sparrows, and many more.

Take Roche Harbor Road out of town and watch for dabbling ducks and Common Snipe in the flooded farmland on the left (FL). After passing Halvorsen Road, turn off onto the next gravel lane to the left and turn right in less than one hundred yards. Follow this to Three Meadows, the finest marsh for bird-watching on the island (FW). This privately owned wetland is open to birders; however, it is recommended that they seek permission to visit the marsh from the Three Meadows Association (see Appendix B). A nearly deafening roar emanates from the wetlands during the spring and summer breeding season—the chorus of countless frogs and birds. The nesting species here include Pied-billed Grebes, Canada Geese, Mallards, Cinnamon and Blue-winged Teals, Wood Ducks, Ring-necked Ducks, Hooded Mergansers, Soras, Virginia Rails, American Coots, Killdeers, Common Snipes, Marsh Wrens, Yellow Warblers, Common Yellowthroats, and Red-winged Blackbirds. Migrants and wintering birds are even more varied, with Greater White-fronted Geese, nearly every type of pond and bay duck, Northern Harriers, plovers, yellowlegs, sandpipers, all varieties of swallows, Mountain Bluebirds, and many more stopping by for a visit. Three Meadows is the Trumpeter Swan's favorite wintering location in the San Juans. The surrounding brush and woods are inhabited by nesting Red-tailed Hawks, Great Horned Owls, Western Screech-Owls, Northern Saw-whet Owls, Band-tailed Pigeons, Bushtits, vireos, and Western Tanagers, to name just a few (ST, DC, RW).

A short way up Roche Harbor Road is Sportsman Lake, utilized by many waterfowl, especially Common Mergansers. In spring, look for Barrow's Goldeneyes among the flocks of Common Goldeneyes. This lake's large size draws Double-crested Cormorants, many types of gulls, and Ospreys, while along the shore are found many of the same nesting species seen at Three Meadows. Huge flocks of migrating swallows feed on insects over the water's surface, and in summer wide-ranging Black Swifts are sometimes seen overhead (AR). Egg Lake, separated from the bigger lake by a narrow swamp, also has many of the species found at Three Meadows. It is reached by turning left off Roche Harbor Road onto Egg Lake Road. Excellent views of the surrounding marsh and riparian habitat are available from the roadway and public dock (FW, RW). Nesting birds around the lakeshore include Pileated Woodpeckers, Willow Flycatchers, Tree Swallows, Hutton's Vireos, Yellow Warblers, and Western Tanagers.

Return to Roche Harbor Road and make a series of right-hand turns onto Rouleau Road, Limestone Road, and San Juan Drive. A short distance down San Juan Drive is Reuben Tarte Picnic Area (on the left side) with access to a small beach and rocky point; often Pelagic Cormorants, Marbled Murrelets, Pigeon Guillemots, and other birds of open salt water are found here

SAN JUAN ISLAND AREA

(SW). Go back to Roche Harbor Road and follow it to its end; here there is a resort with a boat launch and marina. The protected waters of Mosquito Pass (SW) are used as a wintering area for large flocks of Pacific Loons and Western Grebes although they are often farther south down the channel and not visible from the docks in Roche Harbor. Large numbers of Bonaparte's Gulls and Common Terns may enter the harbor from the north during fall migration; and when they do, they are usually followed by Parasitic Jaegers. The formal gardens near the hotel (PG) are abuzz with Rufous Hummingbirds and should be a good spot, especially in winter, to find an Anna's Hummingbird.

Drive back down Roche Harbor Road to the intersection with West Valley Road and follow this to the British Camp section of San Juan Island National Historical Park (SW, WC, DC, OW, DG, ST, PG). This is a rich birding area throughout the year but it is particularly good during spring migration when all of the regularly occurring flycatchers, swallows, wrens, kinglets, thrushes, vireos, warblers, tanagers, sparrows, grosbeaks, and finches may be seen or heard. In winter, the surrounding bays are loaded with Greater Scaups, Buffleheads, Common Goldeneyes, Surf Scoters, Oldsquaws, and Red-breasted Mergansers. From the parking lot (a great place to listen to the sounds of woodland birds) hike down to the historical buildings and check the lawns and shrubs for appropriate species. Scan Garrison Bay from the dock and then walk out to Bell Point for an even better vista. The trail goes through a belt of Pacific Madrone and Rocky Mountain Junipers, which is attended by thrushes of several kinds. Look for wintering and migrating Varied and Hermit Thrushes. Townsend's Solitaires, and American Robins feeding on the edible berries. The glacial banks beneath the trail harbor nesting Belted Kingfishers and Northern Rough-winged Swallows. Also watch for Great Blue Herons, gulls, Ospreys, Bald Eagles, and American Crows along the shore.

Other trails through the park afford good chances of seeing tame Columbian Black-tailed Deer, European Rabbits, and Wild Turkeys, the latter often seen displaying right on the main road. The trail from the parking lot up to Mt. Young may yield sightings of accipiters, Band-tailed Pigeons, woodpeckers, Red-breasted Sapsuckers, Chestnut-backed Chickadees, Red-breasted Nuthatches, Brown Creepers, and Red Crossbills. From the balds and meadows at the top (the best place on the island to watch the setting sun) you may see many kinds of raptors, Turkey Vultures, and Common Nighthawks. At dawn, Wild Turkeys can be heard "gobbling" down below, and in the twilight hours the absorbing sight and sound of displaying Common Nighthawks may be witnessed at eye level.

If you can tear yourself away from British Camp, drive south on West Valley Road and scan the pond and farmland from the roadside for the usual species (FW, FL, RW). Wild Turkeys often roost in the trees in front of the ranch just past the pond. Across the road from the pond are nesting Willow Flycatchers, Cedar Waxwings, and Western Tanagers. Turn right at Mitchell Bay Road and follow that to its end at the Snug Harbor Resort. The protected waters of Mitchell Bay and the half-submerged rocks at the entrance are a good place to view wintering marine birds, especially grebes, cormorants, scoters, scaups, and Harlequin Ducks (SW, RS). Return to the pavement and drive south on West Side Road to San Juan County Park. Many woodland species may be seen here (DC, WC) and there are also views of Low Island

(NWR), often a nesting location for Black Oystercatchers (RS). Barn Swallows have nested in natural caves in Smallpox Bay, and Canada Geese have nested along the marine shoreline. Overhead you might see patrolling Bald Eagles and Belted Kingfishers. Farther south is a narrow pond that parallels the road (FW, RW), a good spot for Barrow's Goldeneyes in the spring, Hooded Mergansers and Wood Ducks in the summer, and Red-breasted Sapsuckers in the winter.

Continuing southward, the next location is Lime Kiln "Whale-watching" State Park (SW), an excellent place for spotting Harbor and Dall's Porpoises, Minke Whales, and Orcas. The birds are here, too, with Pacific and Common Loons, Red-necked Grebes, three kinds of cormorants, Bald Eagles, a plethora of gulls and terns, Ancient and Marbled Murrelets, Common Murres, Pigeon Guillemots, Rhinoceros Auklets, and possibly tubenoses seen from shore. The band of trees that extends from the park to Deadman Bay is an important wintering area for flocks of Varied and Hermit Thrushes, attracted to the fruit of the Pacific Madrone (OW). On the west side of Mt. Dallas you may see Sharp-shinned Hawks, Band-tailed Pigeons, and Pileated Woodpeckers. Flowing into the bay is a lively stream bordered by tall deciduous trees along the road and dense shrubs nearer the beach (RW, ST). Follow the road to some amazing vistas at the foot of Mt. Dallas and gaze uphill for possible Golden Eagles, falcons, Mourning Doves, Northern Flickers, Rock and House Wrens, Townsend's Solitaires, bluebirds, and Vesper, Chipping, and Savannah Sparrows (DG, OW). The shrub-lined fence rows harbor large numbers of California Quails, Bewick's Wrens, Rufous-sided Towhees, Fox, Song, Golden-crowned, and White-crowned Sparrows, Pine Siskins, and American Goldfinches (ST).

The birding continues to be fine along West Side Road until it passes Hannah Heights and becomes Bailer Hill Road. Turn left on Wold Road and head north past several small lakes and ponds used by a fair number of waterfowl, especially Hooded Mergansers, Ring-necked Ducks, Lesser Scaup, and nesting Pied-billed Grebes (FW). Turn right on San Juan Valley Road and begin watching for the abundant birds of prey found in this rich farmland (FL, AR). The valley extends from here to False Bay, and every species of accipiter, eagle, buteo, and falcon known in the San Juans may be observed soaring overhead, gliding between woodlots, or perched on fence posts in this extensive area. In the winter look over the ponds and flooded fields in the valley for swans and dabbling ducks. Ackley Pond and Marsh, located just east of the intersection of San Juan Valley Road and Douglas Road, is an excellent place for wetland species. Many kinds of sandpipers may be seen using the habitat here during migration, and several other species have nested here, including Mallards, Green-winged and Cinnamon Teals, Soras, and Common Yellowthroats (FL, FW). Bald Eagles and Red-tailed Hawks maintain a constant vigil over and around the marsh.

When finished with Ackley's Marsh, drive south down Douglas Road and follow it around a curve where it changes into Bailer Hill Road. Prime raptor territory begins here and sightings may begin with a Golden Eagle perched in the patch of tall firs on the south side of the road. The heart of San Juan Valley is shortly reached at the intersection with False Bay Road. Scan for all raptors, especially Northern Harriers, Rough-legged and Red-tailed Hawks, eagles, Merlins, and Northern Shrikes. At night the valley is haunted by Common Barn-Owls, Great Horned Owls, and Short-eared Owls. Vast flocks of American Crows, Common Ravens, European Starlings, Brewer's and Red-winged Blackbirds, and Brown-headed Cowbirds gather after the breeding season. This is also a good place to find large groups of Water Pipits, Savannah Sparrows, and Western Meadowlarks (FL). Drive down False Bay Road, watching for Northern Shrikes and other passerines along the fences and hedgerows (ST).

Once at False Bay, park at the wide spot and study the shallow waters and tide flats dotted with small rocks (SW, SS, RS). Try to arrive between the low and high water so the birds are not too widely scattered or gone from the area altogether. Don't despair if you arrive here and see nothing. Consult your tide table and return in a few hours or the next day. False Bay is the best shorebird habitat in the archipelago and nearly every species recorded in the San Juan Islands has been sighted here. Some of the more interesting ones include Lesser Golden-Plover, Semipalmated Plover, Black Oystercatcher, both yellowlegs and dowitchers, Whimbrel, Ruddy, and Black Turnstones, Sanderling, and Spotted, Semipalmated, Baird's, Least, Western, and Pectoral Sandpipers. Large flocks of wintering and migrating Black-bellied Plovers, Killdeers, and Dunlins forage on the exposed intertidal zone and in nearby flooded farm fields at high tide (FL). Many loons, grebes, Great Blue Herons, wigeons, scaups, Common Goldeneyes, Buffleheads, and mergansers are seen under normal weather conditions and, during freezing spells, they may be augmented by a variety of swans, geese, and dabbling ducks. False Bay is an excellent place to study and compare Bonaparte's, Mew, Ring-billed, California, Herring, Thayer's, Western, Glaucous-winged, and hybrid gulls in their various plumages. Common and Caspian Terns, Bald Eagles, falcons, and Belted Kingfishers add to the diversity. Rare, casual, and accidental species tend to gravitate to False Bay after arriving in the San Juans so you will really have your hands full on an active day here.

Continue on False Bay Road, and after turning east, check the shrubs, woods, and fields for small owls, Band-tailed Pigeons, Western Wood-Pewees, Bushtits, House Wrens, Northern Shrikes, various warblers and sparrows, Brewer's Blackbirds, and American Goldfinshes (DC, ST, FL). Just before coming to Cattle Point Road you will enter a stand of Red Alders and see a marshy pond on the left. This is Panorama Marsh, an excellent location for the typical fresh-water and riparian species (FW, RW). Pied-billed Grebes, rails, dabbling ducks, Tree Swallows, and Cedar Waxwings nest here. The area has been a source of some interesting records including Green-backed Heron, Trumpeter Swan, summering Ring-necked Duck, Sharp-tailed Sandpiper, Red-naped Sapsucker, and early and late migrant passerines. Turn right on Cattle Point Road and survey the farmland and thickets for many of the same birds found in San Juan Valley (FL, ST).

Take a right on Eagle Cove Road, stop at the parking lot for Eagle Cove Picnic Area, and walk down the wet ravine to the sandy beach. Along the trail look for Great Horned Owls, Rufous Hummingbirds, Downy Woodpeckers, and abundant nesting and migrating passerine species (RW). The beach may have a few Sanderlings and gulls to watch, and offshore there may be large rafts of Red-necked Grebes, scoters, and mergansers (SS, SW). Drive to the end of the road and walk to Eagle Point over rocky benchland inhabited by nesting Savannah and Vesper Sparrows (DG). You may also encounter

Northern Harriers, Short-eared Owls, Horned Larks, Eurasian Skylarks, Lapland Longspurs, or Snow Buntings. The point has superb vistas of the Strait of Juan de Fuca and you have a good chance of seeing everything possible at Lime Kiln State Park and more (SW). Look along the water's edge for Spotted Sandpipers, Wandering Tattlers, and other rock birds (RS).

Go back to Cattle Point Road and turn into the American Camp section of San Juan Island National Historical Park, taking an immediate right turn down a gravel lane to the headquarters. The belt of trees and shrubs along the road is a good place, especially in the fall, for migrating hummingbirds, woodpeckers, and all passerine species (DC, ST). This area is a good spot to seek uncommon migrants such as Red-breasted Sapsucker, Western Wood-Pewee, Hammond's Flycatcher, and MacGillivray's Warbler. Careful inventories may reveal vagrant kingbirds, unusual warblers, rare sparrows, and late and early records for the more common birds. The large south-sloping prairie between the redoubt and Pickett's Lane is a prime spot for nesting Eurasian Skylarks, Vesper Sparrows, and Savannah Sparrows (DG). Migrants and winter birds include Horned Larks, Water Pipits, Lapland Longspurs, Snow Buntings, and Western Meadowlarks. Also look for prowling Northern Harriers, Rough-legged and Red-tailed Hawks, Snowy and Short-eared Owls, Golden and Bald Eagles, American Kestrels, other falcons, and Northern Shrikes.

Down Pickett's Lane is South Beach, the longest sandy stretch in the islands; flocks of Sanderlings forage here (SS). Check the open salt water that spans from the parking area to Cattle Point and on out to the Salmon Bank buoy. In this zone occur some of the densest concentrations of foraging marine birds and mammals in the inland waters of Washington State (SW). Every seabird regularly found in the San Juan Islands may be recorded here, and rarities to watch for include Arctic Loons, Northern Fulmars, shearwaters, storm-petrels, Brown Pelicans, kittiwakes, Sabine's Gulls, Arctic Terns, Pomarine and Long-tailed Jaegers, Tufted Puffins, and Cassin's Auklets. The late summer to early winter concentrations are the largest and richest and offer the greatest chances of an unusual sighting. For more views of this extensive area, periodically stop at pull-outs along Cattle Point Road after turning right at the top of Pickett's Lane.

Another highly productive area is Cattle Pass, accessible from the Cattle Point Picnic Area and Cattle Point Lighthouse Reservation, both obvious from Cattle Point Road on the southeastern tip of the island. The fast and turbulent waters of Cattle Pass are often crowded with Pacific Loons, Red-necked Grebes, Brandt's Cormorants, sea ducks, Red-necked Phalaropes, Heermann's Gulls, Common Murres, and Rhinoceros Auklets. Again, nearly every marine bird and mammal known to inhabit the San Juan Archipelago may be encountered in these waters and rarities are to be expected (SW). Harlequin Ducks, Black Oystercatchers, Black Turnstones, and a variety of gulls perch or forage on the rocks below the lighthouse (RS). Goose Island, owned by The Nature Conservancy and visible from the picnic area, is a breeding site for Glaucous-winged Gulls, oystercatchers, and Harbor Seals. More seabird colonies are visible in the middle of the pass, including Whale Rocks with a huge flock of nonbreeding Brandt's Cormorants, Mummy Rocks (NWR), and Long Island (NWR). This entire area, especially the nesting colonies, is visited by numerous Bald Eagles. Check the nearby trees and shrubs for migrant passerines, especially the copse near the lighthouse (ST, RW). The air overhead is often full of swallows or swifts in migration (AR). The dunes around the lighthouse may yield larks, Savannah Sparrows, Lapland Longspurs, Snow Buntings, and American Goldfinches (DG).

Follow the pavement of Cattle Point Road to its end and look over Fish Creek and Griffin Bay for birds that prefer calmer waters than Cattle Pass (SW). A short trail leads west along the shore of Griffin Bay, passing some rocks good for Harlequin Ducks (RS), to Third Lagoon (SS). Great Blue Herons, Hooded Mergansers, Killdeers, Greater Yellowlegs, and Belted Kingfishers are seen here year-round. Access to First Lagoon and more views of Griffin Bay are found back along Cattle Point Road from a parking lot located just east of the intersection with Pickett's Lane. Scan the lagoon for shorebirds such as Wilson's Phalarope and dabbling ducks. Griffin Bay usually harbors a large assemblage of loons, grebes, cormorants, bay ducks, sea ducks, mergansers, and gulls. Particularly abundant here are Common Loons, Western and Horned Grebes, scaups, goldeneyes, scoters, Oldsquaws, and most alcids.

A trail from the parking lot leads into dense woods occupied by nesting accipiters, Red-tailed Hawks, Great Horned Owls, Pileated Woodpeckers, Winter Wrens, Red Crossbills, and other typical woodland birds (DC, WC). Jakle's Lagoon, very similar to Third Lagoon, and the shore of Griffin Bay are reached via this trail. River Otter families may be seen munching crabs along the beach. Harbor Seals forage within easy view and rest on the offshore rocks at low tide. The glacial banks are pocked with the nesting holes of Belted Kingfishers and Northern Rough-winged Swallows. The trail up from the parking lot, following the ridge of Mt. Finlayson, leads along an interesting ecotone or boundary between prairie and coniferous woods with possible Northern Saw-whet Owls, Northern Flickers, Common Ravens, House Wrens, Hermit Thrushes, and bluebirds (DG, DC). Many birds of prey soar in the updrafts here by day, and a night hike will reveal hunting owls perched in the wind-twisted trees and Common Nighthawks kiting overhead.

One other spot with a lagoon and views of Griffin Bay is located near Friday Harbor and is reached by driving north on Cattle Point Road and turning right on Pear Point Road. Before reaching the gravel pit you will see a lane descending to Jackson's Beach, the divider between Griffin Bay and Argyle Lagoon (SW, SS). The whole regime of marine birds may be seen in the bay, with Marbled Murrelets particularly numerous in winter. The lagoon affords good looks at many diving ducks, a few foraging shorebirds, and gulls and crows dropping clams on the roadway. Continuing around Pear Point Road you may see Golden Eagles perched above the excavations, and also the typical birds of shrubby thickets and woodlands (ST, DC). You can stop at the public boat launch at Turn Point to look at more gulls and shorebirds (SS), and there is often a Bald Eagle perched near its nest on Turn Island State Park, just offshore. The road eventually leads back to Friday Harbor and the ferry terminal.

BOATER'S GUIDE: Very few marine birds and mammals may be seen from a boat that are not visible from shore at one time or another. However, boat trips are the easiest and sometimes the only way to consistently locate a variety of our offshore species. Observing these creatures at sea allows for a fuller appreciation of their life histories and role in the ecosystem. Begin a marine field trip fully aware of the boating dangers that are present in the San

Juan Islands. Powerful currents, sometimes choppy or heavy seas, hull-splitting deadheads and rocks, fog banks and tricky weather, and a high level of commercial and noncommercial traffic may complicate a voyage through the archipelago. The maps and descriptions given in this book are no substitute for federal navigation charts, sea experience, and a sound vessel properly equipped with the necessary safety gear. Be aware that these are cold waters, even in summer, so be prepared to treat hypothermia. Winter trips are especially hazardous.

Some of the places mentioned in this boater's guide are also described in the sections discussing the main islands and the ferry routes. Refer to the appropriate passages in these when viewing such areas. (The index may be helpful in these instances.) Remember to operate your vessel in a manner that does not disturb wildlife, and respect the 200-yard buffer zone around National Wildlife Refuges.

A good place to start is Friday Harbor with its wonderful variety of marine birds and quick access to the intense activity of San Juan Channel. Cruise south down the channel on the alert for flocks of feeding seabirds that seek out the converging currents. Turn Island State Park usually has nesting Bald Eagles and Western Screech-Owls (DC), and hordes of Bonaparte's Gulls during the termite hatch in late summer (AR). The offshore rocks near the park sometimes have resting cormorants, Harlequin Ducks, gulls, Black Turnstones, Surfbirds, and Harbor Seals (RS). Take a look into Griffin Bay, especially during winter when this protected area offers a *relatively* wave-free environment to boaters and attracts vast rafts of seabirds composed of many species. Go through Cattle Pass and survey the Salmon Bank and beaches of American Camp, areas that can all be virtual circuses of bird life (SW). Keep alert for rarities here, especially after foggy weather and storms.

Cattle Pass marks the beginning of a series of small islands (RS) used by breeding seabirds extending all the way to the southeast end of Lopez Island. Easily recognized by large smears of guano and strong odors, these rocks and islets are nearly all owned by The Nature Conservancy or by the federal government as part of the San Juan Islands NWR. Collectively, they account for much of the nesting seabird activity in the inland marine waters of Washington State, and breeding species include Double-crested and Pelagic Cormorants, Black Oystercatchers, Pigeon Guillemots, Glaucous-winged Gulls, River Otters, and Harbor Seals. They are also good places to locate Bald Eagles, Surfbirds, Black Turnstones, Rock Sandpipers, Wandering Tattlers, Brandt's Cormorants. Heermann's Gulls, Western (and hybrid) Gulls, Harlequin Ducks, and sea lions. Worth observing from a respectful distance are Whale Rocks, known for their flock of Brandt's Cormorants that often numbers up to 2000 birds, Mummy Rocks, Long Island, Hall Island, Secar Rock, Swirl Island, and Castle Rock. Colville Island, the jewel of this bunch, has one of the largest Glaucous-winged Gull colonies in Washington and is the only place where Tufted Puffins are known to nest in the San Juan Islands. Use your binoculars to look for puffin burrows in the exposed soil under bushes or grass tufts. Foraging Tufted Puffins are most often sighted near Iceberg Point but may be encountered anywhere from the Salmon Bank and Cattle Pass east to Rosario Strait (SW). They rarely venture west to Lime Kiln State Park and north to Friday Harbor and Anacortes.

Colville Island (NWR) offers a chance to study all three of the archipelago's cormorants and the ways they interact to prevent interspecific competition. On top of the island sit the densely clumped cylindrical stick nests of Double-crested Cormorants. Well below, perched on narrow ledges along the cliffy sides of the island, are Pelagic Cormorant nests made of seaweed and excrement. Brandt's Cormorants, nonbreeders in the archipelago, roost along the clifftops, furthering the cause of peaceful coexistence. A similar community awaits several miles up Rosario Strait at Bird Rocks (NWR), the only other place in San Juan County where Double-crested Cormorants have recently nested. With the exception of Tufted Puffins, you may see all of the same species here as are found at Colville Island (NWR), but in lesser numbers. Across the strait and the county border lies Williamson Rocks (NWR) with the same avian cast as Bird Rocks.

Cruising north up Rosario Strait you will pass by James Island. Watch for a powerful tiderip near the eastern tip of the island; it attracts large numbers of Bonaparte's Gulls, Heermann's Gulls, Common Terns, Parasitic Jaegers, Red-necked Phalaropes, and many more species (SW). Another fine birding area is Pelican Beach on the north tip of Cypress Island, farther up the strait. Numerous Marbled Murrelets are seen fishing only a few feet from shore in the powerful currents (SW), and if you beach your craft, be sure to take the trail to Eagle Cliff. Many forest species will be spotted along this path, such as nesting Sharp-shinned Hawks, Varied Thrushes, and Purple Finches (WC). At the top of the cliff are fine vistas and possibilities of Bald Eagles, Black Swifts (AR), Rock Wrens, and Vesper Sparrows (DG). Obstruction Pass, on the west side of the strait, is known for large numbers of Marbled Murrelets, and the Peapod Rocks (NWR) is encountered farther north. Always search large flocks of seabirds in Rosario Strait for noteworthy pelagic species.

North of Orcas there is a chain of sculptured sandstone islands well worth visiting for the scenery alone. This group includes The Sisters (NWR), Clark Island State Park, Puffin Island (NWR), Matia Island (NWR) and State Park, Sucia Island State Park, and Patos Island State Park. The birds and wildlife found at these islands, although slightly less concentrated, are nearly identical to those found south of Lopez. The larger ones have enough trees to provide habitat for Great-horned Owls, Pileated Woodpeckers, Townsend's Solitaires, Townsend's Warblers, Western Flycatchers, and other woodland denizens (OW, DC). Bald Eagles and Turkey Vultures may be seen circling above or resting on snags along cliffs. Pigeon Guillemots and Belted Kingfishers nest abundantly due to the plentiful fissures in the stone and are preyed upon by Peregrine Falcons (RS). Sea lions haul out in large numbers during the winter months on Patos and Sucia Islands.

Next comes Bare Island (NWR) and Skipjack Island (NWR), both with nesting Pelagic Cormorants. Black Oystercatchers, Glaucous-winged Gulls, and Pigeon Guillemots. Waldron Island's Cowlitz Bay is a shallow eel grass habitat utilized from fall through spring by numerous rafting seabirds (SW). Flocks of Brants drop in here to feed and Yellow-billed Loons have been sighted among the more common species. In the summer months, Cowlitz Bay is notable for nonbreeding loons, grebes, scoters, and Harlequin Ducks, with the sea ducks occurring in large flocks. Sandy Point is often crowded with roosting gulls (SS). Just south of the bay is White Rock (NWR), with the same nesting species as Bare and Skipjack islands. Of prime interest here are the large flocks of Surfbirds, Black Turnstones, and other rock birds (RS). White Rock (NWR) is in the heart of an important Minke Whale foraging area.

Another group of NWR sites, composed of Flattop Island, Gull Rock, Cactus Islands, Ripple Island, and Gull Reef, has well-attended Harbor Seals haul-outs, nesting sites for Black Oystercatchers, and roosts for summering flocks of Harlequin Ducks that have exceeded 100 individuals (RS). The waters surrounding these NWR sites are a good place to observe foraging Harbor Porpoise. Nearby Spieden Island has many Bald Eagles, a large Pigeon Guillemot colony on the north side, nesting American Kestrels, Belted Kingfishers, and Common Ravens. You may think that you've made a major navigational error when you see European Fallow Deer, Japanese Sika Deer, Indian Axis Deer, Indian Blackbuck Antelopes, wild goats, Corsican Mouflon Sheep, or Barbary Sheep on Spieden Island, but these are remnant herds from the days when it was a fee-hunting resort. Of the many game birds introduced here, only Wild Turkeys are still regularly seen.

Spieden Channel is an active wildlife area with extremely strong currents. Minke Whales forage here, as do flocks of Bonaparte's Gulls and Common Terns with their tag-along jaegers (SW). Many sightings of the rare Northern Elephant Seal have come from this area. Sentinel Rock (NWR) and Sentinel Island, owned by The Nature Conservancy, are used by nesting Bald Eagles and a large herd of Harbor Seals. South and west of here, across the fast-flowing waters of the channel, lie Battleship Island (NWR), Barren Island (NWR), and Posey Island State Park. These locations have Harlequin Ducks, breeding Black Oystercatchers, overflying Parasitic Jaegers, and, in summer, numerous Marbled Murrelets (RS, SW). Weather permitting, go through Mosquito Pass in the winter to see large flocks of Pacific Loons, Western Grebes, scoters, Oldsquaws, and other diving species (SW).

Haro Strait and the west sides of San Juan and Henry islands are favorite feeding and traveling areas for pods of Orcas, Dall's Porpoises, and solitary Minke Whales. Bird activity increases in Haro Strait near Turn Point State Park on Stuart Island where a large tiderip occurs, also good for foraging Northern Sea Lions, Dall's Porpoises, and Minke Whales. The cliff at the point is home to a large colony of Pigeon Guillemots that are sometimes attacked by stooping Peregrine Falcons (RS). There is another big breeding location for Pigeon Guillemots on a south-facing cliff near the west end of Stuart Island. Approached from two different bays on opposite sides of Stuart Island are the adjoining Reid Harbor and Prevost Harbor state parks. The riparian and dry coniferous woodlands here support Great Horned and Western Screech-Owls, Western Flycatchers, Black-headed Grosbeaks, and the usual spectrum of San Juan forest birds. Grassy balds on the south slopes of the island are home to nesting Blue Grouse and Common Nighthawks (DG, OW). The shores of Stuart Island are inhabited by many River Otters and Mink (RS).

Point your bow east and cruise to the northern end of San Juan Channel where another marine state park, Jones Island, is situated. The park is a fair spot for locating birds of wet and dry coniferous forests (WC, DC) and is the home of a small herd of Columbian Black-tailed Deer. Several partially or completely albino individuals have resided here and all the deer are tame enough to be hand fed. Note the small physical stature of the local populations of deer in the San Juans.

Yellow Island is a short distance south of here and is famous for its spring wildflower displays (DG). Although it is owned by The Nature Conser-

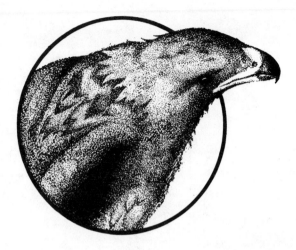

Golden Eagle

vancy, this is one preserve that people are allowed to visit in small numbers if they observe the rules posted on the island. The reef to the west of the island sometimes has Black Turnstones, Surfbirds, and Black Oystercatchers, the latter species nesting on nearby Low Island (NWR). Friday Harbor is only a short distance south from here if you wish to make a loop trip of your boating tour.

FIDALGO ISLAND: Although not part of the San Juan Islands proper, Fidalgo Island lies on the eastern edge of the archipelago and offers excellent birding possibilities for those who don't have the time to take a ferry to Lopez, Shaw, Orcas, or San Juan. The ferry terminal, located on the northwest end of Fidalgo Island, is the starting point of this birding excursion. Leave the ferry parking area and take the first right turn onto Sunset Avenue. In about one mile you will enter Washington Park, a rocky headland laced with recreational trails and roads. There are numerous opportunities to scan the open salt water for marine birds and the rocky shoreline is an excellent place to view Black Oystercatchers and Harlequin Ducks (SW, RS). The dry coniferous forest contains most of the species typical of this habitat in the San Juan Islands (DC). Of considerable interest are the open woodlands of Pacific Madrone, Douglas-fir, and Rocky Mountain Juniper found growing on the steep, south-facing bluffs (OW). A wide variety of birds may be seen here, including House Wrens and Townsend's Solitaires.

The next stop on this tour is Deception Pass State Park. Drive back toward the ferry terminal on Sunset Avenue and turn right onto Anaco Beach Road/Marine Highway, located about 100 feet before the turn-off to the ferry toll booths. Follow this road for several miles to a stop sign and turn right on Havekost Road/Rosario Road. In another few miles you will see signs for

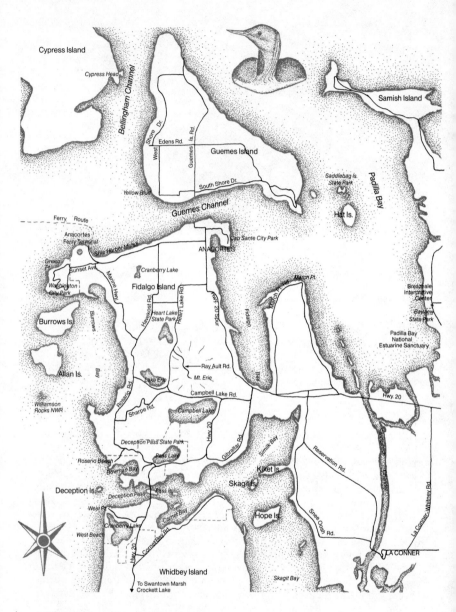

Cypress Island

Cypress Head

Bellingham Channel

Samish Island

Shore Dr.

West

Edens Rd.

Guemes Is. Rd.

Guemes Island

South Shore Dr.

Yellow Bluff

Saddlebag Is. State Park

Padilla Bay

Guemes Channel

Hat Is.

Ferry   Route

Anacortes Ferry Terminal

Ship Harbor Marsh

Cap Sante City Park

ANACORTES

Green Pt.

Sunset Ave.

Cranberry Lake

Washington City Park

Marine Hwy.

Fidalgo Island

Breazeale Interpretive Center

March Pt.

Bayview State Park

Burrows Rd.

Heart Lake Rd.

Havekost Rd.

Heart Lake State Park

Hwy. 20 Spur

Fidalgo

March Head

Padilla Bay National Estuarine Sanctuary

Burrows Is.

Rosario Rd.

Burrows   Bay

Lake Erie

Ray Ault Rd.

Mt. Erie

Allan Is.

Campbell Lake Rd.

Hwy. 20

Williamson Rocks NWR

Sharpe Rd.

Campbell Lake

Hwy. 20

Deception Pass State Park

Gibraltar Rd.

Similk Bay

Reservation Rd.

Rosario Beach

Bowman Bay

Pass Lake

Kiket Is.

Deception Is.

Deception Pass

Pass Is.

Skagit Is.

Snee Oosh Rd.

West Pt.

Cornet Bay

Hope Is.

La Conner–Whitney Rd.

Cranberry Lake

West Beach

Hwy. 20

Cornet Bay Rd.

LA CONNER

Whidbey Island

To Swantown Marsh
Crockett Lake

Skagit Bay

FIDALGO ISLAND AREA

Rosario Beach and Bowman Bay, both with a wide diversity of birding habitats (SW, RS, DC, WC). South of here lies Deception Pass, spanned by a high bridge that is part of Washington Highway 20. The small island in the middle of the pass offers exciting views of churning tidal races, Pigeon Guillemots, cormorants, Bald Eagles, and other marine birds (SW).

Continue south on the bridge to Whidbey Island and take the first right turn. This will lead you past Cranberry Lake (FW) to West Beach and Point (SW, RS, SS). The point is an excellent place to study loons, grebes, cormorants, scoters, Harlequin Ducks, mergansers, gulls, and alcids. The old-growth timber in this section of the state park is impressive and should be a rewarding area for locating owls, Vaux's Swifts, Pileated Woodpeckers, Olive-sided Flycatchers, and other forest species (WC). A bit farther south on the highway, on the left side, is Coronet Bay Road. Following this will take you to a small bay with views of protected salt water and mud flats, visited by foraging grebes, Great Blue Herons, sandpipers, ducks, Ospreys, and kingfishers (SW, SS).

If you happen to be leaving the San Juan Archipelago by driving south down Whidbey Island on Washington Highway 20, be sure to stop at Swantown Marsh, located just south of the naval air station and Crockett Lake, adjacent to the Keystone ferry terminal, for some interesting birding. If you wish to continue your tour of Fidalgo Island, turn north on the highway, recross the bridge, and drive several miles to Lake Campbell Road. This road winds through scenic farmland and past Lake Campbell (FL, ST, FW), which can best be scanned for birds from the public access site. The road splits about a mile and a half from Highway 20, with the right fork becoming Heart Lake Road. Very quickly you will see Lake Erie to the left, often occupied by large numbers of waterfowl such as ducks and coots (FW). The next body of water visible from this road is Heart Lake, perhaps the best location for fresh-water species on Fidalgo Island. Wood Ducks, Hooded Mergansers, and Ospreys nest around the edges of the lake, while scaups, Ring-necked Ducks, Redheads, Buffleheads, and other waterfowl cover the lake's surface in the winter. Ruffed Grouse, a species absent from the San Juan Islands proper, breed in the woods surrounding Heart Lake. Return about a half-mile south on Heart Lake Road and go left on Ray Auld Drive. This winds to the summit of Mt. Erie, a 1300-foot-high promontory with breathtaking views of the islands, lakes, and waterways below. Ravens, Turkey Vultures, Red-tailed Hawks, and Bald Eagles may be watched at eye level as they ride the thermal updrafts. Many common species typical of coniferous forests live on Mt. Erie, and mountain vagrants, such as Rosy Finches, may drop in for a rare visit.

Retrace the route back to Highway 20 and travel north to the large intersection at the head of Fidalgo Bay and turn right. In less than a mile turn left onto March Point Road and follow it along the eastern shore of the bay toward the oil refinery (SW, SS). The shallow marine waters and extensive mud flats are used by rafts of Common and Red-throated Loons, Western, Red-necked, and Horned Grebes, every imaginable species of waterfowl, including Ruddy Duck, and a plethora of shorebirds. Flocks of Dunlin and Western Sandpiper may number in the thousands at certain times of year, and, along with the abundant ducks, attract Merlins and Peregrines. The sloping pastures to the right are home to wintering Common Snipes, Snowy Owls, Rough-legged Hawks, and occasional flocks of Snow Buntings (FL). Dozens of Great Blue Herons hunt voles and roost in the open fields. Scattered thickets shelter numerous wrens, Bushtits, sparrows, and other passerine species (ST). Thayer's Gulls are particularly numerous around the refinery storage tanks and these flocks should always be checked for rarities. From the north tip of the point you can see Padilla Bay and one of the largest wintering concentrations of Brant on the Pacific Coast (SW). Heading south on the east side of March Point you will eventually have to cross some railroad tracks. The shoreline and lagoon here are sometimes rich with bird life and the flocks of American Wigeon may harbor Eurasian Wigeon. Turn left past the tracks and you will meet Highway 20, with options to turn left toward Interstate 5 or right to follow the signs to Anacortes and the ferry terminal.

If you travel east (left) toward the interstate, look for signs indicating Bayview State Park and the Breazeale Interpretive Center located a few miles to the north on the east shore of Padilla Bay (a National Estuarine Area). The interpretive center houses many excellent exhibits and a well-stocked natural history library. The center also sponsors numerous field trips in the area and hosts a variety of educational programs, films, and lectures. The Padilla Bay shoreline and the farmland from the Skagit River Delta to the Samish River Delta is perhaps the best location in the contiguous United States to find large falcons, such as Peregrines and Gyrfalcons (FL). Virtually every raptor known to occur in Washington may be observed in this rich agricultural region, especially during migration and winter. As you drive through the area, be sure to check all suspicious-looking lumps in the flat fields with your binoculars. The dark lumps may turn out to be ground-perching falcons and the light ones Snowy Owls. Sometimes three or four Snowy Owls may be visible in a single glance during "invasion" years.

Species Accounts

Sharp-shinned Hawk

The arrangement and names used to describe birds in this book follow those established in the sixth edition of the American Ornithologists' Union's *Check-list of North American Birds*, published in 1983, and its supplements. The sequence of the descriptions roughly follows what is thought to be their evolutionary path, beginning with older more "primitive" birds and ending with the newly evolved "advanced" species. Each bird is listed by both its common name and a scientific binomial, the latter being universally accepted. This "Latin" name is used by scientists and international birders to prevent confusion that may arise when a bird is known by several titles in different languages.

All birds are members of the **class** Aves, a zoological division that separates them from mammals, reptiles, and other creatures with backbones. The class Aves is then divided into **orders**, broad categories used to lump birds that share the same basic structural patterns of skeleton and other anatomical parts that became established early in bird evolution. The names of orders always end with the suffix "iformes" and are therefore easily recognized. Subdividing an order leads us to the next link in the taxonomic chain, **family**, a grouping that uniformly ends with the suffix "idae." External details, such as bill shape, feather arrangement, and feet are used to determine what family a bird belongs to, making this a very useful classification for the average birder. For instance, gulls (Laridae), woodpeckers (Picadae), and hummingbirds (Trochilidae) are all readily distinguishable families of birds and may be recognized at a glance.

A **genus** is a group of birds that evolved from one common ancestor, and this is the first word listed in every scientific binomial. The second word in a Latin name refers to the **species**. A species is a population of individuals that are similar enough to one another to interbreed naturally. Individuals that are too different to successfully interbreed are separated into different species. Refer to the pages describing gulls to learn about some exceptions to this biological rule.

Example: Sharp-shinned Hawk (Accipiter striatus)

Class: Aves (birds)
  Order: Falconiformes (diurnal birds of prey)
    Family: Accipitridae (broad-winged hawks)
      Genus: *Accipiter* (long-tailed with short, rounded wings and sprinting flight)
        Species: *striatus* (smallest of genus with square-tipped tail)

The terminology used to describe the status of birds is as follows:

resident: a species present throughout the year
migrant: a species making a seasonal transit between wintering and breeding ranges
breeder: a species known to breed
visitant: a species not known to breed; also a species not directly en route between breeding and wintering ranges
local: species occurs in selected sites of specialized habitat only
abundant: species occurs repeatedly in proper habitats, with available habitat heavily utilized, and/or the region regularly hosts great numbers of the species
common: species occurs in all or nearly all proper habitats, but some areas of presumed suitable habitat are occupied sparsely or not at all and/or the region regularly hosts large numbers of the species
fairly common: species occurs in only some of the proper habitat, and large areas of presumed suitable habitat are occupied sparsely or not at all, and/or the region regularly hosts substantial numbers of the species
uncommon: species occurs regularly but may easily go unobserved; utilizes little of the suitable habitat, and/or the region regularly hosts relatively small numbers of the species
rare: species within its normal range, occurring regularly but in very small numbers. "Very" rare is used for a species which occurs more or less regularly, but not every year, and usually in very small numbers
casual: a species beyond its normal range, occurring irregularly and infrequently; usually occurs singly or in very small numbers
accidental: a species so far from its normal range that further observations are unlikely; usually occurs singly
irregular: species shows marked fluctuations in seasonal abundance from year to year; also referred to as "sporadic" and "irruptive."

Footnoted information concerning rare bird and historical records may be found in Appendix C.

LOONS
(Gaviiformes/Gaviidae)

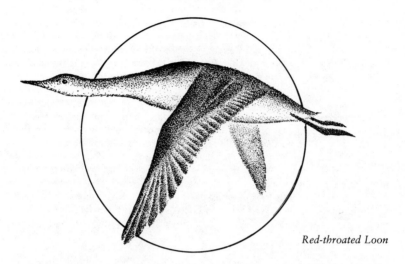

Red-throated Loon

These are living "dinosaurs" of the bird world. Fossils of our modern loons have been found from the last Ice Age. They are members of a very primitive order of diving birds, the Gaviiformes, which evolved perhaps 50 million years ago. Only one family remains in existence from this ancient order, and its members are our present day loons, the Gaviidae. This family has only five living species remaining, and at least four occur regularly within the San Juan Islands. The archipelago is a very important area for wintering and migrating loons; some of the highest concentrations of these birds in North America are found here. From fall through spring loons can be seen frequenting our waters, as these aquatic birds spend about three-quarters of each year in a marine environment. Even during the summer months, when they are normally found nesting on northern lakes, non-breeding individuals and early or late migrants are occasionally found among the San Juans.

The sexes are identically plumaged and the immature birds look very similar to drab winter adults. Loons molt twice a year, each species attaining distinctively different breeding plumages during the spring before departing northward. After breeding, adults molt into a dull winter plumage, and for a brief period all loons become flightless as they regrow their wing feathers. Swift and strong in the air, loons require a long take-off run and often patter 100 yards before they become airborne. When landing, these heavy-bodies birds ski across the water on their breasts for quite a distance. During migration they are often seen flying among the islands with their big feet and heads dangling lending them a hunch-backed appearance. However, overwintering birds may not take flight at all if they can avoid it, preferring to remain in the element they know best.

Beautifully adapted to the water, these virtually tailless birds have their webbed feet placed far back on their bodies, making them nearly useless for walking but very efficient for swimming. When in search of prey, loons start each deep dive with a powerful forward lunge. Equally as streamlined, and even faster than the small bait fishes they feed upon, loons seize food with their daggerlike bills up to 200 feet below the surface. This ability has earned them the name "helldiver" with many local old-timers. In many parts of the world they are referred to simply as "divers." Their awkwardness on land inspired North Americans to call them loons, the appellation being a derivative of an old Scandinavian word meaning lame or clumsy. Regardless of what they are called, the loon's weird and haunting cries are symbolic of everything wild.

Red-throated Loon (*Gavia stellata*). By far the smallest and most slender of the loons, this species can leap directly from the water into flight if necessary. Red-throated Loons are fairly common and seen singly or in small numbers throughout the San Juan Islands. Occasionally concentrations of several dozen birds will gather in favored embayments, and the shallow, protected shores of Lopez and West Sound frequently harbor these interesting flocks. They are often observed foraging only a few feet from shore, even at downtown Friday Harbor's waterfront. Nevertheless, this loon is easily overlooked and is outnumbered by Pacific Loons a hundred to one. Red-throated Loons are present as migrants and winter visitors in our area from late September through early May, and there are very rare summer strays.

Pacific Loon (*Gavia pacifica*). For those hardy persons who venture out onto the leaden winter waters or stroll the deserted shorelines during this unpopular season, flocks of Pacific Loons are a familiar sight. During storms or strong winds,

A Pacific Loon negotiates the strong tidal current of Cattle Pass.

Loons in breeding plumage; clockwise from upper left, Yellow-billed Loon, Red-throated Loon, Common Loon and Pacific Loon

these sleek birds may be seen taking shelter in many of the protected bays, harbors, and passes formed by the San Juan Islands. The flocks always seem to know which side of a land mass is the safest for riding out the coming heavy weather. Depending on the direction of the wind, dense flocks numbering several hundred birds may be seen in favored areas like Griffin Bay, Mosquito Pass, or among the islets south of Lopez. Calmer weather lures them into more exposed locations, and they prefer areas where they can cavort among tiderips, which are a common marine phenomenon among these islands. The Pacific Loon is a specialist in exploiting the feeding opportunities of these temporary but recurring events. Spieden Channel, Cattle Pass, and Rosario Strait are all notable for the numbers of Pacific Loons attracted to the powerful currents converging in these areas. Of all locations in North American, the San Juan Archipelago, including the Gulf Islands, boasts the largest wintering population of this loon.

Starting in late August, southbound individuals or small flocks of Pacific Loons may be seen in the San Juan Islands as fall migration begins. By the last week of September, greater numbers of these birds are passing through the archipelago, continuing southward to winter off the Oregon and California coasts or as far away as the Sea of Cortez in Mexico. The largest flocks aren't seen until mid-October and most of these will remain here throughout the winter months. These new arrivals are still adorned in gleaming metallic plumage, but by early November most have molted into somber winter grays. Beginning in late March, a few Pacific Loons can again be seen displaying their breeding finery. However, the spring molt is more drawn out than the October change of dress and many remain throughout April and into May wearing winter plumage.

As the weather warms during April, and the birds grow new feathers, a careful observer may notice the Pacific Loon flocks dwindling in numbers. At the same time, groups of these divers begin to appear in the major straits, especially along the south shores of San Juan and Lopez islands. These newcomers are birds that spent the cold months farther south and are now resting and feeding before continuing their long journey to the interior lakes of Alaska and northern Canada. Flocks of northbound migrants can be seen at these important staging areas until the summer solstice, although a decline in their numbers is noted before this. For most islanders, these will be the last loons they see until the next fall.

In case you are wondering why you can't find the Pacific Loon in your field guides, it's becuase this is a "new" loon. Ornithologists have long debated over its full status as a species distinct from the **Arctic Loon** (*Gavia arctica*), a primarily Siberian bird. The Arctic Loon is slightly larger than the Pacific Loon and has a greenish instead of a purple throat sheen, a darker gray nape, and a longer bill and wings. Most Arctic Loons winter in Asia and their status along the Pacific coast of North America is unclear. A few green-throated individuals were sighted at Cattle Point, San Juan Island, in mid-May, 1986, near a large flock of purple-throated Pacific Loons. Unfortunately, these green-throated birds could not be conclusively identified as Arctic Loons. Unless a specimen is examined in the hand, it may not be possible to distinguish between these two look-alike species.

Common Loon (*Gavia immer*). Goose-sized and bearing a black dagger bill, the Common Loon is unmistakable on our San Juan waters. It is a common winter visitor and migrant to nearly all bodies of salt water and is seen more often than the other members of its family due to its even distribution in our area. Rarely it is seen in fresh-water habitats, usually in late summer, when newly arrived from its present breeding range. Formerly that range included the San Juan Islands and nesting was thought to occur in the archipelago at least until 1948.[1] Unfortunately, this bird is extremely sensitive to human disturbance near its nest and no longer breeds in most parts of Washington. Listen for tremolo calls when it appears in late July and August, still clad in elegant breeding plumage. For a short time the birds can be coaxed, with a variety of imitations, into making this laughing noise. As autumn progresses, they fall silent and remain so throughout the long winter. Nearly all Common Loons depart our waters in the months of April and May, freshly molted into their crisp summer colors. However, like the Pacific Loon, rare nonbreeders may be seen all summer.

Yellow-billed Loon (*Gavia adamsii*). The largest loon in the San Juan Islands, this primarily Eurasian bird presents another problem in identification. Other than the decidedly yellowish color of the upturned bill and this loon's huge size, apparent in all plumages, look for its brown color and a dark ear patch highlighted by its pale face and neck when in winter colors. Yellow-billed Loons are usually not seen this far south in breeding plumage since the majority of sightings occur from November through March. In extreme cases, this most northerly of all loons could appear in mid-September or linger until mid-May; very rare summer sightings are usually nonbreeding immatures.[2] The San Juan Islands are situated in the middle of what may be one of the most important wintering areas south of Alaska for this species that seeks shallow, protected water.

GREBES
(Podicipediformes/Podicipedidae)

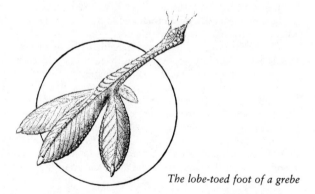

The lobe-toed foot of a grebe

Paralleling each other in evolution, loons and grebes bear a strong superficial resemblance. Like the loons, male and female grebes are usually indistinguishable even when adorned with their showy breeding plumage during the spring and summer. Behavioral clues can be used to tell them apart as they perform elaborate courtship "dances" and other distinctive breeding activities. Also in affinity with the loons, grebes have their legs placed far to the rear of a nearly tailless body, making them superb swimmers. They, too, have great difficulty getting airborne and will spend the entire winter or summer in one small area, never taking flight if they can possibly avoid it. Loons and grebes both prefer to escape danger by diving beneath the water's surface, and in this way they can elude just about any enemy. These two families naturally occupy a similar niche in the ecosystem, with most grebe species spending fall through spring on marine waters and breeding on inland fresh-water lakes and marshes.

Despite this apparent closeness, dissimilarities between the two families are many; thus the grebes, having no known living relatives, are placed in a separate order, Podicipediformes. The grebe family has evolved lobed toes with only partial webbing, unlike the loons and quite different from most other waterbirds, enabling them to propel themselves through the water with great vigor. These unusual feet are frequently displayed by the bird while it preens, partially rolled over in the water, or when characteristically stretching a long leg over its back and waving a big foot in the air. Another grebe trait is the habit of keeping the long, thin wings tucked beneath the body plumage, making them barely visible when not in use. Weak fliers, grebes must flap frantically to remain aloft, and one wonders how they can manage such long migrations. Indeed, one species of grebe in Central American has lost the ability to fly and spends its entire life on the lake of its birth. Also, the grebes' diets are not restricted to fish, and many specialize in catching insects or crustaceans.

The domestic habits of grebes are also unique. On a quiet body of water, the adult pair constructs a nest of decaying vegetation. Often built without any anchoring, this floating platform supports several chalky eggs that can, if necessary, survive total immersion during rising water levels. At first the boldly striped young ride about on the parents' backs, but they are soon able to swim on their own. Starting at an early age, the downy chicks are fed quantities of finely textured body feathers by the adults, an unusual and mysterious behavior. This dietary anomaly will persist throughout the grebe's life.

Grebes are represented in the San Juan Islands by six species, one of which breeds here. Used as a stopover point for migrants and a winter home for the rest, the islands are a haven for this family. Significant concentrations occur from fall through spring on our protected marine waters, making grebes some of our most noticeable visitors. Even during the summer it is possible to see an occasional non-breeding individual remaining among the islands.

Most of our grebes migrate here from the north and east, rising over high mountain passes to gain access to our waters. Surprisingly, you won't see these large flocks actually migrating unless you look for them under the light of the moon. One fall day you will wake up, glance out on the water, and see that the winter contingent has suddenly arrived. Just as quickly, these birds will steal away on a spring night, leaving the bay empty. Without grebes, our winter waters would indeed seem deserted.

Pied-billed Grebe (*Podilymbus podiceps*). Like a little feathered submarine, this bird has the ability to sink beneath the water's surface without a ripple. Compressing its feathers to force out air and reduce bouyancy, the Pied-billed Grebe sometimes swims with only its periscopelike head in sight. The "Dabchick" is found on quiet ponds and lakes, where it is an elusive but common breeding resident of the

The three common species of grebes in the San Juans are distinguished by their size and wing pattern; from right to left, Red-necked, Western, and Horned.

San Juan Islands. It is hard to comprehend the number of eerie, quavering calls that this shy bird is responsible for. Especially on a spring dawn, one can hear these sounds reverberating loudly over Killebrew Lake, Frank Richardson Wild-fowl Sanctuary (Deer Harbor Marsh), Three Meadows Marsh, and other favorite nesting areas. The Pied-billed Grebe is sometimes seen on salt water—this can happen during migration or when its usual haunts have temporarily frozen during a cold spell.

Horned Grebe (*Podiceps auritus*). Sprinkled across our shallow, protected bays, the Horned Grebe forms the matrix of our wintering flocks of marine birds. Locally, they can be quite abundant and number in the low hundreds at choice locations such as Griffin Bay. The most numerous grebe in the San Juan Islands, it appears in late August and September and departs from April through late May. The small size, clear white cheek and neck, and single white wing patch visible in flight separate the Horned Grebe from its neighboring cousins.

Red-necked Grebe (*Podiceps grisegena*). Though slightly less abundant than the Horned Grebe, this bird is found in a wider variety of salt-water habitats. You can see the Red-necked Grebe from the ferry in open channels or from shore in protected harbors. From August through May its stuttering "keeaark" quavers over the water. This common grebe is readily identified in flight by two white patches fore and aft on each wing. Ruddy spring migrants stage in flocks of up to 200 birds along the southern shores of San Juan and Lopez islands, gathering to rest and feed before pushing on to their distant breeding grounds.

Eared Grebe (*Podiceps nigricollis*). The distribution of this smallest grebe in Puget Sound is spotty and localized. The San Juan Islands are one area it has largely forsaken despite the apparent availability of suitable habitat. The low numbers recorded here may be due in part to confusion with the similar Horned Grebe. Look for the Eared Grebe's peaked crown, dusky ear patch, and thin, dark neck from mid-August through early May, when it is here as an uncommon migrant and rare winter visitor.

Western Grebe (*Aechmophorus occidentalis*). The elegant, snowy-white plumage of this bird was nearly its demise. The skin, or pelt, of the Western Grebe's breast was used for decorating women's hats and making ear muffs and hand warmers.

The Western Grebe is distinguished from the very rare Clark's Grebe by the dark feathers surrounding its eye, and by its bill, which is greenish-yellow.

Grebe "fur," as it was called, commanded a high price and led to the slaughter of countless thousands many decades ago. Today these handsome, swan-necked birds are completely protected by law and can easily be seen in the San Juan Islands. Flocks of Western Grebes concentrate in the deeper interior channels and bays and are locally abundant from October through April, although lesser numbers may be found a couple of weeks before and after these months. Several thousand individuals have been estimated to winter in the San Juan Islands and surrounding waters. Rare nonbreeding Western Grebes are more likely to be seen summering in the San Juans than either Horned or Red-necked Grebes.

Clark's Grebe (*Aechmophorus clarkii*). This bird has been a source of controversy for many decades for ornithologists. Originally classified as a full species, it was later lumped with the Western Grebe and given subspecific status. Recent evidence showing that the Clark's Grebe does not interbreed with its look-alike cousin has prompted its return to species status by the American Ornithologists' Union. The Clark's Grebe may be distinguished from the Western Grebe by its white cheeks extending up to surround the eye, and greenish, not orangish, bill. We expect it to be at least a casual migrant and winter visitor in the archipelago among flocks of Western Grebes. Our paucity of records may be attributed to its past anonymity.[3]

TUBE-NOSED SWIMMERS
(Procellariiformes)

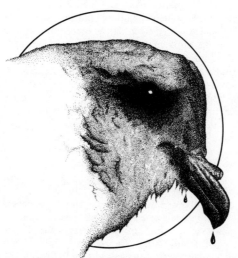

*Fork-tailed Storm-Petrels display the tubular nostrils and
plated bill seen in all members of this order.*

The tubenoses are seldom-seen birds in the San Juan Islands because of their seagoing habits. Extended migratory routes take them over vast tracts of ocean, where they most often forage on the productive continental shelves. Truly pelagic, they spend the greater part of their lives at sea, only coming ashore to reproduce. At colonies originally isolated from all mammalian predators, they raise a single chick that requires one of the longest care periods of any bird. These musty-smelling creatures feed their young very infrequently since the parents need to range over long distances while searching for food. Squid, fish, and small marine organisms are captured by the adults and converted into an efficiently transported stomach oil. This rich, foul-smelling food is regurgitated to feed the young or expelled at raiding enemies, usually humans, as a defense. Having evolved an extremely slow reproductive rate, several tubenose species have not recovered from uncontrolled hunting and exploitation for eggs and feathers.

The best chance one has of observing these seafarers in the San Juan Islands is to diligently scan our major waterways, especially the Strait of Juan de Fuca, from a boat or exposed point. Look for them when strong storm winds and thick sea fogs move in from the direction of the Pacific Ocean. These conditions can overpower and disorient these long-winged navigators, occasionally forcing dozens of them into our waters for a short time. Most often though, individuals or tiny groups are seen feeding among flocks of gulls and can be immediately recognized by their alternating pattern of soaring glides followed by flapping wings. Chunky, subtly colored bodies, and, at close range, tubular nostrils perched atop a heavily plated bill will help alert the birder to an interesting visitor in these islands.

Our transient tubenoses will belong to one of three families, the albatrosses (Diomedeidae), shearwaters and fulmars (Procellariidae), or storm-petrels (Hydrobatidae). The giant albatrosses are very unlikely this far away from the ocean and are considered accidental in the inland waters of Washington. However, there is one species that formerly frequented nearshore marine habitats: the **Short-tailed Albatross** (Diomedea albatrus).[4] This immense bird was recorded on the eastern edge of the San Juan Islands around the turn of the century when a specimen was shot and collected by a Native American and then given to a local naturalist. Now on the brink of extinction due to uncontrolled slaughter at its nesting islands, this bird may never again grace our shores.

The **Northern Fulmar** (Fulmarus glacialis)[5] is an irregular and rare winter visitor from late October through early March. From a distance, this medium-sized tubenose has the appearance of a gull except for its flat, stiff-winged flight and thick, bull-neck. Scavenging habits attract Northern Fulmars to fishing boats and other vessels where they escape notice among flocks of their similar-appearing colleagues. Most individuals are "dark phase" birds in this region. Smaller still is the **Sooty Shearwater** (Puffinus griseus),[6] a dark bird with white wing linings, which migrates in incredible hordes down the outer coast of Washington. They can be irregularly seen in the inland waters at any time of year but most frequently from July through November when a few migrants usually take a "wrong turn" and wind up here. Peak numbers of sightings in the San Juans generally occur in September, coincident with the massive southward movement on the open ocean. Almost identical to the Sooty is the **Short-tailed Shearwater** (Puffinus tenuirostris),[7] a smaller, shorter-tailed bird with more uniformly pale wing linings. Normally they are considered a very rare species but in certain "invasion" years they make small forays into the inland waters and are seen regularly. This shearwater is most often recorded November through mid-February.

The storm-petrels are often referred to as "sea swallows" because of their nearly continuous flapping and diminutive size. When conditions are suitable these lovely birds daintily patter their feet across the surface of the water while picking up plankton and other minute life forms. The pearly gray **Fork-tailed Storm-Petrel** (*Oceanodroma furcata*)[8] is irregularly and very rarely observed from late March through November; sightings are most likely July through October. Both it and the casually occurring **Leach's Storm-Petrel** (*Oceanodroma leucorhoa*)[9] breed at the mouth of the Strait of Juan de Fuca on Tatoosh Island. The Leach's Storm-Petrel is more highly pelagic and migratory in its habits and therefore wanders much less frequently into our waters from mid-April through October.

PELICANS AND CORMORANTS
(Pelecaniformes)

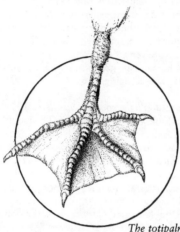

The totipalmate foot of a cormorant

Most people wouldn't think these two families were related at all, much less that they are seen in the San Juan Islands. It is thought that this coast-inhabiting order shares the same ancient ancestor as the tube-nosed swimmers. The pelicans and cormorants display strongly hooked beaks like the tubenoses but their nostrils are sealed to prevent the entry of water when diving. Heavy-bodied fish eaters, they are rather sedentary and forego the long migration of other seabirds. Their distinctively colored throat pouches are quite elastic and will accommodate large prey as well as provide a cooling effect for the bird by gently fluttering. All four toes are connected with webbing and the third claw on each foot is serrated for use as a comb during feather preening.

Pelicans (Pelecanidae) are famous for their high-altitude dives for fish swimming near the surface. To cushion the impact of these dives, the pelican is equipped with shock-absorbing air sacs under its skin. The **Brown Pelican** (*Pelecanus occidentalis*)[10] wanders north from its breeding grounds in California during the late summer. Following the warm current flowing up the coast at this time, the birds invade Washington's outer beaches in force. Not many penetrate inland as far as the San Juan Islands and they are very rarely seen here, most often in the major straits and channels from mid-July through October. The **American White Pelican** (*Pelecanus erythrorhynchos*) is no longer present as a plentiful breeding species or migrant in Washington. It was formerly seen during migration along the outer coast in fair numbers. Today, stragglers or small flocks are occasionally noted migrating through the inland waters. Some have undoubtedly passed through the San Juan Islands; however, no records have been published of the American White Pelican in our area.

In contrast, the cormorant family (Phalacrocoracidae) is very well represented in our islands by three common species. Dark, goose-sized birds, their common name literally translates to "marine crow" and their scientific name works out to "bald raven." They are one of the few marine birds that lack completely waterproof plumage, and often pose with their soaked wings outstretched to dry. Cormorants dive from the surface of the water and will pursue fish to depths of 100 feet or more. Their dense bones and wettable feathers enable them to dive deeply but also make flying a laborious task. The steep, rocky sites chosen for roosting and colonial breeding activities facilitate takeoffs and landings for these birds. When leaving the water, they must patter across its surface for long distances before getting airborne and, once up, will usually barely clear the waves as they fly along. Cormorants never go far from land and return in long lines each evening to their current home. This group movement is reversed in the morning when they disperse to favorite foraging areas.

Double-crested Cormorant (*Phalacrocorax auritus*). When watching a flock of cormorants on the wing, look at their long necks. The Double-crested Cormorant carries its stout neck with a distinct kink at the base, making identification easy. At close range the orange-skinned pouch is obvious, and in breeding season, extremely close scrutiny will reveal startling turquoise eyes and two flaxen crests. Double-crested Cormorants are resident in the San Juan Islands and can be seen in nearly all aquatic habitats. They are the only cormorant found on fresh water and are frequently observed feeding in busy harbors and ports as well as perching on docks and pilings. The Double-crested Cormorant is the only one in our area that builds stick nests, adding new material each year. These cylindrical "haystacks" can be seen squeezed together in dense masses on Colville Island, Williamson Rocks, and Bird Rocks NWRs where over 200 of the birds traditionally breed. Unfortunately, the nesting activities are subject to a variety of disturbing influences, including nearby human fishing and recreational activities as well as the availability of food supplies on a yearly basis. The Double-crested Cormorant rookeries in the San Juans have been occupied off and on for several decades.[11] In some years they are quite productive and raise many offspring but in others no young are ever detected, although the birds may frequent the nest sites. No breeding was observed in the San Juan Islands in 1985 and 1986 despite the initiation of several new colonies in adjacent Canadian waters. While the Double-crested Cormorant rookeries remain intermittent in Puget Sound, the very successful British Columbia population has tripled in the last 15 years.

Brandt's Cormorant (*Phalacrocorax penicillatus*). A visit any time from August through March to the tiny offshore rocks and islets bordering the Strait of Juan de Fuca will reveal large flocks of Brandt's Cormorants. Several thousands of these birds may be seen roosting side by side or foraging in the strong tidal convergences around Cattle Pass. Seeking out the active currents and tidal rips that they specialize in exploiting, smaller groups may be observed feeding in Rosario Strait or San

Cormorants in flight; from left to right, Brandt's, Double-crested, and Pelagic

Juan Channel at the entrance to Friday Harbor. Brandt's Cormorants can also be found in most of the other open salt-water bodies among the San Juan Islands but not in the concentrations listed above. Although they are found all year in these waters, the nesting colonies of this species are located on the shores of the Pacific Ocean and currently only nonbreeders remain in spring and early summer. Past reports of Brandt's Cormorants nesting in the San Juan Islands are viewed with some skepticism today. However, in light of the family's habit of shifting rookeries, it is possible that this species may have actually bred here. To identify this medium-sized cormorant, look for its buff-colored throat feathers and straight neck in flight.

Pelagic Cormorant (*Phalacrocorax pelagicus*). Any small cormorant with white flank patches and a red face is most assuredly this common breeding resident. In flight it also appears to have a pencil-thin neck and an equally long tail. Pelagic Cormorants are found nesting on the steep cliffs of many San Juan Islands where they form small, loosely knit colonies. White streaks of guano and pockets of marine vegetation advertise their constantly shifting breeding sites. Like the Double-crested Cormorant, Pelagic Cormorants have been having reduced nesting success in the San Juans during recent years. Most likely this is a result of the increased boat traffic near nesting colonies. On Colville Island NWR, where both of our breeding cormorants have nested, the Double-crested dominates on the flatter, more level areas and the Pelagic utilizes the vertical rock faces. This cormorant is more solitary than its close relatives and is usually found feeding singly or widely scattered over rocky bottoms. It is the most evenly distributed member of its family in the San Juan Islands and is a familiar sight on any body of water except the most protected harbors and bays.

HERONS
(Ciconiiformes/Ardeidae)

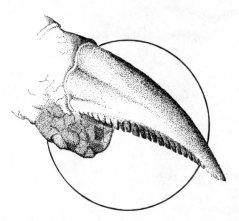

The center toe of many heron species is toothed like a comb and is used during feather preening.

These picturesque hunters are a familiar emblem of our San Juan shorelines. Like a tightly coiled spring, they are always ready to propel their daggerlike bill with a lightning thrust into wary prey. They are skillful spearfishers, and their slender bodies, long legs, and sinuous necks provide high vantage points when looking for animals to impale. Not restricted to daytime hunting, these stealthy waders may continue foraging in the darkness of night.

The herons are joined with one fossil family and four living families in the order Ciconiiformes. This order includes generally carnivorous birds with prominent bills, such as the ibises, spoonbills, storks, and flamingos. Other traits shared by these long-legged and long-necked birds are broad and rounded wings, feet that extend beyond the tail in flight, and feet equipped with four long toes that spread widely for support on mud and algae.

The herons (Ardeidae) have some unique traits which can be used to easily separate them from other families within the order. In flight, herons hold their necks in an S-shaped curve, different from the outstretched posture of other tall birds. During the breeding season they develop showy nuptial plumes on their heads, backs, and breasts. Perhaps most unusual are the three pairs of powder-down feather areas on the body, which are used for cleansing purposes. These special feathers are so brittle they disintegrate with the slightest contact from the bird's bill. During preening this talcumlike dust is distributed throughout the rest of the heron's plumage. It is then combed out of the feathers with the aid of a serrated, flattened claw found on the middle toe of each foot—another distinctive heron feature.

Great Blue Heron (*Ardea herodias*). An inescapable sound along San Juan Archipelago shores is the raucous complaint of a disturbed Great Blue Heron. All intruders are greeted with loud prehistoric-sounding honks as the irritated giant takes flight. Flying away from the potentially dangerous human or eagle, or toward a newly arrived competing heron that has crossed invisible territorial boundaries, this bird loudly declares its rightful place among the denizens of the San Juans.

With a height of four feet and a wingspread of seven feet, the Great Blue is easily the most recognizable and frequently seen heron in the San Juan Islands. This big bird often becomes a dockside neighbor in marinas, and tamer individuals will spend their days stalking the wharfs or patiently waiting on an anchored boat for the tide to turn. During the winter months, several roost overnight in a grove of trees in the town of Friday Harbor, where they calmly gaze down at passing traffic. Some may be seen stalking mice in pastures and farm fields, performing a beneficial service by eliminating unwanted rodents. Others stand immobile against remote rocky shores where they merge beautifully with the irregularly patterned background. Posing like sentries on floating beds of kelp, or, farther offshore, balancing on floating logs, they are visible for miles, sometimes drifting with the tidal currents for considerable distances. The solitary heron allows no other hitchhikers on its raft of debris.

The hundreds of miles of shoreline in the San Juans provide extensive foraging grounds, if not suitable nesting sites, for this big predator. Together with freshwater wetlands, fallow farm fields, and pastures, the marine habitats support several hundred Great Blue Herons in our area for much of the year. Normally very defensive of their hunting territory and quick to chase one another off, temporary truces are declared and concentrations of a dozen or more herons may occur in some of the more productive feeding locations like False Bay or Crescent Beach. They also gather in even larger groups at favored roosting sites, choosing open fields or tall firs that offer long views in order to guard against approaching danger.

In our local area Great Blue Herons are year-round residents, most common from late summer through early spring, when not engaged in nesting activities. Their peak numbers occur during September when a post-breeding dispersal of adults and young sends many wandering away from nesting areas. The population will remain high throughout the winter months but declines as the breeding season gets underway. Documented nesting occurred at Deer Harbor, Orcas Island, in 1928[12] and more recently, there have been reports of small heron rookeries near the Frank Richardson Wildfowl Sanctuary and Point George, Shaw Island. These colonies seem to be unstable and shifting. This may be due in part to human activities, such as logging, which appears to be the case at the Orcas Island site. Other rookeries are found on Sidney Island, B.C., and Samish Island. Coronet Bay, Whidbey Island, may also be the location of breeding activity if nearby logging ac-

Great Blue Heron

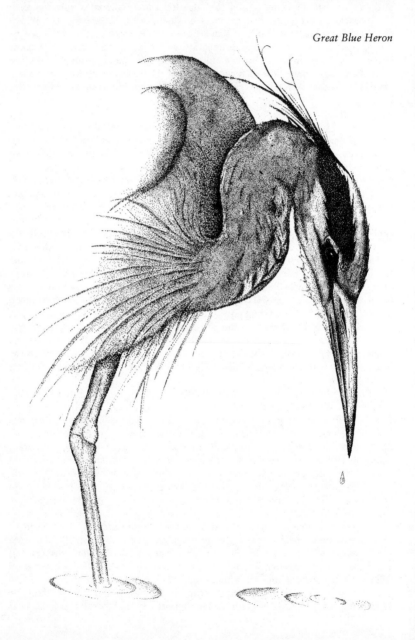

tivities have not displaced both colonies there. Dozens of pairs crowd together at
these communal sites to build large stick platforms that serve as nests, high up in
the canopy of a mature stand of alder trees. Here the young herons are fed the
regurgitated remains of the parents' hard-earned catch.

Consuming a variety of prey, Great Blue Herons are not finicky eaters. Any
small animal that moves within the bird's long reach is likely to end up as heron
fodder. Food is carefully positioned head-first before swallowing, and with larger
fare the task may take up to half an hour to complete. The expandible gullet is able
to accommodate fish up to a foot in length, frogs, snakes, crabs, small birds, and
rodents. Striking and impaling these delicacies with deadly strength and accuracy,
the hunter sometimes has problems removing the mouthful from its bill. The
senior author once observed a Great Blue Heron wearing a large turtle on its beak
for a full day. It had speared the reptile through a leg hole and was effectively
muzzled by the tough shell encircling its beak. Unable to vent its anger by squawk-
ing, the frustrated bird flew off at the end of the day with its heavily weighted head
dangling low.

Other Herons: Besides the Great Blue Heron, there are several smaller and much
less common members of this family that should be carefully watched for in the
San Juan Islands. The **American Bittern** (*Botaurus lentiginosus*)[13] is probably a
very rare migrant and winter visitor and is usually located in cattail marshes and
similar habitats. When approached, this secretive, brown-streaked bittern will
"freeze" with its bill pointing skyward, cloaking itself from view in the midst of
the vegetation. A sure giveaway of this bird's presence is its loud, resonant "oonk-
a-lunk," most often heard at dawn and dusk. Bitterns have been reported calling
from Sportsman Lake during May and June in recent years, possibly indicating
that they sometimes nest in the area.

The crow-sized **Green-backed Heron** (*Butorides striatus*) is a rare visitor and
migrant in the San Juans. Recently established as a breeder in the Puget Trough,
our first record of this species was in 1960. Since then it has become a regular
rarity. As yet there has been no solid evidence of any nesting among the islands, although immature birds have been seen. Look for Green-backed Herons on
lakeshores, ponds, and marshes at any time of year, but mostly during the warmer
months.

Black-crowned Night-Herons (*Nycticorax nycticorax*)[14] are casual mid-
winter visitors to the San Juans, our sightings probably representing stragglers
from the burgeoning population east of the Cascade Mountains. Wandering immatures could potentially find their way to our islands in late summer and fall as
they disperse from their nesting colonies.

Two other herons, the stately **Great Egret** (*Casmerodius albus*) and the
dumpy **Cattle Egret** (*Bubulcus ibis*), have been rapidly expanding their ranges
northward up the coast of Washington, as far as the bordering portions of British
Columbia. Late summer through early winter is the time of the annual post-
breeding dispersal of Great Egrets, therefore offering the greatest probability of
finding this alabaster wader as it temporarily shares habitat with Great Blue
Herons. The terrestrial Cattle Egret has invaded the region in greater numbers and
can be seen in pastures snapping up insects that flee from the ponderous feet of
cattle and other livestock. Documented sightings of either of these two white
herons in the San Juan Islands has been lacking, but they are eagerly anticipated by
the authors, who are offering a six-pack of Grape Nehis to the first birder that
comes forth with a valid record.

WATERFOWL
(Anseriformes/Anatidae)

Northern Pintail drake

For ages waterfowl and humans have shared an intimate connection. Both primitive and modern hunters have been enchanted with the pursuit and eventual consumption of these birds, which were also domesticated early in human history, furnishing a convenient source of eggs, meat, and down. Later, waterfowl provided entertainment in parks, gardens, and aviaries. Today, large numbers of people enjoy observing swans, geese, and ducks in their natural environment, still drawn by their beauty and conspicuousness. In addition, this 80-million-year-old family has had the distinction of being one of the world's most popular literary subjects.

The waterfowl are a world-wide group known for great migratory movements and abundant high-latitude nesting. During migration and winter, waterfowl congregate in vast, garrulous flocks at important staging and wintering locations. They are often seen traveling in long aerodynamic lines and V formations as they propel themselves swiftly with their tapered wings. Their short tails preclude any sharp turns, so waterfowl flight is straight and direct. Ranging in weight from one to 30 pounds, most species can be identified in flight by size and distinctive flight patterns.

Waterfowl obtain their food in three basic ways: diving, dabbling, and grazing. All species heavily utilize aquatic environments, and this choice is reflected by their webbed feet, short legs, long necks, and dense waterproof plumage underlaid with insulating down. The grazers, like swans and geese, frequent cultivated land and pastures, especially during the nonbreeding season. They have retained longer legs that are mounted in a more forward position on the body for better walking ability. The family is also noted for a generally flattened bill, bearing a toothlike fringe on the interior edges and a small terminal hook or "nail." Cygnets, goslings, and ducklings, the young of this varied group, are all precocious and follow the mother soon after hatching.

Swans

Tundra Swan (*Cygnus columbianus*). The "swan song" of legend may be based on truth. Reliable naturalists have heard prolonged and mournful notes issue from stricken Tundra Swans as they plummet to earth after being shot. The usual utterance of this bird is a high-pitched gooselike honking, probably the best way to separate this swan from the other two all-white waterfowl that inhabit the San Juan Islands. Formerly called the "Whistling Swan" from an old description given by Lewis and Clark (the discoverers of the species), it is not known to whistle at all, and the name was recently changed to a more appropriate one. Tundra Swans are quite uncommon as migrant and winter visitors in the San Juans, most often seen and heard flying overhead. When they do occasionally pause to rest or feed, these scarcely encountered swans may be found in small numbers, often in the company of look-alike relatives. Visiting our islands at the same time of year, Tundra and Trumpeter Swans pose an identification dilemma from mid-October through mid-May. The smaller Tundra Swan often shows a tiny yellow "teardrop" in the corner of its eye and a slightly saddle-shaped bill. Distinguishing characteristics of the Trumpeter Swan are thin flesh-colored "lips" near the base of the straight bill and a deep, sonorous, honking call.

Trumpeter Swan (*Cygnus buccinator*). Hunted to the brink of extinction, the Trumpeter Swan has made a remarkable recovery from the mere 35 birds that were counted in 1931. These graceful birds are on the increase and once again range the western United States and Canada. In 1976 they added the San Juan Is-

Trumpeter Swan

lands to their wintering range and have augmented their local population here every year since then. Unfortunately, we haven't been the best host to these birds, as there has been more than one incident of illegal poaching. All swans are fully protected by law in this state and island residents now carefully guard and monitor the Trumpeter Swans distributed through the San Juans.

Our highest count of this, our biggest waterfowl, has been 50 birds in the winter of 1985–86, the majority of them wintering on San Juan Island at a few favored locations such as Sportsman Lake and Three Meadows Marsh. Smaller numbers are seen on Orcas and Lopez islands and migrants can occur anywhere in and over the archipelago. They prefer fresh-water bodies and farmland, but these habitats become useless to them when cold temperatures lock their food sources away in ice, briefly forcing them to use shallow marine shorelines.

Encouraging Trumpeter Swans to remain in the San Juan Islands throughout the summer nesting season can sometimes prove rewarding. The islands are thought to be on the edge of the species' historical breeding range, and already one swan enthusiast claims to have succeeded in tempting a pair to linger for five successive summers, 1977–1981. Buck Gates did this by providing corn throughout the winter months on a secluded ranch lake for both domestic waterfowl and wild birds that included several kinds of swans. Every year in early March the same pair of Trumpeters would drive all other swans from the lake, even Mutes, and trumpet loudly morning and evening. A good observer and judge of waterfowl behavior, Buck felt that the swans attempted to breed in each of those five years. Nests were always located, but only once was one found to contain three eggs. Young were produced several springs but, unfortunately, all of the cygnets hatched by this pioneering pair were taken before they were even half grown. The culprits were Bald Eagles attracted to the hordes of domestic goslings being raised nearby. After failing to raise their offspring the pair would depart in mid-June and return again in August. This remarkable situation ended when waterfowl feeding and husbandry was discontinued on the ranch.

Mute Swan (*Cygnus olor*). The sinuous neck of the swan requires 25 vertebrae for its support, the most of any animal. This is shown to its best advantage in the elegantly curving neck posture of the semidomesticated Mute Swan. The most immediately recognizable swan in our area, its ruffled, upraised wings and large knobbed bill are distinctive. This Old World native was introduced to southern Vancouver Island in the 1950s and has been expanding its range north and east. Mute Swans are considered a locally uncommon resident and rare breeder in the San Juan Islands. In addition to a few territory-defending birds, there are free-flying wanderers and a number of sedentary wing-clipped captives present in the area. Like all swans, these long-lived birds remain mated for their entire lives, displaying more loyalty than most humans. The swan of gardens and city parks, Mutes are particularly aggressive in the defense of their home and young and will attack small animals, children, and even adults, all the while making their only noise, a threatening hiss. Fowler Pond on Orcas Island is a known breeding site for Mute Swans.[15]

GEESE

Greater White-fronted Goose (*Anser albifrons*). Midway in size between swans and ducks are the semiterrestrial geese. The Greater White-fronted Goose is a rather obscure fresh-water species, named for the white band surrounding the base of the bill. These birds are encountered from late August through mid-May as migrants or rare winter visitors. They are most numerous in the San Juan Islands during the month of April and from September through mid-October when they are at best uncommon. As with all of our geese, they are most frequently detected while in flight and they draw attention to themselves with loud, conversational flight calls. Listen overhead for the Greater White-fronted Goose's high-pitched, laughing "wah-wah-wah," since it usually makes only brief stops on small marshes, ponds, or farmland before venturing on.

Snow Goose (*Chen caerulescens*). Immense Vs of Snow Geese can occasionally be seen on crisp, clear winter days, offering a bold contrast to the cobalt sky with their white bodies and black-tipped wings. Navigating at elevations so high that you can almost imagine frost crystals forming on their plumage, these birds must view the islands as so many gems set in the turquoise straits. Lamentably, these handsome geese will continue in their search for extensive deltas and agricultural lands, rarely dropping to more intimate levels in the San Juan Islands. Sometimes a solitary individual will visit a beach or pond from mid-October through May, most likely disoriented or recovering from a wound or illness. The peak of Snow Goose migration, occurring from late October through mid-December and again in April, is the best time to watch for the flocks as they hopscotch between estuarine staging grounds. Most of these flocks are traveling between the Skagit and Fraser river deltas and therefore are most often viewed from the northeastern San Juan Islands.

Brant (*Branta bernicla*). The largest wintering concentration of the Brant on the Pacific coast is found just east of the San Juan Islands in the Padilla Bay National Sanctuary. Like Snow Geese, migrating flocks of Brant are seen over many of the islands, but relatively small numbers will utilize our islands at ground level. There are at least three locations where this small cousin of the Canada Goose will feed and rest regularly in flocks: Cowlitz Bay, Spencer Spit, and Fisherman Spit. These sites all offer shallow offshore waters with eelgrass beds, the most important food for wintering Brants. They also come to these beaches to preen and "gravel up," swallowing grit that enables their gizzards to grind their vegetable diet. The Brant is a true "sea goose," possessing salt-excreting glands that enable it to drink sea water and feed almost exclusively on marine plants. It can be seen in the San Juans from November through mid-May but is common only during the spring movement from mid-March through early May.

Canada Goose (*Branta canadensis*). Long before it comes into view over the Strait of Juan de Fuca, the loud, musical chorus of a northbound flock of Canada Geese may be heard drifting across the water. As spring days grow longer, enticing the birds to return to their place of birth, these rallying cries are heard more frequently. From Cattle Pass it is possible to see flocks of 200 or more "Honkers" stretched out in long lines entering the interior channels of the San Juan Islands. Most often they will follow these "highways" right on through without stopping, but occasionally small numbers will rest in fresh-water and farm habitats or along marine shores. They are fairly common migrants in spring from late March through early May and again in fall from mid-August through mid-November. For the remainder of the year they are decidedly uncommon but are resident in the islands. Formerly the surrounding region had no breeding population of Canada Geese, but recently there have been at least two races of this bird introduced for this purpose to Puget Sound and nearby Vancouver Island. This goose is expected to become a frequent breeder in the San Juans and was first confirmed nesting here in 1986 by the senior author. This pioneering pair constructed its nest on a rocky shoreline just above the high tide line at San Juan County Park and was seen with a single downy gosling on June 24. Two more pairs bred in 1987.

Migrating Canada Geese

PERCHING DUCKS

Wood Duck (*Aix sponsa*). Not many waterfowl, nor any other birds for that matter, can rival the exquisite beauty of the Wood Duck. As its name suggests, this boldly colored perching duck nests in hollow trees over or near quiet ponds and lakes. Amazingly, the ducklings leap from the nesting cavity only minutes after hatching and follow their mother to the water unhurt. Wood Ducks were threatened with extinction in the early 1900s, a result of overshooting and the clearing of wooded swamps. With the establishment of refuges and sensible game laws, their numbers have rebounded and they are slowly expanding their range through our region. In the San Juan Islands they are uncommon migrants and locally common nesters, resident throughout the year but much reduced in the

Wood Duck chicks leap from their nest cavity high in the forest in response to calls from the mother hen.

winter months. Look for these rather ungregarious ducks at Killebrew Lake, Sportsman Lake, Three Meadows Marsh, and other suitable nesting areas.

DABBLING DUCKS

Dabbling ducks are a tribe of waterfowl that prefers shallow water habitats, especially fresh water. "Puddle ducks," as they are also called, seldom dive for their aquatic vegetable and animal food. Instead, they reach down with their bills and point their tails up in the air, a foraging method known as "tipping up." These are the most familiar type of duck and can be seen on nearly every pond, lake, or flooded farm field. They fly well and can burst from the water and immediately become airborne. In the San Juan Islands, poorly drained agricultural land is the most important habitat, especially during winter, and the abundance of these birds will fluctuate with the amount of rainfall. All varieties of dabbling ducks display a bright, iridescent patch of feathers on the wing known as the "speculum." Even though the sexes are plumaged quite differently, both share their particular species' wing pattern.

Green-winged Teal (*Anas crecca*). The Green-winged Teals, bearing a bright green speculum as their name implies, are the tiniest of all puddle ducks. Rare year-round residents, they have been found nesting only twice in the San Juan Islands. A 1985 record came from a rapidly drying farm field in San Juan Valley where a female with her brood of seven young was discovered on July 1 by the senior author. Another brood was found in June 1987. The southward migration of Green-winged Teals commences in mid-August, and they become quite common by late September, remaining so throughout the winter. This hardy little duck declines in numbers in April and the northward movement is over by mid-May.

Mallard (*Anas platyrhynchos*). The most adaptable waterfowl is the Mallard, a ubiquitous bird found in all the usual dabbling duck habitats in addition to farmyards, gardens, and parks. Even tiny Low Island (NWR), a waterless rock in the San Juan Channel, tempted a hen Mallard to make her nest among grass and cacti.[16] It is the progenitor of most domesticated ducks in the world and is the most highly esteemed by the human race, especially for hunting and eating. Despite the fact that four and a half million Mallards fall to hunters' shotguns every year, a figure that does not include those birds that die from ingesting spent lead shot when "graveling up," they continue to survive. In the San Juan Islands, Mallards are a common breeding resident, increasing in numbers during migration and winter. In rainy winters they are downright abundant and outnumber all other dabblers in the wetlands.

Northern Pintail (*Anas acuta*). Northern Pintails are typified by their exquisite forms and conservative dress, their long necks and tails lending them a graceful symmetry lacking in other puddle ducks. These wary birds crane their necks above the stubble of the fall harvest looking for danger in the form of eagles and human hunters. Like Mallards, they are most abundant during wet winters in the San Juan Islands and reach their peak from late October through mid-March. The first fall migrants begin arriving in mid-August and the last spring departures take place in early May. During the summer a few rare birds will remain resident, and nesting is strongly suspected. Northern Pintails range across the Northern Hemisphere and may be the most numerous wild duck in the world.

Blue-winged (*Anas discors*) and **Cinnamon Teals** (*Anas cyanoptera*). Our two summer ducks are the Blue-winged and Cinnamon Teals, two closely related warmth-loving dabblers. Sharing the same farm ponds and marshes for their nesting activities, both species are locally uncommon breeders in the San Juan Islands. Hummel Lake, Frank Richardson Wildfowl Sanctuary, and the Richardson Ponds are all productive locations for these handsome little ducks. Fall departure, often for South America, takes place mainly in August with stragglers occurring through September. Most Cinnamon Teals have returned to the islands by mid-April but early individuals may show up in the last days of March. The Blue-winged Teal, dallying a bit in the tropics, usually arrives at least two weeks later than its cousin and often lingers longer in the fall, too.

Northern Shoveler (*Anas clypeata*). The Northern Shoveler's comically proportioned bill is the paragon of the duck world taken to its extreme. This pond duck is never found in large numbers among the San Juan Islands but is nevertheless a fairly common migrant and winter visitor, especially on Lopez Island. Fall migrants begin arriving in the islands by late August while most northbound birds depart by mid-May, leaving behind a few stragglers for the summer. Breeding is very likely at locations such as the Richardson Ponds where pairs have been sighted in mid-June.

Gadwall (*Anas strepera*). The Gadwall is undergoing a mystifying increase in abundance throughout the region. It was once completely absent from the Puget Trough and probably has not been nesting in western Washington for more than 20 years. It is now regarded as a fairly common migrant and winter visitor in the San Juan Islands, as well as a rare breeder. This resident dabbler was once found nesting on Goose Island in the midst of a Glaucous-winged Gull colony, rather a Mallardlike thing to do.[17] Perhaps this is the secret to the Gadwall's new-found success.

Eurasian (*Anas penelope*) and **American Wigeons** (*Anas americana*). Political bird watchers may be interested to know that every winter small numbers of feathered Russian defectors may be seen infiltrating our local duck flocks. Scanning large concentrations of grazing American Wigeons may disclose the presence of a Siberian emigrant, one that recognizes no national boundaries. Look for a russet-headed duck bearing a creamy crown among the hundreds of green-masked "Baldpates." This will be the Eurasian Wigeon, a bird that visits the North American coast annually from mid-October through mid-April in the company of its American cousin. Despite the apparent profusion of suitable nesting habitat in the New World, this uncommon to rare visitor returns to the motherland each summer to breed. One of our most gregarious dabblers, the American Wigeon is a common migrant and sometimes abundant winter visitor to the San Juan Islands. Having a great tolerance for salt-water habitats, the first and last migrants through our area are usually seen at places like False and Fisherman bays. When the winter rains have flooded the farmers' land, American Wigeons' numbers swell even more, often coincident with the hunting season as many flocks seem to find refuge here from heavy shooting pressure on the mainland. The first American Wigeons are seen in the area beginning in mid-August, but they are not very common until at least mid-September. Winter flocks depart in April, and the last birds are usually seen in early May although a few nonbreeding individuals may remain for the summer. The American Wigeon can be a troublesome bird to its neighbors when visiting ponds too deep for its short reach. To remedy this it will often steal morsels of food from the bills of American Coots and other unsuspecting divers when they return to the surface.

BAY DUCKS OR POCHARDS

Possessing the ability to dive and forage beneath the water's surface, the pochards are found on deep ponds, lakes, and, especially in winter, protected bays and harbors. These birds have largely forsaken the flooded farmland and stubble fields of the dabbling ducks and, as a result, their feet are larger and more widely spaced, giving them more power in the water and less balance on land. Most of our male bay ducks have black chests and rumps, gray bodies, and colored heads. The females are mostly brown. Comparison of the head and bill shape is the most useful tool for identifying these birds. Pochards lack a speculum but they do have wing stripes that help identify the birds in flight.

Canvasback (*Aythya valisineria*). Looking like small, mahogany-headed geese, the Canvasbacks are locally uncommon migrants and winter visitors to the San Juan Islands. They show extreme favoritism toward certain farm ponds teeming with submerged aquatic plants, like the Speers and Fowler ponds. Their largely vegetarian diet has made them one of the most highly esteemed ducks to the epicurean hunter, forcing them to be very alert. Also look for their tiny flocks on shallow bays, where they can appear in late October or rarely in late September. They move north again in March, with the last birds lingering until mid-April.

Ring-necked Duck (*Aythya collaris*). A more appropriate name for this boldly marked bird might be "Ring-billed" Duck. Seldom found on salt water, this bird is more restricted to small lakes and ponds than the other pochards. The only bay duck that has been confirmed as a breeder within the archipelago, the Ring-necked Duck is a rare and local nester on San Juan and Orcas islands.[18] Several locations harbor summering birds and are suspected to be breeding sites, but no ducklings have been spotted anywhere except at Three Meadows Marsh and the Frank Richardson Wildlife Sanctuary. Though only a handful remains present during the warmer months, Ring-necked Ducks are common migrants and winter visitors to the San Juan Islands from late October through early April. Lesser numbers of migrants are seen beginning in late September and through early May before and after the peak migrational movements.

Greater (*Aythya marila*) and **Lesser Scaups** (*Aythya affinis*). These two look-alikes have defeated more bird watchers than any other species, as witnessed by Christmas Bird Count results. Here you will see the Greater and Lesser Scaups listed unceremoniously as "scaup sp.," as few observers will take the time and effort necessary to separate them. If attention is paid to the proper field marks, differentiating between these two bay ducks is not an impossible task. In good light, the males' heads reflect iridescent highlights, green in the Greater and purple in the Lesser. On overcast days, head profile is the most important feature, with the Greater Scaup showing a rounded crown and a slightly larger bill. In comparison, the Lesser Scaup's head has a distinctly peaked crown with a smaller bill. A less reliable guide is their choice of habitat, the common to abundant Greater Scaup preferring marine habitats and the slightly scarcer Lesser Scaup picking freshwater haunts. These migrants and winter visitors are most numerous in the San Juans from November through March. The first to arrive in the fall, around mid-September, is the Greater Scaup; showing up about a month later is the tardy Lesser Scaup. Both species depart simultaneously and are nearly gone by May, with individuals rarely remaining over the summer. Most of these infrequently encountered stragglers are Lesser Scaups, a possible breeder in the archipelago.

SEA DUCKS

The best waterfowl divers are the sea ducks, which have their short legs set the farthest back under the body. They swim deeply in search of their mostly animal prey, principally mollusks and crustaceans. Most of these birds prefer large open bodies of water and, as the name implies, they are most often observed on salt water. Possessing small pointed wings like the bay ducks, they must patter across the water and into the wind for some distance before getting airborne.

Harlequin Duck (*Histrionicus histrionicus*). The San Juan Islands are a center of abundance for this strikingly beautiful bird. These shy little sea ducks are par-

The boldly patterned plumage of a drake Harlequin Duck allows it to blend into its normal background of turbulent water.

ticularly numerous near the multitude of offshore rocks and reefs in the archipelago, where they can be seen all year. In 1985 the senior author observed summering flocks that numbered 90 and 160 individuals; they were found, respectively, at Sandy Point on June 26 and Gull Reef (NWR) on June 20. In the winter, Harlequin Ducks are more evenly dispersed in smaller groups and may be seen frequenting the shores of the larger islands as well. Land-bound birders find them most accessible at Cattle Point, West Sound, and Agate Beach. Although they are common residents here, their actual nesting grounds are on fast, white-water rivers of the Olympic, Cascade, and Rocky mountains.

Oldsquaw (*Clangula hyemalis*). Penetrating the autumn fogs, a loud yodeling across the bay signifies the return of our noisiest sea ducks. Their black-and-white plumage and long, quill-like tails make them unmistakable and easy to pick out from the huge rafts of scoters that they often accompany. These tundra nesters are one of the deepest-diving ducks and will secure foods such as shellfish on rocky bottoms 200 feet below the surface. Late September is when the first migrants may appear in the San Juan Islands, but they aren't usually common until mid-October. Look for the largest wintering flocks of Oldsquaws, up to a hundred or so birds, in the deep fiordlike sounds of Orcas Island. Departure takes place in late April and early May but rare nonbreeders are seen nearly every summer.

The only species of North American duck that possesses distinctive summer and winter plumages is the Oldsquaw. Here a drake is shown in winter garb.

Black Scoter (*Melanitta nigra*). This is the least common of the three scoters that reside in the San Juan Islands. Sometimes called the "Butterbill" because of the swollen orange base of the male's upper mandible, the Black Scoter gathers in large numbers at particular locations. However, none of these is in the San Juans and we only see an occasional bird or two, usually mixed in with other sea ducks. Apparently, we lack the right habitat for this finicky waterfowl, but they are regular just to the east in Lummi Bay. They are seen with the greatest frequency from November through April but nonbreeding individuals are rarely seen throughout the summer months.

Surf Scoter (*Melanitta perspicillata*). One of the most distinctive San Juan sounds is the tremulous whistling of a scoter flock taking wing. At the sight of a Bald Eagle making an aerial reconnoiter across the bay, large rafts of these sea ducks will suddenly take wing in an antipredator defense. By becoming airborne, ducks and other waterbirds are able to foil dive-bombing attacks by hungry eagles. Surf Scoters are among the most numerous of the marine waterfowl and are abundant from August through April when flocks of several hundred birds may be seen in protected waterways and bays such as Lopez Sound, East Sound, and Griffin Bay. At all other times of year smaller localized groups of nonbreeding resident Surf Scoters may be encountered quite commonly in the San Juan Islands.

White-winged Scoter (*Melanitta fusca*). Along with the other two scoters, these birds will stage in migrating rafts that number up to 1000 individuals. Studying these fall concentrations from the high bluffs over South Beach, a fascinating phenomenon may be observed. At an unknown signal, one end of the resting flock will begin scooting across the water and labor into singing flight. Like a wave, the action ripples through the remainder and after several minutes they will all be strung in a long line heading for the Pacific Ocean. White-winged Scoters are nearly as plentiful as Surf Scoters during the winter but are much more localized in distribution. Outnumbered by Surf Scoters nearly everywhere except at Harney Channel, good numbers of these waterfowl are also seen at East Sound and Griffin Bay. White-winged Scoters share the same timetable of seasonal abundance as Surf Scoters and are seen together in mixed flocks all year.

Common Goldeneye (*Bucephala clangula*). A common migrant and winter visitor to our lakes and protected shallow bays is the Common Goldeneye. Also called the "Whistler" because of the vibration of its beating wings, this tree-nesting duck is late in arriving and early in departing. Look for Common Goldeneyes between late October and early May but not in large numbers except from mid-November through March. Occasionally they are sighted during the summer months but these rare birds are regarded as nonbreeders.

Barrow's Goldeneye (*Bucephala islandica*). Easily overlooked because of its similarity to the other goldeneye, this locally common winter visitor and migrant is best looked for at West Sound and protected rocky shores along Crane and Shaw islands. The male Barrow's Goldeneye can be recognized by its crescent-shaped cheek patch, black shoulder mark separating the white of the sides and breast, and an extensively black back. The female is distinguished by its small, sometimes all-yellow bill, and steep forehead. These birds arrive and depart at much the same time as the Common Goldeneye but in this species summering birds may have a greater significance. Barrow's Goldeneyes, which frequent wooded lakes during the spring migration, should be looked for in these same habitats during the summer nesting season. Careful surveys may eventually make it possible to add this bird to our list of breeding San Juan avifauna.

Bufflehead (*Bucephala albeola*). Nearly every pond, lake, lagoon, bay, and hogwallow in the San Juan Islands has at least once harbored a jaunty Bufflehead. This little diving duck is about the size of a Horned Grebe and disappears beneath the surface in a similarly abrupt manner. Bobbing to the surface like a cork, the buoyant Bufflehead is unlike other bay and sea ducks in that it has the ability to rocket directly into flight without a running start. Persistent and animated courters, male Buffleheads can be seen displaying to prospective mates and threatening each other with bobbing heads all spring. The Bufflehead is an abundant migrant and winter visitor in the San Juan Islands from mid-November through April; rarely a nonbreeding Bufflehead will be seen during the summer months. Look for the first fall migrants appearing in late October and the last northbound travelers finally disappearing in mid-May.

MERGANSERS

Adapted for the underwater pursuit of fish, crustaceans, and aquatic insects, the mergansers are streamlined waterfowl that inhabit both fresh- and salt-water habitats. Long, narrow bills equipped with serrated edges and backward-pointing toothlike projections enable them to handle their slippery prey. These crested ducks are recognized in flight by a lean, stretched appearance and straight-line formation when in flocks.

Hooded Merganser (*Lophodytes cucullatus*). When aroused by danger or passion, the male Hooded Merganser raises a hood of startling pattern and proportion. This wonderfully bizarre bird is a common breeding resident in the San Juan Islands and can be found on many secluded ponds and lakes. The broods of this tree-cavity nester are a familiar sight from late May through July on Killebrew Lake, Frank Richardson Wildfowl Sanctuary, and Three Meadows Marsh. In winter Hooded Mergansers are also seen on protected salt-water bodies, and, though outnumbered by the other merganser species, they are the most widely distributed.

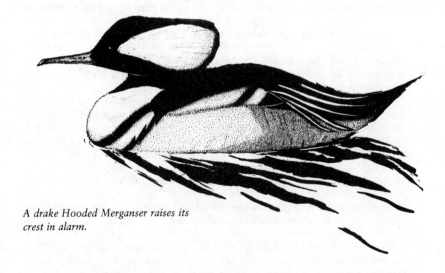

A drake Hooded Merganser raises its crest in alarm.

Common Merganser (*Mergus merganser*). The large "Goosander," as they are called in Europe, is our other resident breeding merganser. This bird is a locally uncommon nester on Mountain Lake, and perhaps other high, timber-fringed lakes, where it lays its clutch of eggs in the cavity of a tree. Starting in October, the Common Merganser increases in numbers and remains plentiful through April. They are encountered with less frequency than the other two mergansers but when they are it is usually in large flocks. The early winter herring run in Friday Harbor draws up to 300 Common Mergansers in huge fishing rafts. At times these birds, in the company of other mergansers, cormorants, and gulls, will drive schools of small bait fish against the ferry dock where feeding frenzies ensue. Other localities that attract flocks of 50 or more Common Mergansers are False Bay, Sportsman Lake, and Cascade Lake.

Red-breasted Merganser (*Mergus serrator*). Shaggy-crested Red-breasted Mergansers are common migrants and winter visitors to salt-water habitats in the San Juan Islands. They will usually make their first appearance in mid-September but some earlier individuals rarely show up in August. Red-breasted Mergansers normally do not become common until mid-October. Over the winter they can be seen more widely distributed in the marine environment than the Common and Hooded Mergansers and are rarely if ever seen on fresh water. Spring migration begins in April when large flocks of Red-breasted Mergansers are sometimes seen staging at South Beach on their way north. Sightings decrease by mid-April until the last birds, other than a few rare summer stragglers, depart in May.

Stiff-tailed Ducks

Ruddy Duck (*Oxyura jamaicensis*). Stiff-tailed ducks are another small tribe of extremely aquatic waterfowl represented in our area by only one species, the Ruddy Duck. They are the best divers in the entire family and share many behavioral traits with grebes. These include the ability to sink below the water's surface without a ripple, night migrations, weak flight low over the water, and an inclination to dive when escaping danger. Supremely adapted to a waterbound existence, their big feet are nearly useless on land and their long tails, providing underwater steerage, are often held erect. Stiff-tailed ducks also differ from other ducks by wearing a dull winter plumage and having male assistance during the raising of young. Ruddy Duck courtship is a weird ritual of piglike grunting accompanied with the slapping of the male's large blue bill against his breast, forcing large quantities of bubbles into the water.

The tameness and flocking habits of these stout little ducks make them a terribly easy target for gun-bearing humans. A list of nicknames given the Ruddy Duck by hunters, often referring to their supposed impregnability to gunshot, is long: steel-head, fool duck, god-damn, hardhead, shot-pouch, booby coot, blatherskite, dumb-bird, dumpling duck, hickory-head, water partridge, leather-back, light-wood knot, sleepy dick, and tough-head. This attention from hunters has resulted in a lot more than just silly names. Populations have declined in many parts of their range, including the San Juan Islands. Formerly, Ruddy Ducks were common migrants and winter visitors in the archipelago, possibly even breeding on occasion. A steady reduction in numbers took place in the 1950s and 1960s and they are now quite uncommon and somewhat localized. Hummel Lake, Richardson Ponds, and the MacKaye Harbor Marsh, all situated on Lopez Island, are the best locations for Ruddy Ducks in the San Juans today. Look for them from September through April or May on ponds, lakes, and shallow bays.

Rare Waterfowl

A number of rare waterfowl sightings have occurred or are anticipated in the archipelago. The **Emperor Goose** (*Chen canagica*),[19] normally a seashore loving bird, was possibly sighted once in the San Juan Islands. This casual species is to be looked for November through May near eelgrass beds, perhaps among flocks of

Brant. Once of the most remarkable waterfowl ever observed in the San Juans was an accidental **Common Pochard** (*Aythya ferina*).[20]. This Eurasian bay duck is seen regularly in the Aleutian and Pribilof islands of Alaska but nowhere else in North America. The **Redhead** (*Aythya americana*),[21] another bay duck, should be found in fresh-water habitats, very rarely, from October through April. **King Eiders** (*Somateria spectabilis*)[22] normally winter in Alaska; however, there are two records of this accidental species in the San Juans. Another amazing record of an accidental species is of two **Smews** (*Mergellus albellus*),[23] an Eurasian merganser. As with most rare waterfowl, this bird would most likely be found in the colder months.

Since waterfowl are such strong fliers and long-distance migrators, it is reasonable that we expect to eventually add several more varieties to the San Juan Islands checklist. Judging by sightings in the rest of the Puget Trough, the following species are quite likely to be added given enough time. The **Black Duck** (*Anas rubripes*), a common species east of the Mississippi River, has been introduced south of Vancouver, B.C., and near Everett, Washington. Birds of this species have been found wandering from these locations and probably visit the San Juan Islands rarely but go undetected among the many Mallards. Another Eurasian species that occurs almost annually in fresh-water lakes and ponds around Puget Sound and on protected salt water on Vancouver Island is the **Tufted Duck** (*Aythya fuligula*). Look for this rare bird in flocks of Ring-necked Ducks and Greater Scaups, where it can easily be missed.

DIURNAL BIRDS OF PREY
(Falconiformes)

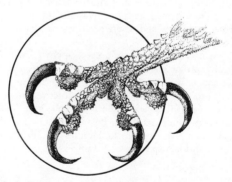

Strongly curved claws, a reversible outer toe, and spiny pads enable Ospreys to grasp and carry live fish.

Strewn across the rolling prairies on the south side of San Juan Island, large boulders stand like silent sentries awaiting the next glacial invasion. Offering a vantage point above the dense carpet of grass and thistles, these granitic erratics lend themselves as perches for sharp-eyed birds of prey. Maintaining a ceaseless vigil, inspired by hunger and caution, hawks and eagles hunt and consume prey atop these pedestals and deposit white banners of nitrogen-rich guano across the rock. Washed down by rain, this fertilizer feeds clumps of primitive plants otherwise starved for nutrients on the stark surface of weathered stone. The favorite raptor watchtowers, commanding the best vistas of the open landscape, are revealed by large splashes of orange, yellow, and lime-green lichens.

Partly because of the availability of suitable habitat and abundant food resources, the San Juan Islands are one of the best places for enjoying and studying birds of prey. Observing these high-strung predators from a considerate distance, one can distinguish between the 17 species that inhabit the archipelago by their size, shape, silhouette, and style of flight. Active by day, the three families of diurnal birds of prey in our area share a few basic similarities: sharp, hooked beaks for tearing flesh, strong, piercing talons, and amazing flying abilities. Usually the female is larger than the male and both wear similar plumage. Probably to compensate for their lack of strength and skill, the immatures are often dressed in feathers much larger than the adults, providing them with extra lift. Many of these species have a world-wide distribution and are often highly migratory or nomadic.

In the San Juan Islands we have New World vultures (Cathartidae), hawks and eagles (Accipitridae), and falcons (Falconidae) patrolling a spectrum of habitats. The vultures, consumers of dead animal matter, are very different from the other two families. Hawks and eagles are the most varied group and show a diversity of size, shape, and hunting strategies. These broad-winged birds are frequently seen soaring overhead or perched on fences and telephone poles throughout the archipelago. Falcons, the swiftest of birds, have long, pointed wings and long, narrow tails.

Around the globe the diurnal birds of prey have been beset with the same inescapable problem—humans. Shot, trapped, and poisoned, raptors have been directly persecuted by misguided ranchers, farmers, and hunters. They have also been hit hard by habitat destruction and massive loss of reproductive capabilities caused by pesticides and other long-lived chemical toxins absorbed through the food chain. Many species are now much reduced in population and occupy only fragments of their former ranges. In Washington State, all birds of prey are completely protected by law and severe penalties are levied upon those who molest or harm them in any way.

Everyone loses when birds of prey disappear. Their sensitive metabolisms act as biological "barometers" to warn us of dangerous levels of toxins accumulating in the ecosystem. They provide a great service to agriculture by removing great quantities of prolific rodents and other destructive pests from the environment. In the San Juan Islands they help to keep the voles and rabbits in check and also remove carrion from our roadsides. Possessing immeasurable aesthetic value, wild free-flying raptors give pleasure to countless people with their spectacular aerial displays and unbridled spirits.

NEW WORLD VULTURES
(Cathartidae)

Turkey Vulture (*Cathartes aura*). Flying high over San Juan Valley, a Turkey Vulture scents a decaying Townsend's Vole. Gliding earthward in response, the "buzzard" alights on the ground and begins to search for its dinner among the freshly mown hay. Finding the dead rodent flattened by a farm tractor, the scavenger prepares for a light meal. Meanwhile, vultures soaring over Cady Mountain and Beaverton Valley, alerted to the sight of their descending colleague and hoping for a banquet in the form of a large carcass, have quickly closed the distance and landed. Disappointed, they begin a silent squabble over the tiny mor-

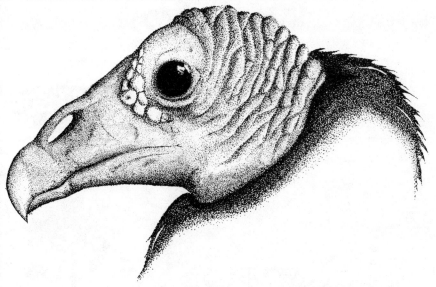

*The naked head of the Turkey Vulture is a hygienic
adaptation to a scavenging diet.*

sel and the ugly, naked-headed birds saunter back and forth over the field in un-
gainly sideways hops. Outnumbered, the finder seeks sanctuary in the air and
departs amid a rush of flapping wings, its prize safely dangling from its beak and
looking like a furry flapjack.

Unparalleled as a soaring bird, the Turkey Vulture is a beautiful sight—from a
distance. It seeks out rising columns of warm air in order to gain altitude in effortless, climbing spirals. Descending in a long glide to the next thermal, it repeats the
process and is able to cover long distances without flapping a wing. Sharing these
aerial escalators with the related hawks and eagles, Turkey Vultures can be recognized by their two-toned underwings, V-shaped wing posture, and tiny heads. The
heads appear small because they are unfeathered. This hygienic adaptation allows
the birds to feed deep within a rotting carcass and not soak their head feathers
with blood and gore. Any putrefying bacteria picked up from the carrion are then
exposed on the naked skin to the sterilizing effect of the sun's ultraviolet rays.

Turkey Vultures are common residents in the San Juans, and this is one of the
few places in western Washington where they have been found breeding.[24] Even
in the middle of winter a few vultures may be seen, especially over Lopez Island.
Most, however, depart in September when flocks may be observed using the San
Juans as stepping stones as they pass from the Canadian Gulf Islands to the mainland. One favorite route begins as they cross Haro Strait to western San Juan Island and from there go to Turn and Cattle points where they glide over to Lopez
Island. As numerous as they are during the fall passage, this is but a trickle of the
main movement down Vancouver Island. Over the city of Victoria, from 300 to
500 a day have been counted during the peak of migration. The return in spring is
more gradual and slowly begins in mid-March. By mid-April they are once again in
full strength and performing their beneficial clean-up for all of the islands.

HAWKS AND EAGLES
(Accipitridae)

Nesting Ospreys are found in the vicinity of large lakes in the San Juan Islands.

Osprey (*Pandion haliaetus*). Hunting from a perch or while hovering over a body of water, this large crook-winged raptor dives from great heights to obtain food. The "Fish Hawk," as it is known to many, is the only bird of prey that may be seen purposely plunging into water, sometimes completely submerging itself. A cosmopolitan species, the Osprey is restricted to a fishy diet and has adapted spiny feet with a reversible toe to help grip its slippery prey. In the San Juan Islands these vociferous birds may be seen nesting at several locations, particularly in the vicinity of large fresh-water lakes, although they also frequent marine shores. At least four of their bulky stick nests may be found on Orcas Island and several more are scattered over the other islands. Ospreys are rather uncommon in the archipelago, probably because of harassment from the bigger Bald Eagle. These pirates often steal fish from the Ospreys and generally make life miserable for them. Ospreys can be seen from April through September; very rarely, later into winter.[25]

Bald Eagle (*Haliaeetus leucocephalus*). Our national bird is unquestionably one of the prime birding attractions in the San Juan Islands. Bald Eagles nest in the archipelago in greater concentrations than anywhere else in the contiguous United States; 58 active nests were recorded in the spring of 1986 by the Washington State Department of Game. This number represents more than one-third of the total breeders in Washington. During the winter the population swells to roughly 250 individuals. The only time of year when the Bald Eagle is not plentiful is during fall when most move to mainland rivers to take advantage of salmon runs.

Live food for these sea eagles is basically anything smaller than themselves, but when found dead, food can be unlimited in size. Content to scavenge, Bald Eagles are not the fearsome predators that many people believe. However, when necessary they will hunt and kill prey with great skill and ferocity. This is sometimes accomplished by a cooperative attack strategy wherein a pair will make carefully timed stoops on a diving bird such as a grebe or merganser until it is exhausted. Young birds often specialize in pirating voles from Red-tailed Hawks and harriers. A flock of 35 immatures and adults was observed by the senior author in a pasture near False Bay on February 2, 1982. The birds were attracted to several rabbit and salmon carcasses that were deposited by researchers in order to observe the eagles' behavior. About a dozen eagles were actively feeding on the carcasses while an equal number bathed and drank from a puddle less than 100 feet away. The remainder of the eagles were perched on fences and telephone poles within one-fourth mile of the food source.

Eagles display extreme fidelity toward their mates and remain together for life. They have been known to live for 50 years in captivity. Charles Nash has watched Bald Eagle pairs defending the same territories in the San Juan Islands for the last 20 years, demonstrating their site loyalty. Most birds make their huge nests near the shore, and an active one is found every two to ten miles. Adding branches and sticks to their favorite nest each season, a couple will maintain one or two other sites as alternatives. Sensitive to logging, building construction, and other disturbing influences, many have been forced to use their alternative nests and others have been driven completely out of their territory. Bald Eagles have been steadily losing ground in the San Juans, and, since the area is presumably already at maximum carrying capacity, there is no place for displaced breeders to go. Only slightly less alarming is their attrition by power lines, a hazard that electrocuted one bird in the summer of 1982, simultaneously igniting a brush fire at American Camp and knocking out power over most of San Juan Island for a short time. If this majestic bird is to remain a symbol of our islands and nation, we must carefully monitor its well-being and protect it from these modern dangers.

Northern Harrier (*Circus cyaneus*). Swooping low over the fields of grass, a slender bird with long wings and tail tirelessly ranges over the pastures and prairies with an eye for mice and other small prey. Suddenly the Northern Harrier will appear close at hand over a rise and then be gone the next minute, its white rump flashing from far across the valley. This lightly built predator can cover up to 100 miles a day in its search for a meal, usually flying back and forth over the same patch of open country. Food in sight, it reacts with a catlike pounce, crumpling up and stabbing talons first into the weeds. Like other birds of prey, it usually scores a kill in only one of ten attempts. When the "Marsh Hawk" does capture a vole it often must face a more difficult problem posed by the larger broad-winged hawks and eagles. Patiently waiting at their perches, they launch into flight the moment a harrier makes a catch and usually are able to commandeer the tidbit without a struggle. No match for these powerful pirates, the harrier goes back to work and tries again.

The Northern Harrier is a locally common migrant and winter visitor in the San Juan Islands from September through April. Its stronghold is the southern halves of San Juan and Lopez islands, and 10 or more may be seen coursing San Juan in a single day. In the September migration, the species follows the same routes as Turkey Vultures but in lesser numbers. Northern Harriers are uncommon and local breeders during the summer, when a few adults can be observed in appropriate nesting habitat on San Juan Island. A nest with three eggs was found July 8, 1987 at American Camp by the senior author. Cinnamon-washed immatures appear in August and outnumber the adults for the rest of the year.

Sharp-shinned Hawk (*Accipiter striatus*). The three accipiters, often called true hawks, are a dashing group of raptors. Their short wings and long, narrow tails allow them to weave in and out of thick vegetation at high speeds. By means of rapid flapping punctuated by short glides, they actively patrol concealing woods and thickets. Hunting almost exclusively for other birds, they are able to capture this difficult game with an explosion of speed. Bold and fierce, accipiters often attack birds larger than themselves. One winter evening on the west side of Mt. Dallas, the senior author watched a male Sharp-shinned Hawk pursuing flocks of robins as they returned to the tall timber for the night. Whenever he made a run at one, a mettlesome Pileated Woodpecker would swoop by and intervene with a loud yammering. Each time, the infuriated "sharpie" would veer in the direction of the big, red-crested bird and pursue it to a snag. A game of hide-and-seek ensued as the Pileated Woodpecker dodged behind the trunk at each pass of the hawk. As it was half the size of the heavily armed woodpecker, it's just as well the little hawk was unable to catch his tormentor. Thwarted, he went to roost that night with an empty crop.

Sharp-shinned Hawks, smallest of the accipiters, are particularly dreaded by thrushes, sparrows, and other songbirds. These hawks are commonly seen migrating and overwintering wherever small birds abound. After April, they decline and retreat to quiet woods. In the San Juan Islands they nest uncommonly in forests unoccupied by their larger relative, the Cooper's Hawk.[26] Sharpies are the most aerial of the accipiters and are frequently seen soaring in small circles rather low to the ground during the fall migration period in September and October.

Cooper's Hawk (*Accipiter cooperii*). Considering how difficult it is to catch a glimpse of this secretive bird, it may be hard to believe that the San Juan Islands boast the highest density of nesting Cooper's Hawks on the continent.[27] The patchwork of forest, field, hedgerow, and woodlot that typifies the island landscape affords ideal breeding habitat for this medium-sized accipiter.

Abundant rabbit and bird populations provide ample food all year. Cooper's Hawks, residents and migrants in the archipelago, can be told from the Sharp-shinned by their bigger build and rounded, instead of square-tipped, tails.

Northern Goshawk *(Accipiter gentilis)*. The largest and rarest of accipiters is the steely plumaged Goshawk. In the San Juan Islands it is a scarce winter visitor and migrant near thickly timbered wood margins. This species is frequently attracted to Rock Dove roosts and feeding areas and may linger near these abundant sources of food for weeks at a time. Northern Goshawks are very rare residents and possible breeders in the summer.[28]

Red-tailed Hawk *(Buteo jamaicensis)*. The highly adaptable Red-tailed Hawk has fared better than any other bird of prey in the struggle to survive civilization's encroachments. While other raptors decline, this broad-winged hawk has been able to hold its own in most regions and even expand its range into areas cleared of dense woods. In the San Juan Islands its solid shape and shrill whistling screams can be noted over any terrestrial habitat. Abundant breeding residents, pairs of Red-tailed Hawks display to each other at any season by diving, talons extended, in mock attack. Like other broad-winged hawks, or buteos, these birds are accomplished soarers and hunt from thermals, as well as when perched on telephone poles and fences. Although they are not picky eaters, their diet consists mainly of rabbits and rodents, captured at the end of sharp-descending glides. An albino Red-tailed Hawk on Lopez Island has enchanted observers there for several years.

Rough-legged Hawk *(Buteo lagopus)*. Like all arctic-nesting raptors, the handsome Rough-legged Hawk is a very tame bird of prey. Halfway between the Northern Harrier and Red-tailed Hawk in form and behavior, this broad-winged

Rough-legged Hawk, a visitor from the far north

hawk is most often seen in the open country of south San Juan and Lopez islands. It is a locally common winter visitor from mid-October through March with some birds present up to a month before and after these times. The Rough-legged Hawk's yearly numbers in the San Juan Islands are affected by local vole populations and the cyclical state of lemmings in the northern tundra.

Golden Eagle (*Aquila chrysaetos*). When strong winds blow off the Strait of Juan de Fuca, the empress of the sky may be seen floating motionlessly on the updrafts over Mt. Dallas. One clear October evening we sat upon a bleached knoll of this mountain and watched the sun set in the misty mosaic of Canadian islands. Sharing this spectacle with us was a Golden Eagle high overhead. Surveying her domain from a lofty vantage point, she had apparently come to watch, not hunt. As soon as the sun plunged below the horizon she wheeled around and went to roost; all was well within her kingdom.

Seldom seen in the rest of western Washington, the Golden Eagle is a distinctive San Juan feature. There are presently at least three resident breeding pairs on San Juan Island and one pair on Lopez and Orcas. Golden Eagles are year-round residents in the San Juans with more than a dozen censused during many recent winters. Some expert observers feel they have been declining in the archipelago lately. Human disturbance seems to be the problem for this bird and at least two pairs had to relocate their nests in 1985. A gravel pit excavation coupled with the building of a nearby home forced the Turn Point birds to rebuild at a nearby, quieter site. A more vivid example of Golden Eagle vulnerability was the loss of an active nest with eggs near False Bay. The nest tree was sawed down by a landowner in a reckless and illegal act, but luckily the birds were able to start over the following spring at a new location, missing only one breeding season. The guilty parties in this episode eventually paid $10,000 in fines, thanks to the stringent laws protecting these noble animals. With the limited amount of suitable nesting habitat on San Juan Island available to these birds, this scenario may be repeated; thus careful monitoring and reporting of violators is recommended to all bird lovers.

The Golden, a species of true eagle, is not closely related to the similarly sized Bald, a kind of sea eagle, with which it is easily confused. Young eagles of both species are mostly dark-colored, but the Golden Eagle at any age possesses a tawny nape. Immature Bald Eagles are heavily mottled and acquire the white head and tail when four or five years old. Subadult Golden Eagles have white "windows" near their wing tips and white tails with a broad, dark, terminal band. Unlike the Bald Eagle, the Golden is a terrestrial bird and spends little time near marine shorelines. It is also a much fiercer bird, depending very little upon carrion for food. It does sometimes scavenge afterbirths and stillborn livestock, a practice that has led to the misconception that Golden Eagles kill healthy animals. At least 20,000 Golden Eagles in the Western United States were gunned from aircraft between 1940 and 1962 before protective laws were enacted. In truth, this beneficial hunter does not normally prey on livestock and exists largely on rabbits, both in the San Juan Islands and throughout its range.

FALCONS
(Falconidae)

*Our tiniest falcon, the
American Kestrel, hunts small
prey such as this Northwestern
Garter Snake.*

American Kestrel (*Falco sparverius*). The diminutive "Sparrow Hawk" introduces us to the falcons, a swift group of raptors recognized by their long, pointed wings and narrow tails. These birds are built for straight, rapid movement and powerful stoops or dives. Falcons are efficient predators and prey principally upon other birds, capturing them in flight at high speeds. Well adapted for the task, these aerodynamically shaped birds have bulletlike heads, short necks, broad shoulders, and tapering hindquarters. Also aiding them in their aerial assaults are heavy brows and dark malar stripes that reduce glare, nostril baffling to prevent the absorption of excess oxygen when stooping, and notched bills for snapping their victims' neck vertebrae.

The American Kestrel applies these tactics mostly in winter, when insects, its main staple, have become scarce. In warmer seasons it hunts from perches or while hovering, a very unfalconlike method. Although kestrels lack some of the dash possessed by the larger falcons, they make up for it with their friendliness and lovely colors. Uncommon breeding residents in the San Juan Islands during the summer months, kestrels may be found nesting in woodpecker holes in open woodland habitats. Wintering birds are fairly common and American Kestrels reach a migratory peak in September and April. Like many raptors, these birds "stack up" at the south end of San Juan Island when passing through the archipelago and sometimes three or four birds will be seen in a single day perched on the wires paralleling Cattle Point Road.

Merlin (*Falco columbarius*). Low tide at False Bay is a time for many birds to forage. On a winter day large flocks of Dunlins probe the mud for sustenance. Spying these sandpipers from a great height, a Merlin tucks her wings and begins a stoop. Ever alert to danger from above, the Dunlins simultaneously burst into flight and begin evasive maneuvers at the approach of the falcon. Moving in concert, the fleeing birds are unable to outdistance their foe. A flagging Dunlin is singled out and is forcefully met with grasping talons. Two opportunistic gulls rush up to mob the Merlin, intending to steal her prize. Dropping the sandpiper to free her formidable talons, the Merlin lashes out at both gulls in an angry response. Recovering from its shock, the wounded Dunlin seeks to rejoin the safety of the flock, now more than a mile away. Spotting the fluttering escapee, the enraged falcon breaks away from the melee and returns to once again pursue her quarry. In a dazzling acceleration she closes the distance and binds to the Dunlin in an explosion of feathers. Laboriously climbing to a safe altitude over San Juan Valley, the Merlin plucks her meal out of the reach of larger raptors. Accidentally dropped in the process, the dead Dunlin plummets earthward but is easily snatched back before striking the ground. The spectacularly agile Merlin, aware of the watchful eyes of larger piratical raptors, will remain aloft to devour her hard-won feast.

This small falcon is a fairly common migrant and winter visitor in the San Juan Islands from September through April. It ranges widely and can be seen over many habitats in the search for small birds. A Merlin routinely spends the winter near Friday Harbor and can be observed attacking European Starlings roosting on the ferry dock. Rarely, individuals are sighted during the summer months, leading to unsubstantiated rumors of Merlins nesting in remote parts of the San Juans.[29]

Peregrine Falcon (*Falco peregrinus*). The swiftest bird in the world is the Peregrine Falcon. Some observers have estimated its speed in a stoop to approach 200 miles per hour. This large falcon feeds on ducks, pigeons, and other medium-sized birds and is seldom found far from water. Peregrine Falcons are an endangered species and have severely declined over most of their range. It is hoped that they are now recovering from their lowest point, as they have returned to many former breeding locations, including the San Juan Islands.[30] In summer, look for these rare birds near Pigeon Guillemot nesting colonies. From September through April, the uncommon migrants and winter visitors are widespread in the islands.

RARE BIRDS OF PREY

To sight one of these four species of raptors in the San Juan Islands is cause for celebration. These birds have a tendency to be observed on San Juan Island, especially in the open habitats found from Cattle Point to San Juan Valley. The **Swainson's Hawk** (*Buteo swainsoni*)[31] is a very rare migrant in the archipelago from February through October. This pointed-winged hawk is not recorded every year in the area, but formerly it may have been more regular. The **Ferruginous Hawk** (*Buteo regalis*)[32] is an accidental vagrant and has been recorded once on San Juan Island for one of the few western Washington records. The **Gyrfalcon** (*Falco rusticolus*)[33] is a rare migrant and winter visitor to the San Juan Islands from November through March. The **Prairie Falcon** (*Falco mexicanus*)[34] is sighted as a casual vagrant from October through mid-April in the San Juan Islands, only briefly visiting our area before venturing on to southern wintering areas. Like the Gyrfalcon, this powerful raptor is most likely encountered in San Juan Valley or at American Camp.

FOWLLIKE BIRDS
(Galliformes/Phasianidae)

A cock California Quail

This family of ground-dwelling birds has lent itself well to domestication. A quick inventory of a barnyard often reveals an array of strong-legged, scratching fowl. Chickens, turkeys, guinea fowl, pheasants, peafowl, and Japanese quail are favorites of farmers and aviculturalists. All are members of the order Galliformes, a widespread group of about 250 species. The cosmopolitan distribution of the wild varieties is surprising as these birds are short-winged and can fly strongly only for small distances. In North America, one diverse family of fowllike birds is found—the Phasianidae. Within this vocal and gregarious family, the males are usually boldly patterned while the ground-nesting females are well camouflaged. There have been nine of these species present in the San Juan Islands at various times, only two of which were native to the area. The others were brought here for sport shooting.

Blue Grouse (*Dendragapus obscurus*). Ventriloquial booming sounds emanating from the dark conifers may lead the birder on a long and fruitless hunt for this very tame but difficult-to-see fowl. Like other grouse, it emits a sound so low in pitch that owls, humans, and other predators are unable to locate the source. It is unique among birds in that it breeds at lower elevations in spring and moves to higher ground in winter. The Blue Grouse, though locally uncommon in the San Juan Islands, displays a particular loyalty to lichen balds. Rising from the surrounding mantle of woods, these open habitats afford the bird ample food in the way of berries, buds, insects, and conifer needles. The backcounty of Orcas Island is the best place for consistently locating this fairly arboreal fowl. Particularly good spots for this resident breeder are Little Summit, Orcas Knob, and Mt. Woolard. Tiptop Hill on Stuart Island also yields frequent sightings of Blue Grouse.

Wild Turkey (*Meleagris gallopavo*). The Wild Turkeys found inhabiting the San Juan Islands are anything but wild. There is almost no difference between their behavior and the domestic turkeys found on local farms. Without seeing their gold-tipped tail feathers, an observer probably couldn't tell the two apart. This doesn't stop large numbers of birders from coming to our islands to check off these tame

A tom Wild Turkey engorges its wattles while displaying to prospective mates.

birds on their life lists. Extremely wary and hard to even glimpse in other areas, Wild Turkeys were introduced to the San Juans, perhaps less than 20 years ago, and are completely protected by law. Even an occasional poacher can't seem to instill a fear of humans in these birds. They are quite common on the west side of San Juan Island, with the center of abundance at English Camp. Look for their leks (communal displays for breeding purposes) in May and June, often conducted in the middle of a roadway. The woods at the base of Young Hill echo with "gobbling" at this time of year. Wild Turkeys are also present on Spieden Island and there may be a handful left in Moran State Park.

California Quail (*Callipepla californica*). Among this entire group of birds, the California Quail has fared the best. Large coveys, or flocks, of this introduced game bird have been a familiar sight in the San Juan Islands since the 1930s.[35] Although they roam widely on San Juan and Lopez islands in every habitat except wet coniferous woods, sightings from Orcas and the other islands are infrequent. When a flock of this common breeding resident becomes divided, listen for worried calls that sound as if the birds are asking "where are you?" This easily imitated phrase often draws a quick response from an otherwise hidden covey. California Quails favor shrubby thickets and are frequently seen scurrying across roadways bordered by this habitat.

Rare Fowllike Birds: Of the three Old World species brought to these islands, **Gray Partridge** (*Perdix perdix*), **Chukar** (*Alectoris chukar*), and **Ring-necked Pheasant** (*Phasianus colchicus*), only the latter persists. Abundant on all of the larger islands until the early 1970s, the Ring-necked Pheasant is now quite rare and probably only survives by being augmented with released captive birds.[36] The other two species were common to abundant in the early 1960s and were probably introduced at least 10 years earlier.[37] Both Gray Partridge and Chukar are now considered extirpated in San Juan County.

The **Northern Bobwhite** (*Colinus virginianus*) is native to North America but not the San Juans. It was brought to the larger islands around the turn of the century. Gunners found this game bird to be fairly plentiful for some time but the last records are now over 50 years old.[38]

The **Mountain Quail** (*Oreortyx pictus*) was apparently introduced to the Puget Trough region. Naturalists wrote that this handsome quail could be found on Orcas and Waldron islands before 1905.[39] Our Mountain Quails disappeared in the 1930s or earlier, although a handful still remain on southeast Vancouver Island.

The last fowllike bird to be discussed here is the **Ruffed Grouse** (*Bonasa umbellus*). Originally native to the islands, it is probably no longer extant in the county, as no records have been brought forward in the last 50 years.[40] Changing vegetational patterns may be the chief contributing factor to the demise of this broadleaf forest bird in the largely coniferous San Juans.

Chilean Tinamou (*Northoprocta perdicaria*), a South American game bird belonging to a completely different order but included here because of its superficial resemblance to fowllike birds, was introduced to Lopez Island and lasted for several years there. This primitive ground dweller is believed to be the nearest relative to the original ancestral bird that spawned all other species. Tinamous bred successfully and were considered common in Lopez farmland and shrubby thickets during the 1970s but abruptly declined at the end of that decade and are presumed extirpated from San Juan County today.[41]

CRANES, RAILS, AND COOTS
(Gruiformes)

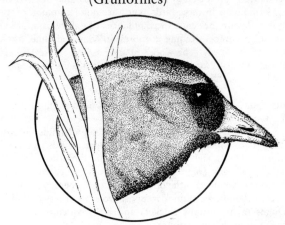

Sora

The Gruiformes are a large and ancient order of birds, probably most distinctive for their lack of a crop, the muscular organ that in other birds stores food. They are represented in the San Juan Islands by only two families, the cranes (Gruidae) and the rails and coots (Rallidae). Seldom seen in this area, cranes are large, long-legged birds that most closely resemble herons. Unlike herons, they fly with their necks outstretched and bugle loudly, having an extremely elongated trachea. They are known for unusual and spectacular mating dances, exuberant displays that provided inspiration to many native cultures. Fossils of cranes dating back 40 million years attest to the antiquity of the bird.

There are only two species of rails found in the San Juan Islands. Both have compressed bodies that allow them to run quickly through dense wetland vegetation. Their long toes prevent them from sinking into the muck as they forage for both animal and vegetable foods. Our one species of coot differs from the rails by having lobed toes and consequently greater abilities as a swimmer and diver.

Shy and rarely observed, our rails are best detected by their frequent and loud calls, often resounding through the night. Together with the insects, frogs, coots, and owls, they are part of the marsh chorus heard on a spring or summer evening. As vociferous and common as they are, many people have never seen a rail, and often the only way to catch a glimpse of these stealthy creatures is to lure them out of concealment with the use of a tape-recorded call. Setting the tape player in a clear spot will usually attract a curious (or even furious) bird as it seeks its rival, or its potential mate. The quiet observer may be rewarded by seeing the mysterious bird slowly and cautiously move into view. Nervously bobbing its head and flicking its tiny tail as it slips through the reeds, the odd-looking rail presents yet another challenge to birders—avoiding fits of uncontrollable laughter.

Virginia Rail (*Rallus limicola*). This elusive bird is a widespread nesting inhabitant of the San Juan Islands. Individuals are concealed in just about every fen, marsh, or flooded farm field choked with canary grass and rushes. Some of the best locations for the Virginia Rail are Egg, Sportsman, Killebrew, and Hummel lakes, and Three Meadows Marsh. Often sharing the areas with Soras, this very common rail is easily distinguished from its neighbors by its long beak, typical of the "marsh rails," and an assortment of distinctive calls. These include a metallic-sounding "kid-dic kid-dic kid-dic," an insectlike whirring, and a descending series of laughing grunts that resembles the noise of a barnyard pig. Though it is a year-round resident of the islands, the population declines some during the winter as most individuals prefer to move south before their watery haunts freeze.

A Virginia Rail emerges from a dense patch of cattails and monkeyflower.

Sora (*Porzana carolina*). If you search for this mouselike bird by hastily crashing through the marsh, your expedition will be fruitless. At best you might get a quick glimpse of the little rail whirring away, dangling its large yellow feet. Quietly waiting at the edge of the fen and appealing to the bird's sense of curiosity with a tape recorder will yield better results. Making a squeaking noise by blowing past a blade of grass is an alternative method of attracting the Sora. It was named after its most frequently heard call but also displays a repertoire of several others. It gives rapid, plucking notes when disturbed and a descending whinny to declare ownership of some soggy real estate. This locally common breeder is usually migratory, though exact fall departure dates are unknown. A few birds may tough it through the winter from time to time, but most fly to warmer climates at least a thousand miles south of the San Juan Islands. Expect to hear this "crake's" sounds mingling with Pacific Treefrogs and Virginia Rails from mid-April through early October.

American Coot (*Fulica americana*). Unlike its marsh-stalking cousins, the American Coot is a raucous clown. An excellent swimmer and diver, the "Mud Hen" is often seen in the company of ducks. This gregarious bird is a fairly common winter visitor and migrant in the San Juan Islands. It prefers marshy ponds and lakes on many of the islands but is found in greater numbers on San Juan and Lopez. When cold spells freeze its favorite haunts, this bird will venture on to shallow salt water. The American Coot is a fairly common nester; the absurdly colored young can be found locally at Three Meadows Marsh, Hummel Lake, Otter's Lair, the Frank Richardson Wildfowl Sanctuary, and other quiet bodies of water with densely vegetated shorelines.

Sandhill Crane (*Grus canadensis*). Like other members of its family, this crane has suffered grave losses over much of its range. Much more common in western Washington before the turn of the century, it was found breeding and migrating in large numbers throughout the region. Today the nesting colony nearest the San Juan Islands is located east of Vancouver, B.C., at Pitt Meadows. Even this relic population is seriously threatened, and it was necessary to augment it in 1980 with Sandhill Cranes from another area. Very rarely, small flocks or individuals can still be seen in the San Juans,[42] especially during the fall migration starting in late August and continuing through October when they are en route to their wintering grounds in California and New Mexico. Even more rare are sightings in the winter and spring months through May. These cranes are easily mistaken for Great Blue Herons, but look for them flying overhead with their long necks outstretched or resting in wet fields and pastures.

SHOREBIRDS, GULLS, AUKS, AND ALLIES
(Charadriiformes)

*A precocious
Killdeer chick*

The high degree of diversity evident in this order is a result of the many specialized ways in which these birds exploit their environment to obtain their animal food. Superficially different, the shorebirds, gulls, auks, and their allies are united by a strong preference for marine habitats, as well as various anatomical characteristics. A careful inspection will reveal that they have a unique bone structure, a tufted oil gland, a reduced hind toe, no crop, and open nostrils. Upon hatching, the downy, camouflaged young are quite ambulatory and are soon able to leave the nest. Adults are densely plumaged and, in most species, the sexes appear nearly identical.

PLOVERS
(Charadriidae)

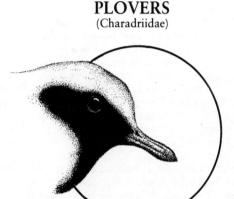

Black-bellied Plover in high plumage

Running rapidly across the level ground, a small, plump shorebird makes brief abrupt stops like a robin. Picking up tiny invertebrate creatures with its dovelike bill, the plover scans the area for food and enemies with its large, dark eyes. The open country that plovers inhabit allows predators very little concealing cover. Falcons are their main foe but even these speedsters have a hard time capturing the wary and fast-flying plovers. Their plaintive and diagnostic calls communicate the presence of danger and also serve to maintain the cohesion of the flock. Plovers seek areas with low topographical relief such as wet farm fields, sandy shorelines, and muddy tide flats. Little of this habitat type is found in the San Juan Islands. Where it does occur, it serves to concentrate and localize the birds. Consistently observed at False Bay, Fisherman Spit, and Spencer Spit throughout the year, plovers are less regular in smaller patches of suitable habitat scattered over the islands.

Black-bellied Plover (*Pluvialis squatarola*). When the first Black-bellied Plovers return in mid-July from their high arctic nesting grounds, they are still clad in black tuxedos and marbled silver topcoats. Our largest plovers, they can always be recognized by their black "armpits," even when wearing the salt-and-pepper winter plumage. These deliberate feeders are often watched by gulls ready to pirate any large prey that the plover may extract from the mud. The senior author once watched an agile Black-bellied Plover shake one pursuing gull after another during a 20-minute chase. Finally it was able to pause long enough to swallow the big marine worm dangling from its beak.

Black-bellied Plovers are common migrants and local winter visitors in the San Juan Islands. Peak numbers occur during migration from late July through

August and again from mid-April through early May. Late May and June are the only times when this species' mournful "tlee-oo-eee" is not expected to be heard in our area. In some years a small flock of up to 100 birds is found overwintering at False Bay and adjacent farmland in San Juan Valley. In 1982 this flock grew to over 500 in late April when its numbers were augmented by migrating plovers.

Lesser Golden-Plover (*Pluvialis dominica*). One of the longest yearly journeys undertaken in the bird world is the annual migration of the Lesser Golden-Plovers. Nesting in the Canadian tundra and wintering in the pampas of Argentina, these birds travel about 16,000 miles each year. At the beginning of this century, this species was nearly exterminated by market hunters. On the rise again today, the Lesser Golden-Plover may soon be divided into two species, with the mustard-colored race, the "Pacific" Golden-Plover, receiving full species status. When identifying plovers in the San Juan Islands, be sure to look for this variety in with our typical Lesser Golden-Plovers. Both races are slightly more delicate than the Black-bellied Plover and can be easily distinguished from their larger relative by their whistled "queedle" call. Lesser Golden-Plovers are uncommon fall migrants usually observed from August through early October; they are less frequent as spring migrants from mid-April to mid-May.

Semipalmated Plover (*Charadrius semipalmatus*). This tiny "ringed" plover is marked with a black breast band, a common camouflage device in the family, which serves to break up the body outline when in open terrain. The name of this bird comes from the fact that it has partially webbed feet, which, like other plovers, it sometimes vibrates or stomps to stir up prey. The Semipalmated Plover is a common migrant in the San Juans from late April to mid-May and again from early July through mid-September. Spring stragglers are seen into June, and fall birds occasionally remain into November; rarely they are seen lingering into January.

Killdeer (*Charadrius vociferus*). The landlubbers of the family, the adaptable Killdeers display very little discretion in the selection of breeding sites. Their simple nests, mere scrapes lined with pebbles, are hidden on golf courses, pastures, beaches, and even gravel lanes. If a pair is nesting in the neighborhood, it is sure to let you know by carrying on at all hours with a loud, repetitive "kill-dee." Should you come too near a nest, the dedicated mother will put on a pathetic broken-wing act to lure you away from her eggs or chicks.

Killdeers are the most widespread and easily observed plovers in the San Juan Islands. Besides the previously mentioned habitats, these common breeding residents are also seen with other plovers along marine shorelines, especially during migration. Killdeers can be extremely frustrating to bird watchers because of their vociferous cries and skittish nature. Attempts to approach a large group of various kinds of shorebirds are frequently thwarted by Killdeers when they take flight, because they flush the entire flock and spoil any chance for careful study.

OYSTERCATCHERS
(Haematopodidae)

The Black
Oystercatcher is a
restless and vocal
denizen of rocky
shorelines.

These interesting shorebirds have evolved a sturdy, laterally compressed bill much like an oyster knife. Sliding this useful tool under limpets and chitons, they are able to pry the mollusks off the rocks at low tide and then slice them from their protective armor. Slipping their bright red beaks into mussels and oysters, they sever the adductor muscles holding the shells together and neatly extract the meat. The oystercatchers' scientific name means "pink-footed"; their clown attire is completed by yellow eyes and chunky shapes. Although gregarious for most of the year, these noisy birds separate into highly territorial breeding pairs in spring when they nest in the comparative safety of offshore rocks and islets. All too frequently, uninformed boaters and fishermen inadvertently disturb the breeding birds and thus provide opportunities for the omnipresent gulls and crows to pilfer the temporarily unprotected nests. The most crucial period in an oystercatcher's life is its first 30 days after hatching. This is when it must learn to fly and forage for its own food. Once these skills are mastered, it may live to be well over 30 years of age.

Families of **Black Oystercatchers** (*Haematopus bachmani*), the only San Juan representative of this family, begin banding together in early fall, sometimes amassing into flocks of several dozen individuals. Never venturing far from their places of birth, these nonmigratory shorebirds are more abundant in the San Juan Islands than anywhere else in the Puget Trough. There are at least 30 nesting locations in the county, among them Goose, Strawberry, Barren (NWR), and Ripple (NWR) islands. Black Oystercatchers will show up on nearly any rocky shoreline or rock-dotted tide flat during the nonbreeding season, September through April, when they are more easily observed and less sensitive to disturbance. Land-bound birders might try Cattle Point, False Bay, San Juan County Park, Obstruction Point, or Washington Park on Fidalgo Island.

STILTS AND AVOCETS
(Recurvirostridae)

*American Avocets skim prey
from the water's surface.*

Extraordinarily long legs and bills typify this family of elegant shorebirds. Small-headed and long-necked, these birds may at times swim like phalaropes. More commonly they probe in mud and shallow water for aquatic prey. The **Black-necked Stilt** (*Himantopus mexicanus*)[43] and **American Avocet** (*Recurvirostra americana*)[44] are both very rare migrants in the Puget Trough and have been recorded in the San Juan Islands.

SANDPIPERS
(Scolopacidae)

*Greater Yellowlegs are
generalist feeders.*

Sandpipers are a large, diverse family of shorebirds showing a great variety of specialized bills and feeding strategies. Most probe or pick with their streamlined bills in moist soil, sand, and mud for small invertebrates and can walk or run quickly on their slender legs. Sandpipers are rather cryptically colored and wear several different plumages, including a breeding, nonbreeding, and juvenile dress. They are very gregarious (while not engaged in nesting activities), resting and foraging in vast, chattering flocks. Sandpipers display great speed and nimbleness in flight, taking off, wheeling, and landing in unison. These dense formations and breath-taking maneuvers serve to confuse predators, which often have a difficult time singling out an individual for attack. The long, pointed wings of sandpipers are made for speed and endurance, abilities they need to migrate long distances and breed in the high latitudes.

Sandpipers within this family that deserve special mention are the phalaropes. These seafarers have largely forsaken the terrestrial habits of their relatives and have adopted aquatic lifestyles. Spending large amounts of their lives over oceans or lakes, they have evolved adaptations that allow them to swim and feed on the water's surface. Among their unique characteristics are lobed toes for propulsion, and dense plumage on their bellies, which provides buoyancy by trapping a layer of air next to the skin. While surface feeding they spin around rapidly, thus stirring organisms into a vortex, so they can secure them with their thin bills. Another distinctive trait of phalaropes is their reversal of sexual roles, whereby the larger, more colorful females defend territories, are polyandrous, and remain aloof from domestic chores. The males are responsible for nest building, egg incubation, and feeding the young.

Sandpipers can be found in many San Juan habitats, including sandy and rocky shores, mud flats, wet agricultural land, lakeshores, and marshes. The phalaropes are seen in the open waterways, often gathering in areas with swift tidal currents. Locations like Three Meadows Marsh, Panorama Marsh, Richardson Ponds, and Swifts Bay Pond are excellent for those sandpipers that frequent fresh water. Rocky shore inhabitants are best sought at Cattle Point, Eagle Point, West Sound, and the Richardson area, unless one has a boat and can visit the many National Wildlife Refuge islands and reefs (from a respectful distance).

Fisherman Spit, Spencer Spit, False Bay, Wescott Bay, and Squaw Bay are all good to excellent for the mud-flat-loving sandpipers. For best results, visit these marine habitats on a rising tide, otherwise you may think that these "hot spots" are very cold indeed. Rising water levels concentrate the actively feeding birds into a narrow band close to shore, providing the best opportunity for study. At high tide, when the birds are roosting quietly, it may seem there isn't a single sandpiper in San Juan County, so be sure to consult your tide tables before planning a shorebird excursion.

Greater Yellowlegs (*Tringa melanoleuca*). Behaving like a hyperactive "mini-heron," the Greater Yellowlegs is our widest ranging sandpiper, both in terms of habitat and season. Showing the greatest favor toward brackish lagoons, birds of this species will eventually make an appearance on nearly every pond, marsh, lagoon, and sandy marine shoreline in the area at some point in a given year. Disjunct from the remainder of their winter range, the northernmost population is found in the San Juan Islands and southern Vancouver Island. Flocks of a dozen or less can be found overwintering at the American Camp lagoons, Argyle Lagoon, Wescott Bay, Frank Richardson Wildlife Sanctuary, Humphrey Head Lagoon, and Swifts Bay Pond. Common as they are in winter, they are even more numerous during migration from mid-April through early May and from July through late September. Greater Yellowlegs are nonbreeding residents in the archipelago; in late May and June they remain very uncommon.

Lesser Yellowlegs (*Tringa flavipes*). Less hardy than the slightly larger and similar Greater Yellowlegs, the Lesser Yellowlegs departs for much warmer regions during the winter months. Although present as a fall migrant from late July through September, this sandpiper is fairly common only in August. Swifts Bay Pond, perhaps the best location for Lesser Yellowlegs in the San Juan Islands, had a flock of 35 recorded by the authors on August 20, 1986. Rare spring migrants occur from mid-April through mid-May. It can be very tricky deciding which species a lone yellowlegs belongs to, and one must pay particular attention to the bill length and call of these leggy birds. The Lesser Yellowlegs, favoring fresh-water habitats to salt, has a proportionately shorter and thinner bill, approximately the length of the head, and a higher, flatter alarm call that consists of one or two "tew" notes. The Greater Yellowlegs is distinguished by its barely upturned bill, longer than the head, and a ringing three-part cry, "dear! dear! dear!"

Solitary Sandpiper (*Tringa solitaria*). Rarely stopping at ponds and fresh-water marshes in the San Juan Islands, these loners migrate through in May and again from mid-July through mid-September on their way to Peru and Argentina. Breeding in northern forests, Solitary Sandpipers are highly arboreal, laying their eggs in the vacated nests of songbirds. Three Meadows Marsh is a particularly good spot to look for the greenish legs, darkly barred rump and tail, and whitish eye ring of this species. When flushed, they emit a high, sharp "peet-weet-weet" and dart off in swooping, swallowlike flight.

Wandering Tattler (*Heteroscelus incanus*). Bobbing and teetering like the familiar Spotted Sandpiper, this bird of rocky reefs and shorelines is an uncommon but regularly observed migrant in the San Juan Islands. Wandering Tattlers are difficult to find during spring migration in May, or, very rarely, June. They are much easier to locate in fall from mid-July through early October. At their peak abundance, Wandering Tattlers are locally fairly common on exposed rocks and points along the Strait of Juan de Fuca from late July through early September, especially at Eagle Point, Whale Rocks, and east to Colville Island.

Spotted Sandpiper (*Actitis macularia*). The "Spotty" is a funny little sandpiper, quite different from the rest of the family. The aggressive females often mate with more than one male and, like the phalaropes, do not assist with incubation or care of the brood. Remarkably, a Spotted Sandpiper was once witnessed carrying a chick to safety by tightly clasping it between its thighs and flying off. Wings bowed in an arc, these birds flap with shallow, vibrating strokes while crying "peet" or "peet weet" in a shrill voice. On the ground, they hold their heads low and pump their tail up and down incessantly. Spotted Sandpipers are rare breeders in the San Juans on ponds and lakes with sparsely vegetated shorelines. They are common migrants in May and also from late July through September, most frequently observed in rocky marine habitats. Straggling birds are seen into late fall, with rare individuals overwintering.

Whimbrel (*Numenius phaeopus*). One of the large and long-legged "curlew type" of sandpipers, the Whimbrel is a striking shorebird with a long neck and gracefully decurved bill. It can be found in a variety of habitats, including rocky shores, tide flats, grassy beaches, and agricultural fields, but in the San Juan Islands it is almost always observed at False Bay. Whimbrels are seen migrating in every month from April to October, with the last spring migrants leaving just as the first southbound birds return. The best opportunity for finding one of these uncommon sandpipers comes during the spring passage in late April through mid-May and, with slightly decreased chances, from late July through early October as they move south. Very rarely a Whimbrel is discovered on isolated beaches or rocks in the middle of winter. Both Williamson and Bird rocks have played host to these hardy individuals, far from their usual California and Mexico wintering grounds.

Ruddy Turnstone (*Arenaria interpres*). Short, squat, and fiesty, the Ruddy Turnstone is a jack-of-all-trades. This versatile bird uses its wedge-shaped bill to overturn rocks, clumps of seaweed, shells, and beach litter, in order to uncover crustaceans and mullusks. Rooting under driftlogs, through wave-tossed algae, and into mud and sand, it finds abundant amphipods, worms, and insects. Ruddy Turnstones snap up flies and grubs from rotting seal carcasses and the senior author has observed them picking bits of flesh from dead sharks and other large fishes. Although these individuals were sitting on a veritable mountain of food they aggressively kept other turnstones at bay with a low head posture and sharp pecks. These harlequin birds are locally fairly common, with nearly all records coming from False Bay. Their spring passage occurs in the first three weeks in May and the southward movement takes place from mid-July through August with some lingering into September. Ruddy Turnstones should be sought in winter as very rare visitors.

Black Turnstone (*Arenaria melanocephala*). Exploring the isolated rocky shorelines of the San Juan Islands by kayak, one becomes well acquainted with this dark and dumpy sandpiper. Occupying offshore islets and reefs, the well-camouflaged Black Turnstone can disappear from sight simply by becoming motionless. If you should paddle too close, this "rock bird" will explode into the air, revealing a boldly striped black-and-white flight pattern and uttering a loud, kingfisherlike rattle. These sandpipers are locally abundant migrants and common winter residents but are observed with much less frequency on the larger islands. Lacking a boat, a bird watcher seeking Black Turnstones should try checking Cattle Point, West Sound, or False Bay at a low tide. Rarely this species can be found residing throughout the year but is most numerous from mid-July to mid-May.

Black Turnstones use their wide bills to overturn rocks and algae in search of prey.

Surfbird (*Aphriza virgata*). At home in the spray of crashing waves, the Surfbird is another one of our rocky shore specialists. Although they are quite tame, "Sea Chickens" usually restrict themselves to the most isolated and exposed islets and reefs along the perimeter of the San Juans, rarely visiting the larger islands. The best locations for observing these stocky birds are found south of Lopez Island and, better still, in the vicinity of Waldron Island. Concentrations of as many as 20 Surfbirds on Bare Island (NWR) and 40 on White Rock (NWR) are commonplace during August and September. These locally common migrants and winter visitors are found in our area from mid-July through April.

Sanderling (*Calidris alba*). The ancient glacial scourings left behind relatively few scattered pockets of sediments in the San Juan Islands. Wherever these deposits of unconsolidated sand and gravel occur, they are subjected to the forces of erosion and are eventually carried into the surrounding waterways. Most of the material is

Sanderlings usually probe for food in wet sand near the water's edge.

swept away by the strong tidal currents, but in some places it collects, punctuating the permanent bedrock shores with sandy crescents. These shifting beaches are rather sterile compared to muddy and rocky shorelines, as marine organisms have trouble locating anchoring sites and keeping burrows from collapsing. Searching along the water's edge at such locations for the relatively sparse pickings, a cluster of ghostly pale sandpipers probes behind each receding wave. The Sanderlings resemble tiny wind-up toys as they mechanically dart away from the next breaking surge and scurry along the beach. Lacking extensive areas of this preferred habitat in the archipelago, Sanderlings are occasionally seen foraging along rocky shores and mud flats. These common migrants and uncommon winter visitors are most often encountered at Sandy Point, South Beach, and the bluffy shores along the east and west sides of Lopez Island. The migratory passages take place from mid-July through mid-October and in April and May when small flocks of a dozen or so birds stop briefly to refuel.

Semipalmated Sandpiper (*Calidris pusilla*). Although very likely North America's most abundant shorebird, the Semipalmated Sandpiper occurs only sparingly along the west coast of the continent. Traveling with large flocks of Western and Least Sandpipers, its presence is usually masked by these other "peeps." ("Peeps" are an infamous group of tiny sandpipers, requiring careful study and a good measure of patience to be correctly identified.) Separating the Semipalmated Sandpipers is done by looking for their black legs, short and stubby bills, and grayish plumage. Most birds seen on the Pacific coast are juveniles with scaly backs, partial whitish collars below the cheeks, chestnut-edged scapulars, and buffy-edged wing coverts. The Semipalmated Sandpiper's diagnostic flight call is a low, short "churk," very unlike the high, drawn-out calls of the Least and Western. Semipalmateds prefer to forage on the drier portions of the tide flat with a picking motion, often along the perimeter of a peep flock since they are harassed by the more aggressive Leasts and fractionally larger Westerns. Passing through the San Juan Islands early, migrating Semipalmated Sandpipers are very uncommon from late June through early September and rare in mid-May, with nearly all records coming from False Bay.

Western Sandpiper (*Calidris mauri*). The longer bill and legs of this peep allow it to forage in deeper water than its look-alikes. Wading into ponds, marshes, and tidal waters, the Western Sandpiper probes deeply with its drooping beak, sometimes immersing its head completely in pursuit of tiny invertebrates. This common shorebird is widely distributed through the San Juan Islands during migration and is locally abundant in flocks of several hundred at False Bay and Spencer Spit. During the fall passage in late June through October, juvenile Western Sandpipers with bright rusty scapulars dominate the mud flats. Occasionally a stubborn individual lingers into November or overwinters in the company of Dunlins. However, they are usually absent until the fleeting spring migration that occurs from mid-April through mid-May.

Least Sandpiper (*Calidris minutilla*). Smallest (but feistiest) of the peeps, the tiny Least Sandpiper is immediately recognized by its yellowish legs and warm brownish mantle. This tame shorebird prefers not to wade in water and is often seen foraging at the high-water mark or in the drier marsh vegetation. Least Sandpipers emit a high, drawn-out "kreep" note when flushed and speed off in erratic

Least Sandpipers make shallow probes
for organisms on exposed tide flats.

zigzag flights. These little fellows are nearly as common as Western Sandpipers in the San Juan Islands and the opening of their migrational windows occurs simultaneously.

Baird's Sandpiper (*Calidris bairdii*). Looking like a big edition of the Least Sandpiper, this uncommon shorebird has a scaly or splotchy back and warm buff foreparts. The Baird's Sandpiper has a low, reedy flight call and a streamlined appearance created by a horizontal stance and long wing tips that extend beyond the tail. Migrating alone or in small groups, the species is seen in the San Juan Islands from late July through September and rarely in early May. Nearly all sightings have come from False Bay, where the birds usually forage by themselves or with bullying Least Sandpipers on dry sections of the tidelands.

Pectoral Sandpiper (*Calidris melanotos*). Pectoral Sandpipers are named for the male's two air sacs found beneath the skin of the upper breast. When courting females on the high arctic breeding grounds, these tundra nesters inflate the sacs and create hollow booming sounds. Pectoral Sandpipers prefer fresh-water habitats over marine shores and are most numerous at Three Meadows and Panorama marshes; False Bay is a good marine location. Craning their long necks when alarmed, Pectoral Sandpipers make a low, guttural "prrrp" much like Baird's Sandpipers as they embark on their dodging and twisting flight. These rare spring and common fall migrants can be seen in mid-April and from mid-July through mid-November. The main fall passage occurs from late August into early October with flocks of 10 to 20 birds a frequent sight.

Rock Sandpiper (*Calidris ptilocnemis*). These uncommon to rare winter visitors and migrants are very difficult to see in the San Juan Islands unless one is equipped with a seaworthy boat or has the swimming abilities of a sea lion. The inaccessible rocks and reefs that they frequent from October through mid-May are surrounded by rough and dangerous waters; this seclusion makes their status somewhat unclear.[45] Flocks of other "rock birds," the turnstones, tattlers, and Surfbirds, should be carefully inventoried for Rock Sandpipers with an ear cocked for their flickerlike whistling. If you really want to see one of these elusive birds, visit Victoria, B.C., and take a stroll along Clover Point; there the Rock Sandpiper is more cooperative.

Dunlin (*Calidris alpina*). The hardy Dunlins are our most consistently seen winter sandpipers, often remaining in flocks of several hundred individuals throughout the winter. They can be locally abundant on San Juan Island from mid-October through late April, shifting from False Bay at low tide to flooded farmland in San Juan Valley at high tide. Generally speaking, Dunlins are common migrants and winter residents that may be encountered at all of the usual shorebird haunts from late September until mid-May. Readily identified at a distance by their gray color, down-curved bills, and nasal, grating "cheezp" flight calls, Dunlins often wheel through the air in synchronized masses, seeming to change shades with every twist and turn.

Dunlins probe tide flats and flooded farmland for invertebrate prey.

Short-billed (*Limnodromus griseus*) and **Long-billed Dowitchers** (*Limnodromus scolopaceus*). Repeatedly stabbing the mud with their extremely long bills, feeding Dowitchers look like feathered sewing machines. Posing a difficult identification problem because of their nearly identical plumages, these two species of chunky sandpipers are easily distinguished from other shorebirds in flight by a white wedge on the back. Listen carefully to their calls when they take wing, as the Short-billed Dowitcher whistles a mellow, low-pitched "tu tu tu" and the Long-billed Dowitcher utters a high, thin "keek." Habitat is also a good clue, with the Short-billed preferring salt-water locations and the Long-billed favoring fresh-water habitats. In the San Juan Islands, however, the Long-billed Dowitcher is often forced to utilize marine shorelines. The Short-billed Dowitcher is a common

Long-billed Dowitchers probe deeply in mud, sometimes even submerging their heads.

fall migrant, its window opening in late June and closing in early October with a few birds straggling until early November. The equally common Long-billed Dowitcher migrates later in fall from mid-July through October with a few birds rarely overwintering. Both species move northward in April and May, although they are much less common in spring migration. If you have a good eye for measurement, you might try telling them apart by their bill lengths, as their names imply. But be warned: there is some overlap between the longest Short-billed Dowitcher's bill and the shortest Long-billed Dowitcher's bill. Confused yet? Wait until you actually see one in the field.

Common Snipe (*Gallinago gallinago*). A loud winnowing sound heard over the moonlit marsh is often the only evidence one ever gets that Common Snipes are present. These secretive bog birds perform a peculiar spring display by flying high and spreading their outer tail feathers during power dives. Rushing over these specialized feathers, the air causes a fluttering "huhuhuhuhu" to warn off rivals. In normal flight, snipes zigzag in a rapid, irregular manner and utter raspy "scipe" alarm notes. Usually remaining well-hidden, these long-billed birds (superficially resembling dowitchers) are heavily streaked to match their reedy surroundings. Probing the mud with their flexible beaks, they are able to seize worms, grubs, and other goodies. Snipes are common residents and migrants in the San Juan Islands in densely vegetated fresh-water habitats and flooded agricultural land. Breeding is assumed in most of our permanent marshes and on those farm fields that remain wet until summer. Their winnowing is heard over Three Meadows Marsh, Fowler Pond, Richardson Ponds, and at least a dozen other locations throughout the nesting season.

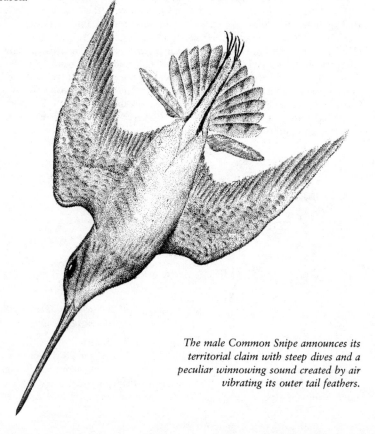

*The male Common Snipe announces its
territorial claim with steep dives and a
peculiar winnowing sound created by air
vibrating its outer tail feathers.*

Wilson's Phalarope (*Phalaropus tricolor*). Pirouetting on the surface of a pond or marsh, the Wilson's Phalarope sometimes spins at 60 revolutions per minute. Stabbing at mosquito larvae and other aquatic organisms with its needlelike bill, this fresh-water species is seldom seen in marine habitats. Wilson's Phalaropes show a decided preference for the open farm ponds and brackish lagoons of Lopez Island, where they can be counted on every spring as rare but regular migrants. Most are recorded in May and the first half of June, with very rare fall migrants occurring in July or August. Eventually, a pair of these birds may be tempted into spending the summer on a quiet, grassy Lopez pond to raise a brood of young.

Red-necked Phalarope (*Phalaropus lobatus*). As the haze of late summer settles over the sparkling inland waters, vast flocks of Red-necked Phalaropes may drift across the straits during their fall passage. However, in other years these sporadic sandpipers may be entirely absent from the San Juan Islands, migrating far at sea as they respond to oceanic winds, currents, and food concentrations. Already wearing conservative winter plumage, Red-necked Phalaropes arrive on our marine waters in mid-July and remain through September, with peak numbers occurring in August. Flocks of at least 1000 birds foraged in the tiderips of Cattle Pass all through August of 1981, and many birds were found dead along the road through American Camp that month. In 1983, the year of the El Niño current, "Northern" Phalaropes were nearly absent from our waters. A small spring passage in mid-May signals the return of these tundra nesters from their pelagic wintering grounds in the South Pacific.

Red Phalarope (*Phalaropus fulicaria*). Riding the high seas of the open ocean, this robin-sized bird feeds upon larval crustaceans, small jellyfish, and other plankton. Sometimes it picks parasites off the backs of whales or scavenges for bits of krill in the eddies of their giant flukes. The highly pelagic existence of the Red Phalarope rarely brings it into the inland waters of Washington, except during persistent westerly gales. Huge flocks have entered the Strait of Juan de Fuca on these occasions, with some individuals dispersing into the San Juan Islands. Their status in the San Juan Islands may be termed casual, or possibly very rare.[46] Fall migrants may occur from mid-August through mid-December, and sightings usually consist of solitary individuals or tiny groups. Records are most numerous in the inland waters in October and November. The Red Phalarope's preference for open straits and channels during this windy and stormy time of year makes it a very difficult bird to observe. Few bird watchers will navigate these tumultuous seas in their own vessels but can look for these hardy sandpipers from the bow of a ferry.

Rare Sandpipers: The San Juan Islands are uniquely positioned in the middle of several shorebird hot spots, including the Fraser and Skagit river deltas, southeast Vancouver Island, and Dungeness Spit. Many birds must pass through the archipelago on their way to or from the Pacific coast. This enhances our opportunities for finding rare sandpipers during the migratory seasons, thereby adding an element of excitement to every visit to False Bay or any other good shorebird location. Sometimes these rarities pop up in unexpected habitats or completely out of season.

The **Willet** (*Catoptrophorus semipalmatus*)[47] heads our list of rare sandpipers recorded in the San Juan Islands. This casual migrant and visitor could appear at any time of year and in a variety of aquatic habitats. Wherever Pectoral

Sandpipers are found in good numbers, birders should watch carefully for a very rare Asiatic migrant, the **Sharp-tailed Sandpiper** (*Calidris acuminata*).[48] Both species have similar habits and markings, but the Sharp-tailed can be distinguished by its rufous crown, buffy breast, and broad, white eyebrows. It may appear from late August through October. The **Buff-breasted Sandpiper** (*Tryngites sub-ruficollis*)[49] prefers much drier habitats than most other sandpipers and is found on golf courses, pastures, dunes, and prairies as a casual fall migrant in the Puget Trough from late July through mid-October.

There are three more species that we feel will eventually be added to our San Juan checklist of avifauna, especially with the growing number of observers in the area. The **Marbled Godwit** (*Limosa fedoa*) is a tall and striking sandpiper that can be found in nearly any watery habitat except rocky shores. It should be looked for from late July until the end of October as it moves toward the Pacific coast from the interior prairies. **Red Knots** (*Calidris canutus*) should occur as scarce migrants along marine shorelines in the fall from mid-August through mid-October and very rarely in spring during late April and May. Another bird that should prove to be a very rare migrant in fresh-water habitats is the **Stilt Sandpiper** (*Calidris himantopus*). Resembling a Lesser Yellowlegs with greenish legs, the Stilt Sand-piper feeds in dowitcher fashion, causing some identification problems, from late August through October.

JAEGERS, GULLS, AND TERNS
(Laridae)

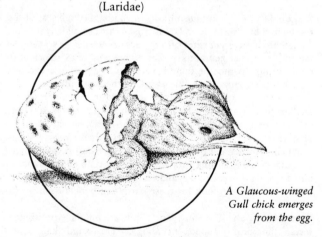

A Glaucous-winged Gull chick emerges from the egg.

A visit to the San Juan Islands would be incomplete without the sight and sound of members of this omnipresent family. From the moment you step foot on the ferry, they will be with you, touching your spirit with their effortless flight and evocative calls. Performing an intricate dance of survival, these quintessential birds leave behind an indelible impression of freedom. Each member of this family has its own part in the ecological tapestry, reflected by its size, form, and behavior. As a family, they possess aerial abilities unsurpassed in the bird world, their long, pointed wings allowing them to course over countless miles during their long lives. Spending part or all of their existence in aquatic environments, they are aided by webbed feet and dense waterproof plumage. More than 20 species inhabit the San

Juans and these are grouped into three distinct subfamilies: jaegers, gulls, and terns.

The powerful, predatory jaegers are the falcons of the sea, their name derived from a German word meaning "hunter." On their tundra breeding grounds they make an honest living by preying on lemmings and birds, but once on the high seas they become pirates. Jaegers specialize in stealing the hard-earned catches of other seabirds, forcing them, after a spectacular chase, to drop or disgorge their fish. Flying with incredible strength and agility, the jaegers' abilities are well known to their favorite victims, the Bonaparte's Gull and Common Tern. Singled out from the flock, many gulls or terns will give up their prize without much fight. Others will flee until they are caught and thrashed by a jaeger's hooked bill or strongly clawed feet. The highly pelagic jaegers follow concentrations of their hosts at sea, often remaining far from shore for months at a time. They accompany the large migrating assemblages of gulls and terns that move through the San Juan Islands in the fall, giving birders a chance to pick them out from the flocks by looking for their burly chests, elongated tail feathers, and marauding habits. Jaegers come in a variety of color morphs, ranging from light and highly contrasting individuals to dark, nearly uniform birds. The three species of jaegers pose great difficulties in identification, especially when the sea is choppy and your stomach is rolling with every wave. Without risk of seasickness, you can safely see jaegers from South Beach, Cattle Point, Davidson Head, the Friday Harbor Marine Laboratories, or any other location that attracts great masses of their hosts.

The gulls are a more easily observed group and can be found in a wide range of habitats. These extremely adaptable birds have evolved into a variety of sizes and patterns and are quick to exploit newly formed niches in the environment. The opportunistic and omnivorous gulls obtain food in as many ways as there are items on their menu. They locate schools of fish and other marine organisms from the air and then swoop down to the surface and dip them out of the water while swimming. Gulls stalk through intertidal zones and plowed fields for invertebrate prey and raid seabird colonies for eggs and young. Some gulls drop clams and other hard-shelled creatures from the air onto rock ledges or roads to break the shells open. This seems like an intelligent thing to do, but often a bird will show very little insight and repeatedly release a food item over soft sand or mud. Most gulls will scavenge dead animals wherever they find them, follow fishing boats for discarded catches, and visit dumps and garbage pits in astronomical numbers. Large gulls are quick to pursue shorebirds, terns, and members of their own kind if they think they have a chance of stealing a coveted morsel of food. Squabbles are a common sight among these noisy, gregarious birds, and their well-developed social behavior has been a favorite subject for many animal behaviorists. In general, gulls are a beneficial group of birds that not only provides a valuable sanitation service and agricultural pest control but may also offer insights into intraspecific aggression.

Many inexperienced bird watchers throw their hands up in frustration when trying to identify gulls, especially when faced with immature birds. Large gulls take up to four years to attain their adult plumage, changing into a different pattern every winter before reaching adulthood. Most mature gulls are white-bodied with a gray mantle across the upper surface of the wings and back, but this is where the similarity ends. When studying a gull, carefully compare its overall size and the shape and proportion of the head, bill, and wings to its neighbors. Also check the coloration of its eyes, bill, feet, and wing tips and add this information to the puzzle. Habitat and season will also help determine which species you are looking at, but always remember that gulls may appear at odd times and in unexpected places. To muddle up the stew even more, many large gulls regularly hybridize with one another and their offspring can display the full spectrum of the parents' field marks. Obviously not every gull is identifiable beyond question, but with patience and practice one can confidently recognize most individuals that live or wander among the San Juan Islands.

The most elegant members of this family are the slender and buoyantly flying terns. These birds seldom soar or swim like the gulls and have more selective diets and refined foraging techniques. Flying over the water's surface, terns spot fishes near the surface and plunge in head first to seize them with their slender, pointed bills. Many terns have long, forked tails and extremely narrow wings that beat rapidly in flight, making them appear distinctive and graceful. They are social and noisy in every aspect of their lives, whether it be foraging, migrating, breeding, or fleeing jaegers.

Researchers have discovered that terns are much more successful in raising young to maturity when they nest in large colonies as opposed to small colonies. They are staunch defenders of their eggs and chicks from raiding predators and will band together to repel raiding gulls, crows, rats, and larger animals. Unfortunately, their combined efforts were not enough to stop pillaging humans, and terns suffered substantial losses at the hands of egg gatherers and feather hunters. Whole colonies were wiped out by this exploitation before it was outlawed in the United States and Canada. Now terns face the danger of pesticides and other toxic chemicals in the ecosystem, which they absorb through their diet of fish. Many contaminants have been proven to inhibit tern reproduction in low dosages and in larger amounts to kill them outright. Usurped from many traditional nesting sites by development projects and competing relatives, terns are declining in many areas. The larger gulls, their exploding populations aided by human garbage disposal, commercial fishing activities, and laws aimed to protect them from human harassment, have taken over many former tern colony sites.

Parasitic Jaeger (*Stercorarius parasiticus*). Bursting into a chorus of raucous complaints and scattering wildly at the sight of a jaeger, Common Tern flocks often give the first clue of this thief's presence. The fleeting movements of a small "skua" require quick reflexes to follow, complicating the task of deciding which one of the three species is being observed. Within the inland waters of Washington, it is nearly always the Parasitic Jaeger, the least pelagic of the subfamily. The first fall migrants usually appear in the San Juan Islands by late July, coincident with the return of their favorite host, the Common Tern. Parasitic Jaegers become more numerous by late August and then hit a peak lasting from mid-September through mid-October, with up to a dozen birds seen terrorizing a single stretch of water at a time. By early November most Parasitics have departed except for rare stragglers that may linger into early winter. Rarely observed spring migrants in the month of May, Parasitic Jaegers probably take a more oceanic route on their way north. The larger **Pomarine Jaeger** (*Stercorarius pomarinus*)[50] is a very rare fall migrant this far from the open Pacific but may show up from mid-July through early November. Another species that is always a surprise to see is the small and graceful **Long-tailed Jaeger** (*Stercorarius longicaudus*),[51] a very rare fall migrant occurring from mid-August until late October.

Franklin's Gull (*Larus pipixcan*). As fur trappers and settlers steadily pushed westward during the early 1800s, they were often accompanied by naturalists who were hungry to explore the diversity of the New World. A common practice of these field scientists was to name newly discovered organisms in honor of their wives, best friends, or even their best friends' wives. The Franklin's Gull, originally thought to have been discovered on the prairies of Canada where it breeds, was named *Larus franklini* in praise of the arctic explorer Sir John Franklin. Unfortunately for Sir John, it turned out that this small black-headed gull had already been named on its wintering grounds in Mexico. The International Board of Zoological Nomenclature, a group of academicians that deals with these issues, determined that *Larus pipixcan* was the proper appellation as it was the first name given the species in publication. Being good sports though, they maintained the common name of Franklin's Gull as one way of keeping everyone happy and themselves out of controversy. Today in the San Juan Islands, this rare fall migrant still causes problems as bird watchers try to pick it out of the enormous flocks of Bonaparte's Gulls. The best time to do so is from late July through the first half of November, and sometimes, but very rarely, a few weeks earlier or later. Look for the Franklin's Gull's partial hood and white "goggles," dark gray mantle, black wing tips, and, as most sightings are of first winter birds, dark secondaries and narrow, black terminal tail band.

Bonaparte's Gull (*Larus philadelphia*). Attracted to localized concentrations of small schooling fishes, Bonaparte's Gulls visit the San Juan Islands in vast numbers. Abundant migrants from mid-July through early October, they remain fairly numerous until mid-December and sometimes overwinter in small flocks. Adorned with black hoods and white eye rings, large numbers of these gulls again move through the area during the spring passage in April and May. Hard-working Bonaparte's Gulls are often harassed by jaegers, and voice their collective displeasure with querulous froglike croaks. The small size and ternlike behavior of these dainty and attractive birds allow them to secure food from sources that are unavailable to larger gull species. When not resting on floating beds of kelp, they search over the marine waters for finned prey, especially in areas with strong tidal currents. Over 1000 Bonaparte's Gulls may congregate to feast on a mass of surface-running fishes, their white wing patches flashing like windblown confetti. Each bird repeatedly plunges into the water headfirst, seizing the slippery prey in its tiny black bill and quickly gulping it down to make room for another. Sometimes Bonaparte's Gulls patter across the surface in storm-petrel fashion, picking at small crustaceans while dancing on their red feet. In late summer when termites are hatching, these buoyant fliers gather in towering spirals over old tree snags, silently plucking the winged insects out of the air just as they leave the colony.

Heermann's Gull (*Larus heermanni*). Certain aspects of this bird make it our "antigull." Unlike its relatives, the Heermann's Gull has a red bill and sooty body as an adult and travels a reverse migrational pattern. Breeding on offshore islands along the Pacific coast of Mexico, the species disperses northward after the spring nesting is finished and takes advantage of rich feeding areas in the middle latitudes. Adult Heermann's Gulls arrive in the San Juan Islands in late June and become locally abundant fall visitors to our marine waters by late July. The chocolatey immatures appear in late September but are always far outnumbered by the handsome adults. These powerful fliers move rapidly and directly from one feeding frenzy to another and aggressively join in the melee with much larger gulls. Even more audaciously, some individuals have learned to trail after jaegers in the hopes of beating this parasite at its own game. Seeing a harried tern or small gull release its catch, the agile Heermann's Gull attempts to intercept the falling prize before the jaeger. Remaining one of the most numerous gulls along the Strait of Juan de Fuca and in the southern half of San Juan Channel until mid-October, concentrations of 2000 birds are not uncommon. When foraging is less productive, the species lines the rocky shores in pure flocks, pale heads lending an ashy sheen to the waterline. Less than 20 miles to the north, Heermann's Gull reaches the limit of its normal postbreeding range and is considered fairly rare along the border of the Strait of Georgia. This species begins to depart our area in October and becomes scarce by mid-November, although occasional stragglers remain long enough to be tallied in our Christmas Bird Count.

Mew Gull ((*Larus canus*). This medium-sized gull, named for its high, soft call, is a familiar denizen of the San Juan Islands. Restricted to the west coast when not breeding, the Mew Gull is a common migrant and abundant winter visitor that rarely tarries through the summer months. The first birds usually appear in late July and the last ones depart in early May for their usual nesting grounds in the northwest corner of the continent. This species has recently begun nesting on islands in fresh-water lakes on south Vancouver Island. Mew Gulls, like their smaller relatives, shun the rigorous competition of large gulls at dumps and landfills. Instead, they actively forage on plowed soil, flooded farm fields, and exposed mud flats, where they run about and probe like plovers with their short bills. Over open salt water, harbors, and bays, the Mew Gull snags floating items from the surface and only occasionally plunges or dips into the water for food.

Ring-billed Gull (*Larus delawarensis*). Uncommon fall migrants and rare winter visitors in the San Juan Islands, Ring-billed Gulls are much less numerous here than on the mainland. Many times observers have reported large concentrations of these birds that invariably turned out to be immature Mew Gulls with dark-tipped bills. To avoid a tragic loss of social status within birding circles, pay close attention to the young Ring-billed Gull's whiter body, more sharply defined, narrower tail band and wing markings, and larger bill. Although they can be seen in any typical gull habitat, "Ring-bills" favor fresh-water situations, farmland, and garbage dumps where the large-gull pressure is not so intense. They are most frequently recorded in late July and August, with some fall migrants moving through the area until early November. The last of the rare spring migrants are observed in April, but it is possible to encounter this species in any month.

California Gull (*Larus californicus*). One of the few bonafide heros in the bird world, the California Gull is credited with rescuing a fledgling religious colony in Utah. In 1848 the Mormons' crops and lives were threatened by a plague of crickets, but the timely arrival of a multitude of California Gulls saved the day. The grateful citizens have since named this species their state bird and erected a giant statue of their feathered saviour in the state's capitol. Although less celebrated in the San Juan Islands, the California Gull's role in this area has been only slightly less heroic. One hundred thirty-five years after the Mormons' plight, a great flock of these birds descended upon a huge pile of rotting fish offal being used to fertilize a pasture, thereby freeing the residents of San Juan Valley from a horrible and growing stench.

California Gulls forage in a broad range of habitats, including open salt water, farmland, mud flats, and dumps and are one of the most beneficial of gulls. Common fall migrants and rare winter visitors in the archipelago, they migrate from late June to early November with the peak passage occurring mid-July through September. In March and early April they are uncommon spring migrants but may rarely linger through the summer. This medium-sized gull is separated from its relatives (as an adult) by its dark mantle, greenish yellow legs, and black and red dot on the bill. On immatures look for the double-barred secondaries (first year only), two-toned bill, and gray-green legs (second year only).

Herring Gull (*Larus argentatus*). A cold yellow "cat's-eye," like that of the Ring-billed and Glaucous Gulls, helps identify this large bird. Some individuals have demonstrated the family's longevity by living to 31 years of age in the wild and 49 in captivity. Over 100,000 Herring Gulls were slaughtered by feather hunters for the millinery trade around the turn of the century, but this species has more than made up for these past losses and has benefited from human expansion more than any other gull. Although Herring Gulls dominate on the east coast of North America, they are uncommon migrants and winter visitors in the San Juan Islands. Most arrive in September and depart by mid-April, but they may rarely be recorded throughout the year. This quintessential gull can be found wherever there is food, be it farmland, bays, open salt-water channels, dumps, or ferry docks.

Thayer's Gull (*Larus thayeri*). This hardy, high arctic breeder thrives on cold, blustery weather and is one of our most numerous winter gulls in the San Juan Islands. Thayer's Gulls only become common after mid-October, although they begin trickling in during mid-Septemer or, rarely, late August.[52] Departure takes place in April and the last birds are seen in the latter half of this month. Thayer's Gulls are easily seen from the ferry as they forage over the open salt water but may also be observed sitting on pilings in Friday Harbor or resting on the tidal flats of False Bay. This bird was recently split off from the superficially similar Herring Gull and is distinguished from it and the Glaucous-winged Gull by its smaller head and bill, darker pink feet, and distinctive wing tips. These are colored dark gray or black, with large white spots on the upper surfaces, and are uniformly white on the under sides. The full species status of the Thayer's Gull may be short-lived; eventually it could be designated as a race of the Iceland Gull (*Larus glaucoides*).

Western Gull (*Larus occidentalis*). A very large, heavy-billed bird, the Western Gull is a strictly marine species that uncommonly visits the San Juan Islands from mid-Septemer through mid-March. At other times of year it is a rare visitor, totally absent only from April through mid-June. A fairly pelagic bird, the Western Gull prefers to forage in the Strait of Juan de Fuca and other large open bodies of salt water where it is most often observed in very small numbers. Breeding along the Pacific coast of the United States, this terrible predator of seabird eggs and chicks loses its dominance as a nesting species in Washington and is replaced by the Glaucous-winged Gull of the Pacific Northwest. Overlapping their breeding ranges on the outer coast of Washington, these two closely related species share many nesting colonies and interbreed heavily. The hybrids, showing various blends of both Western and Glaucous-winged traits are more frequently observed than pure Western Gulls in the Puget Trough and pose a challenge to birders. Most of them can be separated from other large gulls by their dusky, rather than black, wing tips, darker mantle, and bulbous bills.

Glaucous-winged Gull (*Larus glaucescens*). Named for its frosty wings, the ubiquitous and abundant Glaucous-winged Gull is the only member of this family that

A hungry Glaucous-winged Gull chick stimulates its parent to regurgitate food by pecking at the red spot on the lower mandible.

breeds in the San Juan Islands. Up to 5000 pairs, spread over more than 20 locations, nest within the archipelago. Rarely breeding on the major islands, Glaucous-winged Gulls prefer to congregate in colonies on isolated offshore rocks and islets that receive relatively little disturbance from humans or other terrestrial predators. One aberrant pair has repeatedly tried to raise broods on a rocky point near Olga on Orcas Island but has met with little success. There has also been one or more pairs nesting atop a set of pilings at the Shaw Island ferry dock since 1978. The "average" Glaucous-winged pair chooses to construct its nest among those of several dozen other pairs and will utilize the same site year after year. Popular San Juan Archipelago breeding locations (all NWRs) are Colville Island (with more than 1000 pairs), Hall Island (about 350 pairs), and Bird Rocks (a few hundred pairs). Widespread mortality of the young has occurred at the Colville Island colony during several nesting seasons, apparently the result of human disturbance.[53] Despite these temporary setbacks, the breeding population in the San Juan Islands has grown substantially over the last two decades.[54]

It is a fascinating experience to observe these noisy, bustling colonies, although it is difficult to approach them unless one has a seaworthy vessel. Naturally it is strictly forbidden to set foot on any seabird breeding island since even the most well-intentioned visits, including those of wildlife watchers and researchers, may prove disastrous to the survival of eggs and chicks. To prevent damaging effects on the reproductive success of marine birds, maintain a discrete and respectful distance from a colony. Perhaps the most easily and safely studied gullery in the San Juans is on Goose Island. This fair-sized colony may be observed through a spotting scope from the Cattle Point Picnic Area without negative impact.

Mated Glaucous-winged Gulls return to their favorite nest site in early spring and reestablish their old pair bonds and territorial boundaries. New couples usually start somewhat later, but whether the pair is new or old, it employs a variety of postures and vocalizations to accomplish the task. Ceremonial parades, bowing, neck arching, and grass pulling are accompanied by loud, rolling trumpet calls as the birds compete to secure the choicest real estate within the colony. Nests are constructed or repaired in early May, with the first eggs laid at the end of the month. In late June nearly all of the nests contain eggs and a few will be occupied by freshly hatched chicks. Within a month most of the eggs have hatched and cannabilism prevails throughout the colony. Glaucous-winged Gulls are their own worst enemy; a large number of the chicks that are less than three weeks old get killed or eaten by neighboring adult gulls, this being the major cause of mortality within the colony. Young gulls, and even adults, may end up in the talons of Bald Eagles, one of the few creatures other than humans that prey upon these birds. All summer long eagles may be seen visiting the gull colonies in the San Juans, usually selecting tender chicks to feed themselves or their own nestlings. Sometimes three eagles at a time may be seen perched amid the densely spaced nests, casually looking over the day's menu while the adult gulls scream their displeasure.

The oldest and most experienced Glaucous-winged Gull pairs are also the most successful at raising chicks to an independent age. Practice enables them to obtain the largest territories, a very important factor in the survival of young gulls since this helps to prevent them from straying into the homes of hostile neighbors. They are also able to better defend their chicks, forage most efficiently, and cooperate throughout the breeding cycle. Inexperienced pairs usually acquire smaller territories, lay fewer and lighter eggs later in the season, and have less success in raising young.

To survive in the competitive atmosphere of the gullery, the chicks are camouflaged in a mottled downy coat and possess many instincts that help keep them alive. They recognize their parents by voice and stimulate them to regurgitate a meal by pecking at the red spot on the lower mandible of either adult. When their parents are absent, the young gulls compress themselves into cracks and depressions and try to escape being noticed. The parents may identify their offspring by the individualized pattern of spots that each chick has on the back of its head. This recognition, along with appropriate behavior on the part of the chick, helps prevent the adults from attacking their own brood or feeding unrelated chicks, as both of these events are detrimental to successful breeding.

With nesting finished by the end of September, some adult Glaucous-winged Gulls remain resident in the area while others disperse as far south as southern California. Mature birds often return to the same wintering locations every year just as they show fidelity to the same mates and nesting sites during the summer. Prior knowledge of specific areas and food resources is valuable to the survival of these birds, and is possibly a key to their longevity. One Glaucous-winged Gull in the San Juan Islands was found to be 22 years of age. Abundant throughout the year, this species is unquestionably the most familiar and obvious "sea gull" in the San Juans.

Black-legged Kittiwake (*Rissa tridactyla*). The highly pelagic kittiwakes differ from typical gulls by exhibiting some very tubenoselike features and behavior. Well-suited for agile gliding in high winds, the slimly built kittiwakes swoop rapidly over the waves on their long, slender wings. Buoyant and graceful in flight, they are readily distinguished from other gulls by their short, rapid flapping and wing tips that appear to have been dipped in black ink. Hunting and scavenging over the open ocean, these large-headed and short-billed birds drink only sea water and are able to excrete excess salt by means of special glands. Kittiwakes breed on northern sea cliffs in astronomical numbers, thus escaping the rigorous competition for nesting sites with other members of their family.

Within the San Juan Islands, the Black-legged Kittiwake is usually rare but occurs as a nonbreeding summer visitor, spring and fall migrant, and winter visitor.[55] Like other pelagic birds, this species is most likely to be seen in the Strait of Juan de Fuca after storms have blown it into the inland waters. However, on several occasions Black-legged Kittiwakes have been recorded from other marine locations inside the archipelago, including Friday Harbor. Look for them in small numbers in any month except August and September, with adult birds dominating in winter and immatures prevailing in summer. Occasionally a flock of several dozen Black-legged Kittiwakes may turn up, giving testimony to the sporadic nature and unpredictability of sightings of this, the most numerous of all the world's gulls.

Very Rare Gulls: With their strong powers of flight and propensity for long migrations, the gulls have a tendency to peregrinate around the globe. In the San Juan Islands we have one species that is a first-class wanderer, the rare **Little Gull** (*Larus minutus*).[56] This primarily Old World bird strays to the west coast of the United States and Canada in small numbers, usually being discovered among flocks of Bonaparte's Gulls. Little Gulls are most likely to be encountered during the fall passage from September through November but may also be seen from late February through early April. The adults, which far outnumber immature birds, can be separated from our commoner gulls by their tiny size, rounded wing tips, and sooty wing linings.

Scanning the enormous concentrations of Glaucous-winged Gulls from November through mid-May may disclose the presence of a giant, pale visitor from the far north. The **Glaucous Gull** (*Larus hyperboreus*)[57] very rarely ventures this far south and usually only when immature. This highly raptorial bird is a close relative of the Glaucous-winged Gull and hybridizes with it in Alaska where their breeding ranges overlap.

The pelagic **Sabine's Gull** (*Xema sabini*)[58] is a rare to very rare species in the San Juan Islands as it prefers to avoid the inland waters and normally migrates over the open ocean far from shore. It is most likely to be encountered in the Strait of Juan de Fuca during strong westerly winds from mid-August through October. Although not as likely, sightings are possible from late July through mid-December. Less frequently, Sabine's Gulls may be observed in Rosario and Haro straits or in the smaller interior channels of the archipelago. This small, ternlike gull may even be seen in Friday Harbor. Its forked tail and constantly flapping wings boldly marked with large white triangles make it an utterly distinctive bird.

A single hypothetical record of a **Red-legged Kittiwake** (*Rissa brevirostris*)[59] was received from the San Juan Islands, but it is very unlikely that this Bering Sea breeder, which rarely leaves its stormy home, will ever be confirmed in our area.

If all of these gulls aren't enough to keep you busy, try keeping a look out for **Common Black-headed Gulls** (*Larus ridibundus*), casual stragglers from Eurasia. Not yet recorded in the San Juans, they have been observed several times on southeast Vancouver Island as fall migrants from late July through mid-November. Common Black-headed Gulls may easily hide among flocks of Bonaparte's Gulls, but their larger size, sooty underwings, and reddish bills will betray their presence to the alert bird watcher.

Caspian Tern (*Sterna caspia*). Expanding its range up the west coast of the United States, the cosmopolitan Caspian Tern is becoming increasingly common in the inland waters of Washington. Perhaps this stunning bird will continue its population growth and begin a new nesting colony somewhere in the Puget Trough. This largest North American tern made its first reported appearance in the San Juan Islands in 1949[60] and is now an uncommon summer visitor from mid-April through September, with the bulk of the sightings occurring in June, July, and the first half of August. Caspian Terns may be seen resting at False and Fisherman bays or flying over any part of the archipelago, including the interior valleys. Drawing attention to themselves with their harsh, grating calls, they search for food with their blood-red bills pointing down, wings steadily beating, and forked tails spread wide. Caspian Terns usually prey upon small fishes they capture by diving from 30 feet or so in the air. Weighing in at slightly over one pound each, they penetrate the water deeply enough to exploit food resources that are unavailable to the smaller tern species. Cutting through both air and water with great power, Caspian Terns sometimes use their talents to pirate food from smaller seabirds in jaeger fashion.

Common Tern (*Sterna hirundo*). When gazing across the Salmon Bank at a swirling cloud of Common Terns, it is hard to imagine that this species was once nearly extirpated from the North America continent. Like so many other white-plumaged birds, they suffered from the greed of feather hunters and were used primarily to decorate hats. In 1913 Common Terns received full protection and now live up to their name as one of the most numerous and widespread members of this subfamily. In the San Juans they are rare spring migrants from late April through early June and frequent fall migrants from mid-July through early November. The peak southbound passage occurs from mid-August through Septem-

Common Terns gather over a school of juvenile Pacific Herring.

ber, when Common Terns become locally abundant in areas that are well supplied with sandlance, herring, and shrimp. Flocks of 500 birds have been sighted in Friday Harbor and Spieden Channel, and groups of 200 or more have been seen in the north Mosquito Pass/Roche Harbor area. Rosario Strait is sometimes thronged with over 1000 Common Terns, and over 3000 individuals have been observed fishing along South Beach. When feeding in these large concentrations they may be accurately termed "jaeger bait" for they seem to be the favorite host of these parasitic birds. Only when hawking termites or resting on the kelp beds do Common Terns get any relief from the unwanted attentions of jaegers.

Rare Terns: Flying approximately 22,000 miles every year, the **Arctic Tern** (*Sterna paradisaea*)[61] is the world's champion long-distance migrator. One healthy individual, discovered to be 34 years old by its leg band information, may have flown about three-quarters of a million miles up until that point in its life. This is enough distance to make a round-trip journey to the moon with enough miles left over for a one-way trip back. Arctic Terns also see more sunlight than any other animal by breeding in the high arctic and wintering during the southern summer in the Antarctic Circle. Seldom straying far from the open ocean while not actively breeding, they are considered very rare migrants over the open straits and channels of the inland waters of Washington and British Columbia.

Strangely enough, an extremely disjunct breeding colony of this pelagic species was discovered in 1978 on Jetty Island near Everett, Washington, hundreds of miles from the nearest nesting sites in Southeast Alaska. Since that time, a tiny group of Arctic Terns has returned each spring to reproduce at this amazing location, perhaps increasing the chances of seeing this bird in the San Juan Islands. Any small tern sighted in late June or early July, a time when none at all should be present in the archipelago, may prove to be one of these pioneers foraging far from the Jetty Island colony. It is more likely that these local birds, and the northern breeders, will be recorded during migration from late May to early June and again from late July through early October. Any suspected Arctic Tern should be carefully scrutinized while airborne to see if it has translucent flight feathers, very narrow black trailing edges to the undersides of the wings, and a neckless appearance. If the bird in question perches for a moment, look for very short legs, a rounded head, and, if a breeding adult, gray underparts, and a slender bill colored red its entire length. These field marks may be used to distinguish the Arctic Tern from the nearly identical Common and **Forster's Tern** (*Sterna forsteri*), the latter bird a frost-winged species that has been recorded a few times from Puget Sound but never from the San Juan Islands.

The **Elegant Tern** (*Sterna elegans*) has also eluded observers in the archipelago, although there are late summer records of it from Dungeness Spit, Boundary Bay, and Victoria, B.C. These 1983 observations coincided with the warm-water El Niño current and were a part of the first documented invasion of Elegant Terns into Washington and British Columbia. This species normally ranges only as far as northern California after dispersing from its Mexican nesting colonies.

The **Black Tern** (*Chlidonias niger*)[62] is a very rare spring and fall migrant through the archipelago with windows opening in late May through early June and mid-August through mid-September. So far, this dark and tiny tern has only been seen over marine habitats in the San Juans, but it is possible that this marsh-loving species may pause in its long journey to hawk low-flying insects from a fresh-water location in the islands.

ALCIDS OR AUKS
(Alcidae)

A Pigeon Guillemot displays the erect perching posture of this family.

This unique family is the Northern Hemisphere's answer to the penguin. Although completely unrelated and separated by a wide barrier of tropical seas, the ocean-inhabiting alcids and penguins share many obvious similarities and offer an excellent example of convergent evolution. Both families have a conservative black-and-white dress, an upright posture on land, a chunky build, and short wings that are flapped to provide swift propulsion under water. Other shared traits are a dense, waterproof plumage, gregarious habits, and a diet that consists of fish, crustaceans, or plankton. Alcids and penguins have legs placed far back on their bodies, making surface swimming more efficient, and use their large webbed feet like rudders when diving to depths of over 100 feet. Countershading, a type of camouflage that employs a dark upper surface and a lighter underside, has been adopted by these two groups to provide concealment from their prey and aquatic predators like Orcas and sea lions.

In contrast with the penguins, alcids still retain the power of flight except when molting and regrowing their primary wing feathers. Their small wings do dual duty and are designed to function both above and below the water's surface. Not surprisingly, some of the larger species are believed to be evolving toward total flightlessness, and it is calculated that with the addition of a few more ounces of body weight they will be unable to get airborne. Alcid flight is low and direct and is accomplished with furiously beating wings and stiffly held feet, which replace the short tail as a steering device. Since so much effort is required to become airborne, they usually prefer to dive or "toboggan" across the water's surface when faced with danger. Before entering the submarine world, an alcid gives a characteristic "karate chop" to the water with its forehead and submerges with a flick of spreading wings.

Choosing isolated islands and steep cliffs close to abundant food resources for breeding, most alcids are highly colonial during the nesting season. Several species may share the same island, and nesting competition is reduced by specific site requirements each kind has evolved. Alcid courtship rituals tend to be elaborate, with aquatic "dances," head bowing, and bizarre moans, grunts, and whistles all playing a role in pair bonding and territorial defense. Members of this family are adorned with a breeding plumage differing greatly from the basic or "winter" plumage, and several species brandish fantastic head and bill ornamentation that is shed after nesting is completed. Having finished the reproductive cycle, many alcids disperse to neighboring waters for the winter and, in most cases, do not engage in true migrations.

In former days, alcids were endangered by feather hunters and egg collectors. One species native to the Atlantic Ocean, the Great Auk (*Pinguinus impennis*), was slaughtered by the millions, suffering extinction in 1844. The original penguin (note the scientific name), the Great Auk was discovered long before any sailors ventured into the Antarctic, but unfortunately, its complete flightlessness and nearness to commercial markets made it susceptible to exploitative fishermen and whalers. Today's alcids face the danger of spilled oil, a pollution hazard that destroys their waterproofing and poisons them when ingested during preening. Even more disastrous are the losses caused by gill nets used in commercial fishing operations, with hundreds of thousands of alcids estimated drowned every year by American, Canadian, Russian, and Japanese fishermen on the high seas. Much of this "by-catch" is taken within 200 miles of the United States, inside the Fisheries Conservation Zone. Pesticides in the ecosystem have been linked to reduced populations of Common Murres in Oregon and California. Land development and/or disturbances of nesting sites often ruin the success of a given breeding season and have frequently led birds to completely abandon the area, with no alternatives available. The delightful and captivating alcids are candidates for careful protection and monitoring in all parts of their range, but here in the San Juan Islands where they live in such close proximity to humans we must be particularly conscious of actions that may affect these sensitive and highly specialized seabirds.

Common Murre (*Uria aalge*). Outnumbering all other alcids in the Pacific Ocean, the Common Murre is the largest and most colonial member of the family normally occurring in our area. Breeding in a limited number of inaccessible seacliff colonies along the outer coast, multitudes crowd together on narrow ledges almost within reach of one another. A pair's single huge egg is deposited on bare rock and must be held safely between either parent's feet during incubation. Murre eggs are sharply pointed at one end and will roll in a tight circle if nudged, a marvelous adaptation designed to reduce losses caused by high winds or panicked parents. After reaching the age of about three weeks, the chicks do "Kamikaze" leaps from the confined shelves to the sea that may lie 1000 feet below. Until it is able to fly, a young murre apparently follows its male parent, demanding with a shrill voice to be fed. Around mid-July, Common Murres will begin dispersing from their coastal colonies and many gather in the San Juan Islands. Chicks in tow, they catch fish in open channels, straits, and deep bays, while constantly maintaining a dialogue of alternating whistles and groans with their young depen-

A Common Murre pursues its fast-swimming prey with powerful wing beats.

dents. By mid-August the Common Murres begin to outnumber all other alcids in the area, and huge flotillas of several thousand may gather along the Strait of Juan de Fuca and near Cattle Pass. Many of these birds nest in Oregon and northern California and migrate north to Washington after breeding. Moving from one school of bait fish to another, these flocks fly at a rapid clip in long lines only a few feet above the water. Remaining abundant throughout the winter, Common Murres begin to leave the San Juans in April and eventually become uncommon, or even rare in some years, from May to early July. Unfortunately for this species, there is a large amount of gill-netting in the inland waters of Washington, and in late summer dozens of drowned murres will line our San Juan beaches or be seen floating in lines of drifting debris.

Pigeon Guillemot (*Cepphus columba*). When male Pigeon Guillemots dispute with rivals, they chase each other about as if attempting to stitch the air and water together. Bursting out of the sea, they fly a short distance before plunging back beneath the surface, and continue in this undulating pursuit without ever hesitating at the interface between the elements. Resident in the San Juan Islands, Pigeon Guillemots can be observed all summer long as they fish in shallow waters or sit on steep shores near their nests, displaying their bright red feet and mouth linings while uttering shrill whistles. More than 300 pairs breed in small colonies located on nearly every offshore rock and uninhabited island in the archipelago. Guillemots lay their two eggs in a deep crevice or burrow, safe from most predatory birds and mammals. While ferrying fish back to the nest site, these birds are susceptible to the attacks of Peregrine Falcons, perhaps their greatest enemy other than gill nets. The chicks fledge under cover of darkness when slightly over one month old and are immediately independent from their parents. Many will join with adult guillemots in small convoys that soon depart the area. During September, Pigeon Guillemots may be difficult to find in the San Juans, but for the remainder of the year they are one of our most common alcids and can be seen on nearly every stretch of salt water.

Marbled Murrelet (*Brachyramphus marmoratus*). The most mysterious alcid of all is this miniature version of the murre. No one has been able to find a single nest of the Marbled Murrelet in Washington State despite its being a common resident in the San Juan Islands. Oddly enough, considering the rest of the family's habits, one downy chick was found 130 feet above the ground in a Douglas-fir growing in California, and another nest was found at ground level on a rocky slope of a small Alaskan island. Both of these habitats abound in the San Juans, but no one has been able to track the adult birds' movements to any conclusive breeding site in our area. Marbled Murrelets may be seen gathering in small groups at locations with abundant food from April through July, and we estimate that 200 pairs nest in the archipelago. Adults are often observed flying quickly across the water with fish in their bills as if to feed a hidden youngster, and several individuals with brood patches have been collected in the San Juan Islands. Murrelet chicks gain weight fast in order to fledge quickly and minimize their chances of being found by a predator away from the safety of the sea. Just before leaving the nest, they expose their feathers by plucking and eating the overcoat of down from their bodies. In the San Juans, the first juvenile Marbled Murrelets are seen accompanying their parents in mid-July and by mid-August flocks of several dozen may be seen. Late summer concentrations may be observed in Obstruction Pass, Rocky Bay, President Channel, and near the Richardson dock. Their numbers seem to be augmented during the winter months; the senior author observed a string of over 200 Marbled Murrelets foraging along a tiderip in Cattle Pass on February 5, 1982.

Ancient Murrelet (*Synthliboramphus antiquus*). Invading our marine waters at about the same time as the first fall storms, Ancient Murrelets are sporadically common to uncommon winter visitors in the San Juan Islands. Readily distinguished from Marbled Murrelets by their gray backs that contrast strongly with their black napes and crowns, Ancient Murrelets also have yellowish bills and black bibs and lack the white scapulars of the Marbled's winter plumage. Ancients also act more nervous and flighty than Marbled Murrelets and forage in a rather spastic manner, sometimes poking just their heads above the surface between dives. They are a fairly pelagic alcid that eats a large percentage of invertebrate food, and within the inland waters of Washington the largest concentrations are found in early winter far from shore in the Strait of Juan de Fuca. Smaller numbers can be seen closer to shore and among the interior waterways of the San Juans from late September through early April, but more often from mid-October until late March.

Rhinoceros Auklet (*Cerorhinca monocerata*). When enjoying summer boating in the San Juan Islands, beware of charging "Rhinos" hurtling past like little bombs with wings. But don't worry, the horns of these bizarre birds are used strictly for courtship purposes and have no offensive or defensive capabilities. Busying themselves during the daylight hours with capturing sandlance and herring, Rhinoceros Auklets fill their beaks with a half-dozen fish apiece before heading home. Both "Rhinos" and puffins possess especially stiff tongues which they use to pin fish against their upper mandibles. This enables them to open their bills and seize more prey without losing the previously captured food. Thousands of Auklets gather in our marine waters when they are actively raising young, most often foraging in areas with strong currents in the southern half of the archipelago. The majority of these birds makes its home on Protection Island where there are nearly 18,000

A Rhinoceros Auklet speeds over the Strait of Juan de Fuca in search of schooling fish.

pairs nesting; it is the largest breeding colony of "Rhinos" south of Alaska. Another 600 pairs nest on Smith Island (NWR) and 300 more are present on Tatoosh Island, all together comprising 60 percent of the entire breeding seabird population in the inland waters of Washington. Using their strong claws and bills, Rhinoceros Auklets burrow into the soil of steep, grassy slopes, and each pair raises a single young at the end of a tunnel that may be 25 feet long. In order to avoid being attacked by gulls, ravens, or eagles, the adults visit the chick only at night and deliver a billful of fish once or twice each evening. Juveniles, resembling winter-plumaged adults, appear among the islands in early August and quickly outnumber the older birds by the end of the month. Auklets of all ages decline sharply in September as they move offshore or disperse southward along the Pacific coast. A few scattered individuals remain resident throughout the colder months, and an isolated flock overwinters near the entrance of Friday Harbor. By late March, Rhinoceros Auklets return to the area in force and by July are once again putting on an amazing wildlife spectacle.

Tufted Puffin (*Fratercula cirrhata*). One of the most sought-after birds by wildlife enthusiasts, the Tufted Puffin is outrageously adorned during the breeding season,

The colorful bill plates and head plumes of the Tufted Puffin are shed at the end of each breeding season.

with a massive orange and yellow bill, a white face contrasting strongly with its all-black body, and flaxen-colored plumes that stream from behind its head. Like the Rhinoceros Auklet, the puffin's head feathers and bright bill sheath are shed in the fall and regrown every spring. We see puffins in the San Juan Islands only when they are in their finest courting attire because every winter they range the open ocean and seldom approach land except during storms. From mid-May until mid-September, "Sea Parrots" are uncommonly seen in small numbers throughout our marine waters, often discovered with other seabirds in feeding frenzies. Tufted Puffins are locally common along the south shore of Lopez Island, especially at Iceberg Point, where up to three dozen may be counted in a single day. The great majority of these birds is likely to be breeders from Smith and Protection islands (NWRs) visiting the rich waters of the San Juans proper to forage. The others are likely to be individuals that nest on Colville Island (NWR), the last site within the archipelago where puffins are still thought to breed. Formerly, they bred at about 10 different San Juan locations, mostly on smaller islands in the northern half of the county that had sufficient soil to burrow into. For reasons not fully understood, a steady decline took place and only a relict population of puffins is left today. Some of their old sites have eroded, leaving them without the necessary three to six feet of glacial deposits for a secure nest. Other factors that may have caused the local disappearance of Tufted Puffins are increased human disturbance of their isolated breeding colonies and, most likely of all, incidental drownings in gill nets. The United States Fish and Wildlife Service has estimated that 27 percent of the Tufted Puffin population in the North Pacific Ocean Fishery Conservation Zone is caught and destroyed by the gill nets of commercial fisheries every year.

Rare Alcids: Considering the large numbers of alcids that utilize the San Juan Islands for breeding, migrating, and overwintering, it is not surprising that two species were first recorded in Washington State from this area. A single **Thick-billed Murre** (*Uria lomvia*),[63] an accidental bird this far south, appeared in San Juan Channel at the entrance to Friday Harbor one December day. Another far-northern accidental, the **Kittlitz's Murrelet** (*Brachyramphus brevirostris*),[64] popped up inside Friday Harbor in the dead of winter, continuing the list of bird anomalies at this location. **Cassin's Auklet** (*Ptychoramphus aleuticus*),[65] a highly pelagic species that nests as close as Tatoosh Island off Cape Flattery, is a very rare migrant and visitor to the San Juan Islands. During the spring months individuals have been observed at the entrance to Friday Harbor (where else?) and at other places in the San Juan Islands but are most likely to be seen in the Strait of Juan de Fuca far offshore from October through February. The **Horned Puffin** (*Fratercula corniculata*)[66] recorded once in the San Juan Islands, should be looked for during the warmer months in areas frequented by its close relative. It has been observed in the inland waters of Washington several times and has apparently investigated some nearby islands during the nesting season.

DOVES AND PIGEONS
(Columbiformes/Columbidae)

Band-tailed Pigeon

This unique family has developed a rather mammalian method of nourishing its young. Pigeons and doves possess special crops that produce "milk" when they have dependent offspring. This fat- and protein-rich mucous is regurgitated into the throats of the squabs, or chicks, and is their food supply while in the nest. Pigeons and doves also have the unusual ability to siphon and swallow water without having to tilt their heads back like other birds do. These seed- and fruit-eating birds spend a lot of foraging time on the ground, where they strut about with their heads bobbing at every step.

The names "pigeon" and "dove" have been handed out arbitrarily among the family and there is no definitive difference between the two, but the general trend has been to name the smaller species doves. As a family they all have plump bodies, short legs, and short bills, each with a swollen waxy cere (the fleshy base of the upper mandible). Swift and powerful fliers, these birds have pointed wings and pointed or fanned tails. The sexes are very similar and often feathered with some iridescent plumage. The many varieties of pigeons and doves have distinctive calls or cooing notes that readily identify them. Unfortunately, this family and its relatives have been heavily exploited by hunters, sometimes to the point of extinction. The casualty list includes the Passenger Pigeon, Dodo, and Mauritius Pink Pigeon.

Rock Dove (*Columba livia*). The "City Pigeon" was introduced to this country by the French in 1606, and over 300 years later it made its debut in the San Juan Islands. Much more familiar in its urban habitat, this semi-domesticated bird has been a locally common resident of island farms and towns since the 1950s. Many docks and wharves, like those in Friday Harbor, provide homes to large flocks of roosting and breeding Rock Doves. When hungry they may be seen commuting to nearby agricultural lands to forage in plowed fields or pastures for grain and seeds. These variably plumaged birds are often beset by Peregrine Falcons or other predatory birds, forcing them to flee, which they do at speeds approaching 95 miles per hour. This swiftness and their homing ability have made them very useful to humans. "Homing Pigeons" have been used for centuries to carry messages and were utilized during World War II for this purpose.

Band-tailed Pigeon (*Columba fasciata*). Nearly suffering the same fate as the Passenger Pigeon, this overhunted species was close to extinction early in the twentieth century. The Band-tailed Pigeon has recovered to the point where it is once again a common bird over most of its range. In the San Juan Islands, it finds a niche as a woodland bird for most of the year. However, flocks of 200 or more have been seen foraging in farm fields during the peak of migration in September. Numbers decrease gradually until only a handful is present in December, usually on the west side of San Juan Island on Young Hill or Mt. Dallas or at feeding stations anywhere in the islands. By the first of the year, nearly all have departed for warmer climates, leaving only a straggler or two this far north. The first few Band-tailed Pigeons are seen returning in late March and the species is found commonly by mid-May. This bird's mellow call, "whoo-whoo-hoo," may be heard high in the forest canopy, especially where there are fruit-bearing trees such as Pacific Madrone. When making a hasty takeoff, a series of loud snapping sounds results from the wing tips colliding beneath the body. Sometimes a very peculiar flight display can be noted when the pigeons stiffly vibrate their wings and utter nasal "kree kree" sounds while circling above the treetops.

Mourning Dove (*Zenaida macroura*). Humans ascribe a sad tone to the call (a low "who-ah, who, who, who") of the Mourning Dove, a slender bird with a long, tapering tail. It is an uncommon breeding resident in the archipelago, with most records coming from open habitats on San Juan and Lopez islands between April and September. Formerly, it was much more common in this area and the rest of western Washington. Observers reported it to be common in the San Juans through 1959.[67] The reason for the decline is unknown. Like other pigeons, this bird is a favorite target for hunters, and throughout the country approximately 30 million Mourning Doves are shot each year.

OWLS
(Strigiformes)

Searching for Townsend's Voles, a Short-eared Owl soars over the American Camp prairies.

Birds more often seen in myth than reality, the owls are a widespread group that has captured the imagination of humans. Superstitious folk have long considered the hooting of an owl a sign of bad luck or an omen of death. For many small creatures this may be true, but not for humans. If it were fact and not fiction there would be an uncommon number of people dying in the San Juan Islands. These nocturnal birds of prey are found in a variety of island habitats and may be heard at all seasons. Capturing numerous destructive rodents and rabbits, owls are a very welcome and necessary part of our avifauna.

Like other raptors, owls have strongly hooked bills and talons, and keen senses. Each surrounded by a funnel of sound-directing feathers, owl ears are asymmetrically shaped and positioned unevenly on the skull as aids in determining the location of a rustling animal. Owls' extremely large eyes are fixed in binocular stares, giving them excellent depth perception but requiring flexible necks to direct their gazes. Owls have good daytime vision, but it is at night when their eyes perform extraordinarily, as they have a very high percentage of dark-adapted retinal cells.

Once an owl pinpoints its prey's position, it quietly swoops in for the kill, its soft plumage and finely fringed flight feathers allowing for a nearly soundless approach. After devouring a meal, the hunter regurgitates a pellet of undigestible fur, bones, or feathers, depending on the diet. Such pellets can be used to identify the owl species, as well as to analyze the bird's role in the ecosystem.

These cryptically colored birds of prey go unobserved more often than not. They choose hidden roosts to sleep in by day and their presence is often revealed only by pellets or nocturnal calls. If you should see an owl, it is best identified by its size, shape, and habitat. However, these elusive and secretive birds are usually located and recognized by their distinctive voices. By playing taped owl sounds at night, you can probably stimulate one or more birds into showing off its repertoire. A successful "owl prowl" on a moonlit evening is an experience not quickly forgotten.

BARN-OWLS
(Tytonidae)

Common Barn-owl *(Tyto alba)*. Belonging in their own family, Tytonidae, barn-owls are superficially and taxinomically distinct from the "typical" owls, Strigidae. These ghostly pale birds have heart-shaped facial discs and very long legs. Common Barn-owls are frequently found nesting in church steeples, barns, and attics and are perhaps the most beneficial birds in the world because of their nearly exclusive rat diet. They were first detected in the San Juan Islands in 1947 and are now an uncommon breeding resident.[68] Listen for the eerie hissing of Common Barn-owls near abandoned buildings, farmland, and residential areas, especially on San Juan and Lopez islands.

TYPICAL OWLS
(Strigidae)

Western Screech-Owl *(Otus kennicottii)*. Betraying its presence with a deep, bouncing-ball hooting, the Western Screech-Owl is found in open woodlands wherever dense vegetation shelters it from marauding Great Horned Owls. This little mottled brown bird is able to "disappear" against the trunk of a tree by erecting its "horns" and stretching itself thin, thereby distorting its outline. Western

Screech-Owls eat mostly insects and mice, which they swallow whole. They are common breeding residents at low elevations (below 1000 feet) in the San Juan Islands and can be assisted by placing nesting boxes in appropriate habitat.

Great Horned Owl (*Bubo virginianus*). The Puget Sound race of this fearsome predator, the "Dusky" Horned Owl, is the largest owl in North America, outweighing even the Snowy. Great Horned Owls prey on nearly anything that is smaller than themselves, successfully attacking large or dangerous animals by grasping their heads in steely-clawed grips. The remains of Red-tailed Hawks, Short-eared Owls, and Barn-Owls killed by these audacious hunters have been found on various parts of San Juan Island. Usually they hunt the bountiful rabbits and, largely because of the availability of this excellent food resource, are quite abundant in the San Juan Islands. Their deep, booming calls reverberate from nearly every patch of trees and, after a bit of practice, it is possible to have "hooting contests" with them. The Great Horned Owl nests earlier than almost any other bird, sometimes incubating its eggs in an old hawk nest or hollow tree as soon as February.

Snowy Owl (*Nyctea scandiaca*). In years when the lemmings of the arctic tundra have nearly disappeared, giant white wraiths irrupt into the northern tier of the United States. Wandering along beaches, farmland, dunes, and prairies, the Snowy Owl regularly ventures as far south as northwestern Washington and can be very common during "invasion" winters. However, the wide straits seem to be fairly effective barriers to this big predator and it is rather rare in the San Juan Islands from mid-November through February, occasionally being recorded in October or early April. Our sightings have all come from the open parts of San Juan and Lopez islands, especially the America Camp and Iceberg Point areas, where this species is seen sitting on driftwood, boulders, or small rises of ground. Back on its high arctic nesting grounds, the Snowy Owl's breeding success is also affected by the number of lemmings present. When this cyclical rodent is abundant, a bird will lay up to 13 eggs. When the lemming population has crashed, the Snowy Owl may not attempt to nest at all, and these are the years when we are most likely to see this bird visiting our islands.

Northern Pygmy-Owl (*Glaucidium gnoma*). The pygmy-owl has eyes in the back of its head, at least it must seem so to the small birds that come to mob this despised enemy. Two black nape patches that resemble eyes help to ward off harassing woodland neighbors unappreciative of this feared little hunter. By imitating the Northern Pygmy-Owl's repetitive tooting, it is possible to lure many otherwise concealed birds into view, even the owl itself. Often seen in the light of day, the diurnal pygmy-owl has been known to attack prey much larger than itself, although it usually prefers game ranging in size from insects to robins. Its favorite hunting grounds are thick mature stands of coniferous timber with clearings, especially above 1000 feet in elevation. In the San Juan Islands this bird is a rare resident with breeding probable, particularly on Mt. Constitution.[69] Northern Pygmy-Owls are considered uncommon during their migrations in March and September through November.

Short-eared Owl (*Asio flammeus*). When the sun sets on San Juan Island and the diurnal birds of prey settle down for the evening, the night shift comes out and takes over the unceasing patrol of the America Camp prairies. Flying low with mothlike wing beats, the Short-eared Owl is the nocturnal counterpart to the Northern Harrier, sharing the same terrestrial nature and a diet of voles. Even more closely tied to this food source than the harrier, Short-eared Owls are quite uncommon when the vole numbers are low. Conversely, when the population of these rodents is high, the owls become common and small flocks may be flushed from communal roosting areas. Breeding is assumed to have occurred at American Camp in recent years;[70] otherwise, this bird is an irregular migrant and winter visitor from September through April.

Northern Saw-whet Owl (*Aegolius acadicus*). Old-time loggers named this bird for one of its distinctive calls, which resembles the sound of a saw being sharpened with a file. It is one of the tiniest and tamest of all owls and is guaranteed to charm anyone lucky enough to see this most elusive bird. In the San Juan Islands Northern Saw-whet Owls are rare breeding residents and uncommon migrants, most frequently recorded during the fall passage from September through mid-November and in April when they are again moving. The most productive locations for this bird have been the Friday Harbor Marine Laboratories, the forests near Three Meadows Marsh, the south tip of San Juan Island, and the southwest portion of Lopez Island.[71]

The tiny Northern Saw-Whet Owl inhabits woods in order to avoid marauding Great-horned Owls.

Rare Owls: Only the most die-hard "owler" or an extremely lucky one is going to find one of these four birds. The **Northern Hawk-Owl** (*Surnia ulula*)[72] is a casual species recorded only once on San Juan Island. This daylight-loving owl of the far north occasionally wanders into Washington State during the coldest months. More likely to be repeated in the near future is a sighting of a **Burrowing Owl** (*Athene cunicularia*).[73] This very rare stray migrant from eastern Washington has been seen twice on San Juan Island. The **Barred Owl** (*Strix varia*)[74] is rapidly expanding its range south into the Puget Trough from northern British Columbia. Recorded only once on San Juan Island, at the Friday Harbor Marine Laboratories, this large owl is expected to become more numerous in the archipelago. Listen for its "who cooks for you, who cooks for you all?" in moist woodlands and even in residential areas. A very rare winter visitor and migrant to the Puget Trough, the **Long-eared Owl** (*Asio otus*)[75] was formerly listed in the San Juan Islands solely on the basis of some recognizable feathers found below a Bald Eagle nest on Lopez Island several years ago. However, an owlet of this species was recently found at the south end of San Juan Island and brought to the Wolf Hollow Wildlife Rehabilitation Centre. This bird, a helpless downy chick when discovered, is evidence of Long-eared Owl breeding activity in the San Juan Islands, an exceedingly rare event anywhere in western Washington.

GOATSUCKERS
(Caprimulgiformes)

Common Nighthawk
"nest" and eggs

This order of nocturnal birds derived both its common and scientific names from the mistaken belief that its members suckled goats at night. The other frequently heard common name, "nightjar," is a reference to loud and persistent moonlight serenades. A close look at a goatsucker would reveal a tiny bill belying the size of its enormous maw. When opening its mouth, the head splits open beyond the eye, giving the impression that the bird has met with serious trouble. Another interesting feature of nightjars is their large eyes that shine redly in the dark when struck with a beam of light. The single species represented in the San Juan Islands is the **Common Nighthawk** (*Chordeiles minor*), a common migrant and summer breeder. Found ranging our skies from late May through September, this masterful flier hunts for airborne insects, usually at dusk and into the night. Its distinctive fluttering flight, long pointed wings, each marked with a white band near the tip, and long tail visually identify this bird at great heights. The sounds made by the Common Nighthawk are also diagnostic; a nasal, frequently given "peent" call and a resonant "vvroom" of the wings at the end of a male's courtship dive cannot be confused with any other bird noises. When you spend a sum-

*Flying in the darkness, a Common
Nighthawk captures nocturnal insects in
its gaping maw.*

mer night atop Cady Mountain, Tiptop or Young hills, or Mt. Constitution, these
notes will be with you until sunrise. The same locations are good examples of the
Common Nighthawk's open, rocky breeding habitat. This cryptic bird is so well
camouflaged that it lays its two eggs on the ground without any nest.

Swifts and Hummingbirds
(Apodiformes)

These wizards of flight display some of the most amazing aerial feats seen in
the bird world. Both hummingbirds and swifts have stiff, pointed wings equipped
with extremely long primary feathers. To withstand large amounts of stress, the
bend of the wing is located close to the body and the bones are very stout. Sacri-
ficed for the sake of lightness, their legs and feet are very small and barely visible
when tucked against their streamlined torsos. These birds are very sensitive to cool
temperatures because of their rapid metabolisms and have adapted two basic
methods to deal with this problem. During temporary cold snaps the birds become
torpid, a dormant condition that prevents starvation, and in the winter they
migrate long distances to warmer climates.

The swifts (Apodidae) look like cigars outfitted with scimitar wings. Spending
more time in the air than any other land bird, some species in this family even sleep
in flight. Some observers report that these gregarious birds are able to attain

speeds of 200 miles per hour or more, but they usually cruise at 30 to 80 miles per hour when capturing food. Flying with wide mouths agape, swifts feed upon clouds of airborne insects that they often follow for miles along the edges of frontal weather systems. Swifts are recognized high overhead by their sustained chittering notes and rapid, twinkling wing beats interrupted by short glides.

Hummingbirds (Trochilidae), despite being the smallest birds in the world, possess a bold spirit. These insectlike jewels are able to fly in any direction, including backward and straight up. When they hover near flowers for nectar and insects, their long, needle-shaped bills and extrusible, brush-tipped tongues enable them to probe deeply for these energizing foods. The polygynous males, dressed in brilliant iridescent feathers, perform dazzling courtship displays that involve steep dives and pendulumlike arcs in front of admiring females. The hummingbirds are one of the largest families of birds, with over 300 species, all restricted to the New World. Easily attracted to patios and gardens by tubular flowers or special feeders, these animated bundles of energy need to constantly refuel, so keep your hummingbird feeders filled with a clear sugary solution. Honey has caused disease in hummingbirds' mouths, so stick to sugar water without any synthetic red food coloring. And remember, these birds aren't on reducing diets so don't feed them any artificial sweeteners.

SWIFTS

(Apodidae)

Foot of Vaux's Swift

Black Swift (*Cypseloides niger*). Over the summit of Mt. Constitution, a shrill chattering drifts down from nearly invisible heights. A flock of Black Swifts is frolicking in the cresting waves of wind deflected from the barren cliffs. Darting back and forth through the aerial habitat, the birds are making one of their sporadic visits to the San Juan Islands in pursuit of drifting insect masses. From mid-May until early October these opportunists may be seen anywhere over the straits and mountain ranges of the Puget Trough and are easily missed unless one makes a habit of looking skyward. In the San Juan Islands they are erratic but sometimes fairly common nonbreeding summer visitors and migrants, often sighted over Cattle Point, Sportsman Lake, San Juan Valley, Eagle Cliff, and Mt. Constitution. From their mountain and coastal breeding areas, they may make forays of several hundred miles, especially during nasty weather. When insects

Black Swifts forage for airborne insects in the updrafts over Mt. Constitution.

have become scarce and food for nestlings is unobtainable, the young birds become torpid, surviving in that state for several days without ill effect.

Vaux's Swift (*Chaetura vauxi*). A smaller and browner edition of the Black Swift, the Vaux's Swift is believed to be breeding on Orcas and Blakely islands, probably in the vicinity of fresh-water bodies like Mountain and Spencer lakes. These birds build nests of twigs and saliva in hollow trees or, rarely, in chimneys in more settled areas. Preferring heavily wooded country, they forage over openings in the forest canopy. The earliest and latest migrant Vaux's Swifts in the San Juans are seen in late April and early October, but the majority of these locally common birds are observed from mid-May through mid-September.

HUMMINGBIRDS
(Trochilidae)

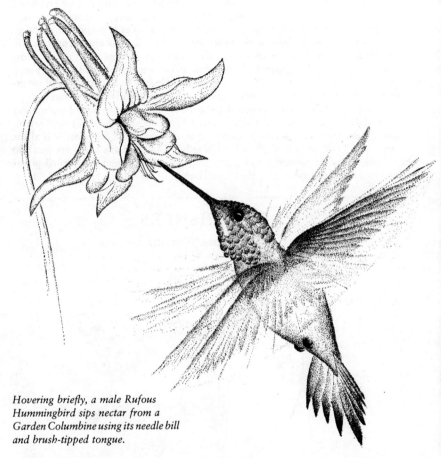

*Hovering briefly, a male Rufous
Hummingbird sips nectar from a
Garden Columbine using its needle bill
and brush-tipped tongue.*

Rufous Hummingbird (*Selasphorus rufus*). Twin badges of spring, the Red-flowering Currant and the Rufous Hummingbird are the first indicators that winter is in full retreat. The coral-pink blossoms and the warm, glittering birds appear simultaneously, as if bound by the same internal clock. Each seeking a flowering bush or tree to defend from all other rivals, male Rufous Hummingbirds arrive in mid-March before the duller females. These aggressive mites are fearless and will often attempt to drive away all intruders, including robins, crows, hawks, and humans. The male bird's mercurial movements can be followed if you look toward the high ringing trills the wings make and the loud, sharp "chewp" notes. Finding a female audience, he will engage in a dizzy flight display, rocketing through large J-shaped arcs climaxed with a sudden popping noise at the bottom of each parabola. Once inseminated by the male, the female gathers spiderwebs and lichens to build her camouflaged nest. Shaped like the stub of a broken branch, this nest is usually placed on a drooping conifer limb. A devoted single parent, the female bird will incubate her two eggs and raise the young alone, often not budging from the nest until gently nudged with a finger. Abundant breeders in the San Juan Islands, Rufous Hummingbirds do not remain long after nesting and begin departing in late July. Normally the last ones depart from the islands in early September, but a few stragglers have lingered through October at geraniums, fuchsias, and hummingbird feeders. Attracted to anything red, Rufous Hummingbirds will readily investigate bright scarves and other objects of clothing worn on the body. This curiosity has been their undoing when it comes to the scarlet insulators used on electric fences. These death traps are responsible for the electrocution of countless hummingbirds and should be repainted a color less appealing to this family.

Careful observation may reveal a slightly different hummingbird visiting our area. **Anna's Hummingbird** (*Calypte anna*) has been undergoing a range expansion up the west coast of North America in recent years. This rosy-headed bird has been seen a few times in the San Juan Islands.[76] Look for this hardy resident and possible breeder, especially during the winter, near flowering ornamental plants and feeders in residential areas like Friday Harbor, Lopez Village, and Eastsound.

KINGFISHERS
(Coraciiformes/Alcedinidae)

A Belted Kingfisher kills a captured Prickleback by striking the fish against its perch.

Most of us who have spent time vagabonding through the San Juan Islands have learned that when sleeping in a quiet bay or cove, it is unnecessary to set an alarm clock to get up in the morning. The irascible **Belted Kingfisher** (*Ceryle al-*

cyon) sees to it that you don't linger in your warm bed beyond the break of dawn. Rattling incessantly, the shaggy-crested bird is easily angered by intruders, human or otherwise. This solitary predator is seen along all of our protected shorelines and fresh-water lakes, where it hunts small fishes while hovering or perched. With a quick dive and a splash of water, the chunky, large-headed bird seizes prey just below the surface with its prominent bill. Returning to a favorite promontory, it will subdue the squirming fish by slapping it against a hard object before gulping it down.

Belted Kingfishers are common breeding residents in the San Juan Islands, seeking steep-walled glacial deposits. Burrowing into these sandy bluffs with their sharp bills, a pair will then shove the dirt out with their feet. These distinctive feet, possessed by all types of kingfishers, have the two front toes fused together. After excavating a three- to seven-foot-long tunnel, they form a chamber that is often carpeted with their disgorged pellets of indigestible scales and bones. The female Belted Kingfisher, bearing a rufous band across her chest, is one of the few North American birds that is more brightly colored than the male.

When cold weather strikes, kingfishers become more plentiful, apparently augmented by birds from frozen northern lands. In the winter, when things quiet down in busy harbors and marinas, they become familiar dockside neighbors and are seen standing watch from sailboat rigging and pilings. The sight and sound of their winter battles are constant along the waterfronts of Friday Harbor, Eastsound, and many other shoreline locations.

WOODPECKERS
(Piciformes/Picidae)

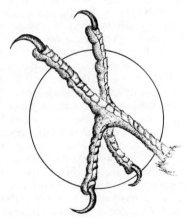

Woodpecker feet have two toes pointing forward and two pointing backward, a useful adaptation for clinging to vertical surfaces.

The woodpeckers belong to the order Piciformes, a group of families that includes the toucans, barbets, honey-guides, and other unusual tropical birds. These families are united by their yoke-toed feet and internal anatomical characteristics that include a special leg musculature. All members of this order also possess specialized bills and corresponding feeding habits. The woodpecker family is known for bills that are straight and strong, a design meant for boring and chiseling. The vigorous hammering of this powerful tool would quickly kill most other birds. To prevent a short life, a woodpecker has not only a reinforced skull, but powerful neck muscles to drive its head in a straight line, thus preventing any torquing and damaging motion to the brain. To compensate for the wear received from this strenuous work, woodpecker beaks continually grow, much like the teeth of gnawing rodents.

All woodpeckers have startlingly long tongues, that in some species, like the Northern Flicker, extend up to two inches beyond the tip of the bill. The extendible tongue is supported by equally lengthy hyoid bones that reach from behind and then over the skull to anchor at the base of the bill. Strong muscles attached to the hyoid bones enable the tongue to dart in and out when feeding. The tip of a woodpecker's tongue indicates its favored diet. The tongue of those species that chisel into trees after boring insects and grubs possesses a sharp horny point for spearing prey. A barbed tip and sticky adhesive saliva are traits shared by many of the ant-eating varieties. Brush-tipped tongues are found in the sapsuckers, a group of woodpeckers that specialize in feeding on tree sap. Other foraging techniques include hammering open hard-shelled seeds and nuts for food and hawking slow-flying insects out of the air.

Some more traits shared by woodpeckers are a strong-clawed grip for clinging to bark and stiff tail feathers for tripodlike support on vertical surfaces. All types of woodpeckers have harsh, strident calls but lack true songs. Instead, they "drum" loudly on hollow trees, or sometimes even houses, to stake out a territory and attract a mate. Just as other birds' songs are distinctive, each kind of woodpecker has its own rhythm, pitch, speed, and duration to its drumming, and these qualities can be used to identify the species without ever seeing the bird.

In spring, when the woods are echoing with territorial drumming, the mated pairs select trees and begin digging out cavities in which to raise their young. The solid white eggs, laid on a few chips of wood, lack camouflage since they are so well concealed. After the eggs have hatched, the adults maintain cleanliness in the nests by carrying away encapsulated fecal sacs. As they get older and more active, the nestlings jockey for position at the entrance holes in order to be first in line for food on the parents' return. Because of the confinement within the close quarters of the nest cavities, some young woodpeckers make their first flight from the nest without ever having stretched or flapped their wings in practice.

Since a pair always excavates a new hole each spring, the old nests are available to different cavity-nesting creatures such as American Kestrels, Western Screech-Owls, Chestnut-backed Chickadees, and chickarees. Without woodpeckers to provide ample breeding sites, many of these other creatures' nesting densities would be greatly reduced. The cavities are also life-saving refuges for other species in times of severe winter weather. Woodpeckers contribute as well to the health of a forest by helping to keep tree parasites in check. Even the sapsuckers take insect pests and do little permanent harm to the trees that they drill for sap.

Unfortunately, in recent years there has been a decline of these beneficial birds in many areas. A large part of this decline has been attributed to the population explosion of the introduced European Starling across the continent. Starlings aggressively compete with woodpeckers and other cavity nesters for breeding sites and usually drive out the native birds. Another problem that woodpeckers face is the cutting of old-growth and dead or dying trees, the favored nesting and foraging habitat for this family. By leaving these critical trees intact and discouraging European Starlings from over-running a woodlot, the woodpecker's continuing presence among these islands will be assured. They can also be aided by feeding stations provisioned with suet through the winter months. In this way these some-times shy and solitary birds can be easily brought into view and enjoyed by all.

Lewis' Woodpecker (*Melanerpes lewis*). This bird was named after Meriwether Lewis, the intrepid explorer of the Louisiana Purchase, for bringing the first specimen back to be scrutinized and labeled by ornithologists. Breaking all of the family "rules," this very unwoodpeckerlike bird has some strange habits. First of all, it spends very little time hammering on trees. Instead, it chooses to swoop from high, dead limbs to hawk beetles, wasps, and other large bugs out of the air. Large and sociable, it is sometimes mistaken for a crow, especially if the lighting fails to highlight its dark green and pink hues. Lewis' Woodpeckers were formerly un-common summer inhabitants of dry wooded habitats in the San Juan Islands, fa-voring open areas for their fly-catching habits. They are now very rare visitors to our area, most likely encountered during migration and winter.[77] Having also un-accountably disappeared from the rest of western Washington and Vancouver Is-land, this beautiful woodpecker may be a victim of the European Starling invasion.

Red-breasted Sapsucker (*Sphyrapicus ruber*). Shy and retiring, the Red-breasted Sapsucker is much quieter and harder to observe than our other woodpeckers. More often seen than the sapsucker itself are the many parallel rows of small holes drilled into trees by this bird. Well maintained and visited regularly, these tiny wells provide the sapsucker's main diet of sap and insects attracted to the sweet substance. Several other kinds of birds utilize these pantries, such as humming-birds, warblers, and less industrious woodpeckers. Migrants begin trickling through the archipelago in late September and are noted as late as early April. Ir-ruptive and sporadic, the greatest numbers are present between November and February when extreme cold weather drives them down from the mountains. Even at their peak, Red-breasted Sapsuckers are an uncommon bird in the San Juans.

When people poke fun at bird watchers, the Yellow-bellied Sapsucker's name usually gets brought into the conversation. It is a very close relative of our normally occurring sapsucker, so close that the two species were once lumped to-gether as one. The Yellow-bellied Sapsucker was further divided by ornithologists in 1985, with the intermontane race present on the eastern side of Washington re-ceiving full species status. Rarely this "new" bird, the **Red-naped Sapsucker** (*Sphyrapicus nuchalis*), will venture over the high crest of the Cascade range and drop into the Puget Sound lowlands. One sighting has been made of this vagrant in the San Juan Islands, where it is most likely to be encountered in winter and during migration.[78]

Downy Woodpecker (*Picoides pubescens*). Equality of the sexes has been achieved in at least one species, the Downy Woodpecker. Females and males will both drum in an attempt to attract mates and will also engage in luring potential partners to a favored nesting site. Looking like a smaller edition of the Hairy Woodpecker, this bird is found ranging in a wider variety of habitats than its larger cousin. Any wooded area can provide a home to this fairly common nesting resident, but it does show a strong preference for broadleaf forests and thickets.

Hairy Woodpecker (*Picoides villosus*). This sedentary bird usually remains in one patch of woods its entire ife, often with the same mate. More wary than the Downy Woodpecker, it is nevertheless easier to locate due to its noisy, active na-ture and greater numbers. The conifer-dominated San Juan Islands provide more extensive tracts of habitat for this larger counterpart. Besides its greater size and unspotted white outer tail feathers, the Hairy can be distinguished from the Downy by the intensity of its call. The "peek" note of both species is uttered singly or in series, but the Hairy's rendition is sharper and more piercing. The Downy's yammering is less sustained than the Hairy Woodpecker's and gradually dwindles into silence.

Northern Flicker (*Colaptes auratus*). Strolling along any wood margin in the San Juan Islands, hikers are sure to flush a bird from the ground that displays a white rump and deeply undulating flight. Upon landing, a sharp single "klee-yer" will ring out assuring travelers that they have just observed a Northern Flicker. Depending mostly on ants for food, this bird spends most of its foraging time on the ground and prefers areas with nearby fields, prairies, or open woodlands. This most terrestrial of our woodpeckers will also feed upon grasshoppers, caterpillars, beetles, grubs, berries, and rose hips. In the winter it may range miles from any trees, and small flocks may be seen venturing onto sand spits and beaches in search of sustenance, making them more susceptible to swift birds of prey. Besides being

Northern Flickers are woodpeckers of
open habitats.

the most social woodpecker we have in the islands, it is also the most abundant member of this family, especially in winter, and can be found year-round. During the breeding season the "wicka wicka wicka" of the adult flickers may be heard in every patch of woods with trees large enough for nesting holes.

Nearly all of our Northern Flickers are the "Red-shafted" variety, which was formerly considered a separate species from the "Yellow-shafted" Flicker nesting east of the Rocky Mountains. The major difference between these two subspecies of birds is the color of the feather shafts and undersides of their wings and tails. Often interbreeding in the overlapping portions of their ranges, they were lumped together as a single species, along with the southwest's "Gilded" Flicker. A careful observer may notice a bird displaying yellow or orange shafts here in the San Juans, the latter being a hybrid of the two races. Occasionally these strays find their way here from Alaska during the fall migration or winter months and reward the persistent woodpecker watcher.

Pileated Woodpecker (*Dryocopus pileatus*). The largest of our woodpeckers is this crow-sized bird with the flaming red crest. Dependent on old trees for its sur-

Rectangular holes and finger-length wood chiselings are sure signs of the Pileated Woodpecker's presence.

vival, the Pileated Woodpecker is fond of destroying termite and carpenter ant colonies. Often it will locate a profitable nest of these destructive insects and return to it daily. Its work is immediately recognizable for it chisels out large rectangular holes and leaves piles of huge wood chips on the ground below. One winter, while writing this book, we were lucky enough to have a Pileated Woodpecker visit a Douglas-fir next to our residence every morning. Each day we gathered enough tinder from his scrap pile to light our wood-burning stove. The San Juan Islands boast an excellent population of this otherwise scarce bird. Our Christmas Bird Count totals are some of the highest in the state, averaging around ten Pileateds each year. Although it is a common breeding resident and frequents all of the islands with mature timber, its presence often goes undetected unless one is familiar with its powerful "kuk-kuk-kuk-kuk-kuk" call.

PERCHING BIRDS
(Passeriformes)

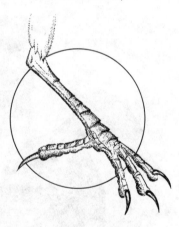

The uniting feature of this order is the perching foot.

All of the bird species and families that follow in this book belong to the "superorder" Passeriformes. Nearly three-fifths of all living birds belong to this group, also known as the perching birds. As they form the bulk of terrestrial bird communities, they are very prominent in a variety of habitats. Passerines are considered the most evolutionarily advanced order of birds and have radiated into myriad forms with widely divergent foraging habits and strategies for existence. All share one feature, a foot with three toes pointing forward and one pointing back, attached with special tendons that utilize the weight of the bird to provide grasping strength. Varying in size from the tiny Golden-crowned Kinglet to the Common Raven, the passerines are renowned for their vocalizations and are often referred to as songbirds. Raising altricial (helpless) young in carefully made nests, perching birds are staunchly devoted parents. It would be a very dull world indeed without the active, colorful, and omnipresent songbirds.

TYRANT FLYCATCHERS
(Tyrannidae)

*A Western Wood-Pewee
waits for a flying insect
to pass by its lofty
perch.*

The name tyrant is a reference to the aggressive behavior of some members of this gigantic family, numbering over 400 species. These primitive passerines are known for their simple vocalizations, large heads, and broad bills surrounded with sensitive rictal bristles. Tyrant flycatchers are usually seen perch ng in alert upright postures on exposed branches. From such platforms they launch themselves into the air and capture winged insects with audible snaps of their beaks, frequently returning to the same branches to swallow their prey. Most of the flycatchers present in the San Juan Islands are rather demure and inconspicuous, often going unnoticed unless sought after. As they are similarly plumaged, many of these birds are extremely difficult to identify and must be separated by their breeding habitats, calls, and songs. Especially tricky are the *Empidonax* flycatchers, a genus of lookalike species that even the most experienced students of birds have trouble distinguishing.

Olive-sided Flycatcher (*Contopus borealis*). "Quick three beers!" an exultant song shouted from every patch of mature conifers in the San Juan Islands, is the sound of the Olive-sided Flycatcher. This bull-headed bird likes to sit on the highest snag in the forest to declare his message of territoriality. Listening for its call, a sturdy "pip-pip-pip," is perhaps a better way of locating this species after the breeding season. A common migrant and breeder, it is present from early May through mid-September.

Western Wood-Pewee (*Contopus sordidulus*). Feasting on flies, bees, wasps, ants, and termites, this olive-brown bird is a fierce predator of certain unwanted insects. The Western Wood-Pewee is an uncommon migrant in the San Juan Islands and breeds sparingly in our dry coniferous forests. For unknown reasons, Lopez Island seems to be the best location to see this species. A burry, descending "fereer" song is its most distinctive feature.

Willow Flycatcher (*Empidonax traillii*). This flycatcher prefers brushy patches of vegetation, riparian woodlands, and shrubby thickets bordering forest margins. The Willow Flycatcher delivers its bussy "fitz-bew" from a prominent perch where its distinguishing marks, such as the lack of an obvious eye ring, help confirm its identification. It is the last flycatcher to arrive in spring and the first to beat a retreat in the fall. This fairly common breeder and migrant is usually in evidence from mid-May through early September, although a few individuals may be seen up to two weeks earlier or later.

Hammond's Flycatcher (*Empidonax hammondii*). Constantly flicking its wings and tail, this nervous open-forest inhabitant usually remains well hidden in the upper canopy. The Hammond's Flycatcher's low, burry "seput tsurp tseep" song, loud "bick" call, and whitish throat are the best guides for separating this species from the Western Flycatcher, which is often found sharing the same habitat. Hammond's Flycatchers are distinctly less common in the San Juan Islands than on the mainland. They are possibly rare breeders, most likely nesting at high elevations like Mt. Constitution. Uncommon during spring and fall passages, this bird's migratory windows are late April through May and again in late August through September.

Western Flycatcher (*Empidonax difficilis*). The almond-shaped eye ring and yellowish wash on the underparts of the Western Flycatcher readily distinguish it from all other "Empids." Its sharp, snappy "suwheet" is heard from every patch of moist wooded habitat and constantly punctuates the chorus of other passerine songs. This abundant migrant and breeder is found from mid-April through late September in the San Juan Islands.

Rare Flycatchers: There are several other tyrant flycatchers that may be encountered in the San Juan Islands. All of them are highly noticeable birds because of their bold plumage and preference for highly visible perches. Since they are migrants and pass through our area quickly, they may pop up in a wide variety of habitats. The **Say's Phoebe** (*Sayornis saya*)[79] is a rare bird in the Puget Trough, regularly passing through in late March and early April and again from mid-August through September. Usually going unreported in the San Juan Islands, this dry-country bird is considered a very rare migrant in our area. Another bird of arid lands, the **Ash-throated Flycatcher** (*Myiarchus cinerascens*)[80] barely extends its range into Washington at the south-central part of the state. Strangely, one showed up in a backyard on Orcas Island during a fall migration.

Leaving their Mexican breeding and wintering grounds far behind, some **Tropical Kingbirds** (*Tyrannus melancholicus*) annually do a "reverse" migration up the west coast of the United States in fall. The few birds that make it this far north are usually seen in October and November before they get wise to the fact that they made a wrong turn at the border. Not yet recorded in the San Juan Islands, they are expected to be found here some autumn day in the future. The **Western Kingbird** (*Tyrannus verticalis*)[81] is a very rare migrant from late March through late October. However, most sightings take place in the last half of May and the first part of June. **Eastern Kingbirds** (*Tyrannus tyrannus*) are expected as very rare migrants from June through August; however, there is only one hypothetical record of this species in the islands.[82]

LARKS
(Alaudidae)

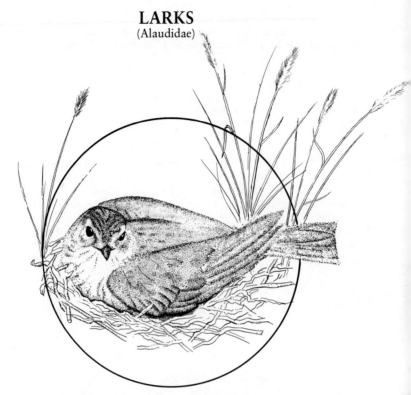

Ground nesters, such as the Eurasian Skylark, depend on cryptic plumage and egg color to avoid detection by predators.

Famed for their vocal abilities, larks rain down their endless, complex tinkling songs from aerial locations. Their territorial display flights and songs end with the birds plummeting toward the ground for several hundred feet, braking at the last moment. Inhabiting barren country, larks are terrestrial feeders equipped with stout, pointed bills and elongated hind claws. When danger approaches, these cryptic birds need only to crouch close to the ground for concealment, and they seem invisible while running across the dunes and grasslands. During the non-breeding season they are gregarious, and flushed flocks will swirl through the air to their next stop, never attaining a great height. They almost never alight in bushes or trees but may be seen standing on rocks or the low wood fences at American Camp.

Eurasian Skylark (*Alauda arvensis*). Its song unequalled by any other bird, the Eurasian Skylark serenades its listeners with incredibly beautiful and sustained melodies. The redoubt at American Camp is a perfect bandstand for enjoying the spectacle of the Olympic Mountains and the larks' courtship flights from March through July. As the birds often appear as mere specks in the sky, it can be difficult to get a glimpse of a singing bird. Watch for one as it terminates its song and dives earthward, or for the males chasing each other near ground level. Introduced on Vancouver Island across Haro Strait in 1903, this Old World bird colonized the San Juan Islands through its own efforts. The first one was seen on San Juan in 1960 and the first nest was discovered 10 years later.[83] Today it is a locally common breeding resident with its center of abundance located in an area bordered by South Beach, the redoubt, and Pickett's Lane. This is the only location in the contiguous United States where the Eurasian Skylark is known to breed. Occasionally strays are seen west to Eagle Point or east to Iceberg Point on Lopez Island.

Horned Lark (*Eremophila alpestris*). This native lark has disappeared from the San Juan Islands and the rest of the Puget Trough as a breeding species. It was formerly a locally common nester in farmland and prairies at Richardson, Davis Bay, Cattle Point, and the south side of San Juan Island.[84] A different subspecies now occurs as an uncommon to rare migrant through the archipelago, sometimes dropping in on the summit of Mt. Constitution in the subalpine habitat. It is most numerous during the fall passage in September and October but may also appear as a winter visitor and spring migrant through May, foraging on beaches, dunes, prairies, and agricultural fields.

SWALLOWS
(Hirundinidae)

Cliff Swallow

These aerial acrobats with their gay chattering voices are among the most familiar and loved of all birds. Swallows adjust well to the activities and habits of humans and often nest in man-made structures, perch on wires and fences, and forage over towns and cities. Their tame nature and insectivorous diets make them a welcome sight when they return in early spring, signaling the end of the long, blustery San Juan winter. Outwardly resembling swifts, swallows differ by their flexible wing beats, lower-altitude foraging habits, and lack of facial bristles. These slender streamlined birds often amass in large, talkative flocks when preparing for their long southward migration. With practice, it is possible to identify all the swallows by their call notes alone.

Purple Martin (*Progne subis*). Despite the removal of nesting snags and the influx of aggressive European Starlings, the Purple Martin remains a breeding species in the San Juan Islands. This large swallow is a vanishing species in the Pacific Northwest and only a handful of widely scattered nesting colonies still exists in the region. Our remnant population is found breeding on Mt. Dallas and Cady Mountain of San Juan Island, and on Waldron Island at Point Disney. These small colonies utilize dead trees, especially Garry Oaks, with natural cavities, a habit that is quite rare now for this species over the rest of its range. Purple Martins have also been seen investigating docks and fishing boat smokestacks in Friday Harbor and Cowlitz Bay for breeding sites. Besides being extremely localized breeders, Purple Martins are uncommon migrants observed in the islands from mid-April through mid-September, especially at Cattle Point. These birds need special help from people in the form of artificial nest boxes and antistarling programs. Without such assistance we may not enjoy the liquid, bubbling notes of the Purple Martin much longer.

Tree Swallow (*Tachycineta bicolor*). High over Sportsman Lake, a pair of Tree Swallows, barely visible through binoculars, drifts on the cool February wind. These hardy scouts are the first swallows to arrive, routinely before the first of March. Tree Swallows are able to subsist on berries and seeds if they arrive too early or cold weather has made insects scarce. These locally common cavity-nesters can be enticed to make their homes under the eaves of houses or in boxes if adequate foraging sites are nearby. Wet habitats with plenty of standing dead trees, such as Killebrew and Egg lakes, are the best places to find Tree Swallows. They are widespread migrants and are often seen in large flocks of Violet-green Swallows, which usually greatly outnumber them. The last Tree Swallows are usually seen in mid-August, although a few may linger into September.

Violet-green Swallow (*Tachycineta thalassina*). Violet-greens are the most abundant and widespread of the swallows in the San Juan Islands and are the most numerous breeders and migrants, often appearing in spring flocks of a thousand or more. These cavity-nesters are semi-colonial at times and can be easily enticed into using nesting boxes. They are frequently seen investigating holes and dark crevices around homes and often nest under eaves or in more unusual spots, like a rolled up piece of carpet stored in the rafters of a garage on San Juan Island. A few of these wonderfully iridescent birds nest in sandstone cavities along our shores. Violet-green Swallows are seen from late February through September with some migrants appearing up to two weeks earlier or later.

Northern Rough-winged Swallow (*Stelgidopteryx serripennis*). Burrowing into sandy glacial banks for nesting purposes, the Northern Rough-winged Swallow is a locally common breeder in the San Juan Islands. This rather solitary bird may be found along many of our shores where erosive forces have exposed layers of these easily excavated deposits. Much more widespread in migration, it is often seen with other swallows from early April through early September. Its raspy, harsh

Northern Rough-winged Swallows excavate their nest cavities in glacial bluffs.

"brrzzt" notes are the deepest in the family and will betray its presence in swirling mixed flocks. The **Bank Swallow** (*Riparia riparia*) is at present a hypothetical migrant in the San Juans with several unconfirmed reports. It might be picked out from among the swallows gathering at American Camp or other staging areas in spring, but it is more likely to be here or on southeast Vancouver Island in fall from mid-August through mid-September.

Cliff Swallow (*Hirundo pyrrhonota*). Crafting ingenious gourdlike nests from pellets of mud, the Cliff Swallows are the potters of the bird world. They favor man-made structures located near water for construction of their colonies but occasionally are found nesting on the rocky cliffs along the shores of Haro Strait. This species has clearly benefited from human activities and is a common migrant and localized breeder in the San Juan Islands, present from early April through mid-September.

Barn Swallow (*Hirundo rustica*). Most familiar of all swallows, these friendly birds are rarely observed nesting away from buildings, docks, or bridges and live in close association with humans. If feathers are tossed in the breeze during the breeding season, these engaging birds become very excited and will perform amazing feats of aerobatics. Trilling and chirping, they will vigorously compete against and chase each other for the prizes, strongly desired for nest-lining material. Barn Swallows are rarely found nesting in natural habitats on the rest of the continent, but in the San Juan Islands they frequently build their mud and straw saucers beneath rocky overhangs. This behavior may be observed along the west-facing shores of San Juan, Matia, Henry, and Stuart islands. Common migrants and abundant breeders, Barn Swallows are present from mid-April through early October, with some strays lingering later.

CROWS, JAYS, AND ALLIES
(Corvidae)

The distinctive flight profiles of a
Common Raven (top) and American
Crow (bottom)

Woven into the myth and folklore of many cultures, this uncanny family has fascinated humans for millenia. Noisy, gregarious, and rather large, these conspicuous birds have always been present near settled areas. Their bold, inquisitive, adaptable, and opportunistic natures have positioned many species to benefit from human activities. Many ornithologists and naturalists consider crows and jays, referred to as corvids, the most intelligent of all birds. They have excellent memories and show an amazing capacity to learn and solve puzzles. A captive Blue Jay was observed using "tools" such as paper clips and straws to rake food into its cage. Many wild birds use a complex vocabulary of calls that may be termed a language, and pet birds frequently become skilled in mimicking the human voice. Crows and ravens, the largest and shrewdest of the corvids, post sentries while the main part of the flock forages. They quickly mob any enemy that captures one of their bunch. In order to obtain food some have learned to pry the lids off milk bottles delivered to doorsteps, and others do the same with garbage containers. Other intelligent performances by these birds include pulling up ice-fishermen's unattended lines and retrieving the baited hooks by reeling in, inch by inch with their bills, and holding the coils in their claws until the morsel is secured.

This family is poorly represented in the San Juan Islands, perhaps because of its unwillingness to cross large bodies of water.

Steller's Jay (*Cyanocitta stelleri*). Puzzling indeed is the paucity of Steller's Jays in the San Juan Islands. Only in the last two decades have these crested black-and-cobalt birds established a beachhead in the archipelago. Steller's Jays are presently locally uncommon breeding residents in the northeast portion of the islands. Radiating from the Eastsound area, they have recently spread to all parts of Orcas Island, with the best chance for locating one in the northwest section. They occur as very rare vagrants on islands to the south and west, and we believe they will eventually succeed in colonizing all of the available thick coniferous habitats and bordering residential areas. Their relative scarcity here and on southeast Vancouver Island could be attributed to a mistrust of crossing open water, stiff competition from our small and abundant race of crows, and heavy predation from a large accipiter population.

American Crow (*Corvus brachyrhynchos*). While dining outdoors at one of Friday Harbor's restaurants, be aware of a sneaky black bandit. Unattended fish and chips will quickly disappear down the gullet of the cunning crow. Also known to Friday Harbor residents as the "San Juan Chicken," this bird may be seen strolling across the fairgrounds and streets in legions. Not restricted to stealing from humans, it pays frequent visits to seabird colonies to snack on the eggs and nestlings of gulls and cormorants. Our little "Northwestern" Crow is well adapted to beachcombing and forages along shorelines for any animal matter, dead or alive. It has learned to drop clams and mussels from a height in order to get at the protected meat. American Crows are widespread in many habitats and may be found throughout the interiors of the islands as abundant breeding residents. Once the summer's young are able to fly, they band together in flocks of 100 or more, often in the company of ravens. As the sun begins to set, some crow flocks may be observed flying to small timbered islands to spend the night in large communal roosts. We consider the "Northwestern" Crow a small subspecies of the America Crow, a treatment widely accepted by Pacific Northwest ornithologists. The larger mainland race does not occur in the San Juans.

Common Raven (*Corvus corax*). The largest "songbird" on the continent, the Common Raven is a powerful predator and scavenger that is found in greater numbers in the San Juan Islands than anywhere else in the Puget Sound lowlands. Like crows, Common Ravens eat grains and other plant materials but prefer foods of animal origin. In the San Juans they are often seen carrying voles in their massive beaks, having pounced, hawklike, on these little rodents. Common Ravens displace the much smaller "Northwestern" Crows in less inhabited portions of the islands and drive them from any area that they choose to nest in. Common breeding residents in rural areas, Common Ravens are not seen cavorting around town like their garrulous cousins. They are by far the best fliers in the family and will soar in thermals for hours, not finding it necessary to flap every few seconds, as do crows. Some aerial maneuvers of these very intelligent birds include high-speed falconlike stoops and barrel rolls, seemingly performed for sheer pleasure. When ravens fly overhead, their massive size, slightly diamond-shaped tails, and deep, croaking voices will distinguish them from other birds.

Rare Corvids: Sightings of these vagrant species are few and far between. All nest in either the high mountains or east of the Cascade range, usually appearing in the San Juan Islands from fall through spring. The **Gray Jay** (*Perisoreus canadensis*)[85] and **Blue Jay** (*Cyanocitta cristata*)[86] are both casual species in the San Juan Islands and generally appear in the colder months. A very rare fall migrant and early winter visitor in the San Juans, **Clark's Nutcracker** (*Nucifragus columbiana*)[87] is most often seen from late September through December at high elevations like Mt.

Common Ravens are perhaps our most intelligent bird.

Constitution and Cady Mountain. Very rare during the nonbreeding season from late September through early March, the **Black-billed Magpie** (*Pica pica*)[88] could show up in any open valley or agricultural area in the islands.

TITMICE
(Paridae)

*Chestnut-backed
Chickadee, one of
our most abundant
woodland species*

Titmouse is a combination of an Old Icelandic word, "titr" meaning small, and a corrupted Anglo-Saxon word for bird. Tame and friendly, these tiny gregarious birds will roam the woods in large flocks, often visiting feeders and residential areas. While actively foraging through the vegetation, they maintain contact with each other by constantly calling, each species with its own distinctive notes. "Pishing" is a great way to attract droves of titmice, along with their cohorts, the kinglets and nuthatches. Resembling fat puffs of down, the rotund titmice are acrobatic foliage gleaners and seed crackers.

Black-capped Chickadee (*Parus atricapillus*). You can count on one hand the number of times Black-capped Chickadees have been sighted in the San Juan Islands. This songbird is quite common on the mainland but has yet to invade the archipelago in appreciable numbers.[89] Its slow westward expansion has apparently been stymied by Juan de Fuca and Rosario straits and the species was just recently confirmed on Vancouver Island. The rare individuals that do venture out to the islands are further hindered by the lack of deciduous forest that they prefer for nesting and foraging. With the expansion of residential areas, the Black-capped Chickadee may eventually gain a foothold in the San Juans. Detecting a wandering or pioneering bird is best accomplished by listening for its diagnostic call, an emphatic "chick-a-dee-dee-dee." A similar-sounding bird, perhaps indistinguishable to someone not familiar with their notes, is the **Mountain Chickadee** (*Parus gambeli*).[90] This casual winter visitor to the islands might be found with other chickadees or visiting feeders from mid-October through mid-March. Mountain Chickadees usually visit the Puget Sound lowlands only when failing food supplies and severe weather drives them down from the high country.

Chestnut-backed Chickadee (*Parus rufescens*). One cool and windy September day, we decided to cross from San Juan to Stuart Island by kayak. Buffeted by strong gusts racing unhindered over the open water, we noticed we were not alone in our struggle against the elements. A tiny flock of Chestnut-backed Chickadees was fighting its way into the headwind and making little progress toward its destination. Obviously exhausted, one caught a glimpse of the following kayaks and, in desperation, turned with the wind and tried to land for a rest on the head of a paddler. Unfortunately, during its descent a sudden gust rocketed the poor bird past its chosen perch and into the frigid, gray water. Scooping the soaked and bedraggled chickadee up before it was swallowed by a whitecapping wave, we placed it within the calm and shelter of a kayak. There it remained, still and quiet, for the remainder of our crossing. When safely upon the shore of Stuart, we brought the wet bird out to see if it was recovering from its shock. Seeing land and trees all about, the chickadee immediately perked up and gazed defiantly at its concerned rescuers. We didn't need to worry; this tiny bundle of feathers possessed an incorrigible spirit that was quickly displayed. Uttering a few scolding notes backed up with some sharp pecks to its finger perch, the ungrateful bird fluttered heavily off to a nearby bush and vanished in the woods soon after.

Probably nowhere else in the Puget Trough is there a higher density of Chestnut-backed Chickadees than in the San Juan Islands. These small but very vocal cavity nesters are abundant year-round residents, with Christmas Bird Count records averaging among the highest in the state of Washington (400+ per CBC). During cold weather they are very gregarious and join large flocks of roaming woodland birds that seek locations with mild conditions for foraging. They are often the most visible members of these winter flocks as they seek dormant insects or seeds at the tips of conifer branches or while danging upside down from an alder cone. This habit, combined with a bold and curious nature, makes them one of the most familiar of our birds.

Occasionally they can be found nesting in the cavities of deciduous trees such as oak or alder, a habitat that in other parts of their range they will shun completely and leave to their more aggressive cousin, the Black-capped Chickadee. As this latter species is not yet present as a breeder in the San Juan Islands, the Chestnut-backed are able to overflow into this alternative habitat without any competition.

Expect to meet these friendly neighbors in any wooded area or even in residential shrubbery. Listen for their wheezy call, a high-pitched conversational "seek-a-dee-dee," as they maintain contact with their family or flock. This same call doubles as their song during the breeding season, when it is uttered with more gusto. Frequent patrons of backyard feeding stations, these cheerful birds are easily attracted to seeds or suet and will provide unceasing entertainment with their energetic antics.

BUSHTITS
(Aegithalidae)

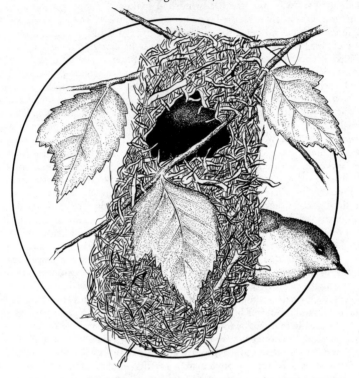

The Bushtit constructs an elaborate gourd-shaped nest of plant fibers.

The single North American representative of this insect-gleaning family is the diminutive **Bushtit** (*Psaltriparus minimus*). Very similar to the titmice in many ways, Bushtits are small, drab birds with tiny bills and comparatively long tails. They are expanding their range into the Pacific Northwest from warmer climates and were first reported from the San Juan Islands on Lopez in 1938.[91] They are now locally common breeding residents in extensive shrubby areas on all the larger islands. Usually seen traveling in small groups, they leisurely drift from one clump of Oceanspray to the next, easily outdistanced by other small flocking birds. Lacking the ability to sing, Bushtits make an endless racket with their sputtery, metallic "tsit-tsit-tsit" note as they flutter from bush to bush. These curious and friendly birds will approach to within arm's reach when "pished" at, affording close observation of the female's yellow eyes and the male's dark eyes. Suspended in plain sight from a bush or sapling, the gourdlike nest is enormous for the bird's size and takes about a month and a half to weave. Bushtits seem to be most numerous in the hedgerows of San Juan Valley and along its periphery in scrubby woodlands.

NUTHATCHES
(Sittidae)

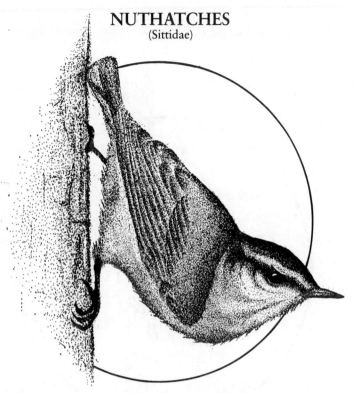

The upside-down posture of a Red-breasted Nuthatch enables it to peer into bark crevices hidden to other birds.

Hopping headfirst down the trunks of trees, nuthatches, with their slightly upturned chisellike bills, pry into bark for insect prey. From this upside-down position they are able to see many morsels that the upward foraging woodpeckers and creepers have missed. To cling at such a precarious angle, the big-headed nuthatches have evolved very long toes and stout bodies, appearing almost neckless and tailless. Their name is a reference to a family habit of wedging nuts and seeds in bark crevices and hacking them open. Nuthatches are frequent patrons of bird-feeding stations, eating both suet and grains. The only species in this group found in the San Juan Islands is the **Red-breasted Nuthatch** (*Sitta canadensis*), a common breeding resident in coniferous woods and residential areas. Like all members of this family, the Red-breasted Nuthatch nests in rotting tree cavities, old wood-pecker holes, and nest boxes. In all cases, this species has the peculiar behavior of smearing the edge of the entrance hole with sticky pitch. After breeding, small family groups of Red-breasted Nuthatches will roam the woods with chickadees and creepers, uttering their nasal "nyak, nyak, nyak" over and over. To be looked for among these flocks is a related bird, the **White-breasted Nuthatch** (*Sitta carolinensis*). Reports of this larger species from the San Juan Islands have never been received; however, the Garry Oaks and Lodgepole Pines of the archipelago may eventually attract a wandering individual.

CREEPERS
(Certhiidae)

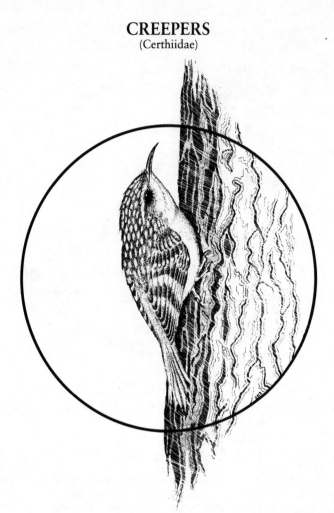

Having begun at the base of a Douglas-fir, a Brown Creeper spirals up the deeply fissured trunk in search of hidden prey.

North America's only representative of this family is the **Brown Creeper** (*Certhia americana*), a slender, cryptic bird with a long, decurved bill. Creepers fly from tree to tree, landing at the base of each trunk and spiraling upward while probing for insects. Like woodpeckers, they use their stiff tails as props against the bark and have strong, clinging feet. In the San Juan Islands the Brown Creeper is a common breeding resident and is found in nearly every patch of trees. This bird is probably the most overlooked woodland species and is best detected among flocks of kinglets and nuthatches by its high lisping "tssee" call and sibilant spring song.

WRENS
(Troglodytidae)

House Wrens are common inhabitants of the Olympic Mountain rainshadow.

A loud, militant scolding coming from the underbrush is likely to be issuing from the cast-iron throat of a wren. Bold and brazen, wrens will readily confront an intruder, human or otherwise, and quickly respond to "pishing." They are highly territorial birds and both sexes sing their bubbling tunes in defense of the nesting area. Male wrens are prolific nest builders and sometimes build up to half a dozen, a habit that decoys enemies and aids their sometimes polygamous nature. Wrens are characterized by their small, rotund bodies with conspicuous barring on the wings and tails. All have slender decurved bills, long legs and toes, and brownish plumage. They are usually seen on or near the ground, actively searching for insects, with their tails cocked at jaunty angles. Their flight is weak and fluttery yet some species undergo long migrations.

Rock Wren (*Salpinctes obsoletus*). Clinging to life on the dry slopes of Mt. Dallas, patches of Prickly Pear Cactus and Death Camas endure the arid conditions. Barren knobs of bedrock, devoid of vascular plants, protrude from the hillside like

A Rock Wren and Prickly Pear Cactus eke out an existence on a dry, rocky outcrop.

steps in a giant staircase. Drifting down on the morning breeze, a variable series of loud, clear couplets, "ke-ree ke-ree ke-ree, deedle deedle deedle," carries across the benchland. An alert and lucky bird watcher may be able to get a glimpse of a Rock Wren dodging among the lichen-encrusted knobs on the steep slope. This irregular migrant and visitor to the San Juan Islands is primarily a bird of the dry interior portions of the continent and is practically unknown elsewhere in western Washington. Rock Wrens seem to be rather cyclical in the islands as they can be numerous in some years and absent in others. A nesting pair was found on Mt. Dallas in 1960 and singing birds have been heard there in many succeeding years.[92] Other locations where singing Rock Wrens have been detected are Mt. Constitution and Eagle Cliff, both likely locations for this species. Migrants have been encountered in a wider variety of places, including the rocky shorelines on the south side of Stuart Island and the western edge of Orcas Island. A few individuals have been found during the winter months on Protection and Vancouver islands, suggesting that Rock Wrens may also winter in the San Juan Islands.

Bewick's Wren (*Thryomanes bewickii*). As a woodland flock percolates through the brush, it will bring to the surface the sedentary Bewick's Wren. Sharply objecting to intrusions on its privacy, this noisy fellow is our most abundant breeding wren. The "Seattle" Wren is found in dense tangles of vegetation throughout the year but is harder to detect from November through February. Its songs are highly variable and may be confused with the vocalizations of many other species, especially the Song Sparrow's. However, a practiced ear will easily pick them out and can even recognize individual birds defending their territories, as each Bewick's Wren sings its own trademark version.

House Wren (*Troglodytes aedon*). Another sun-loving species attracted to our dry San Juan climate is the House Wren. It is quite scarce elsewhere in the Puget Trough with the exception of southeast Vancouver Island and the Tacoma prairies. This aggressive little songster prefers open Douglas-fir and Garry Oak woodlands with sufficient brushy understories. The House Wren is a common breeder in this habitat, often selecting artificial nest boxes over natural cavities. Cocking its tail straight down, the House Wren perches on an exposed branch or fallen tree and tirelessly delivers a bubbling song. This migratory bird arrives as early as mid-April and departs in August, with stragglers remaining until at least mid-September.

Winter Wren (Troglodytes troglodytes). With its head tipped back and throat pulsating, the Winter Wren belts out a rich and marvelous song comprised of over 100 notes. Despite being one of our tiniest songbirds, this little mite has one of the biggest avian voices. An explorer of cavelike enclosures, as its scientific name suggests, the Winter Wren boldly enters buildings through open doors or structural cracks. This brazen bird can be caught napping in surprising places, especially during cold snaps. Winter Wrens have been found in old clothing hanging in garages, woodpiles on porches, and in outhouses where they huddle by warmth-giving lightbulbs. These birds are common nesters in the darkest, moistest conifers during the summer months. They become abundant from late October through April when mountain breeders augment our local population. Throughout the winter, when the entire archipelago is dark and damp, Winter Wrens skulk about like mice in thickets and residential shrubbery, as well as their usual woodland retreats. Sometimes large groups behave like a kinglet flock and move from bush to bush in an energetic search for chilled insects and larvae.

Marsh Wren (*Cistothorus palustris*). With all of the terrestrial habitats occupied by the other wrens, these birds have adapted to breed in flooded meadows and marshes. In the San Juan Islands they are locally common breeders in the limited number of areas with extensive cattail growth. At favored locations like Three Meadows Marsh, Hummel Lake, Sportsman Lake, and Frank Richardson Wildfowl Sanctuary the polygamous males can be seen fluttering a short distance above the reeds to deliver their gurgling songs. Each male builds several dummy nests in his territory, but his mates will lay their eggs only in nests of their own construction. Each large woven sphere of aquatic vegetation is suspended by several cattail stalks and lined with soft feathers and shredded plants. Although the majority of Marsh Wrens departs in September and returns in late March, some individuals are year-round residents in the islands and expand their ranges into salt marshes during the coldest months.

DIPPERS
(Cinclidae)

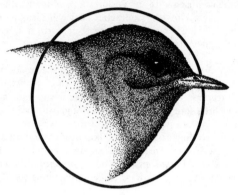

American Dipper

Bridging the gap between wrens and thrushes, the dipper family contains the only truly aquatic songbirds. Leaping or flying directly into a raging torrent, their long legs and big, unwebbed feet allow them to weakly swim on the surface or tenaciously cling to the bottom in search of insect larvae, snails, and beetles. Pumping their wings under water, dippers are able to travel in calm lakes for distances of up to 20 feet with a single breath. These plump gray birds have evolved a variety of physical aids for submarine foraging, including flap-covered nostrils and well-developed and conspicuous silver nictitating membranes, or third eyelids. Their dense, musty-smelling plumage is underlaid with thick down and heavily waterproofed by oil from preen glands that are ten times larger than those of other similar-sized passerines. A dipper is mostly a solitary bird and can be seen defending its territory, a half- to one-mile stretch of mountain stream, throughout the year with musical songs and bobbing displays. Only one species from this unique family is found in North America, the **American Dipper** (*Cinclus mexicanus*). An uncommon to rare resident in the San Juan Islands, most observations of this bird are made on Orcas Island from September through April when mainland birds have dropped to lower elevation streams and lakeshores. Breeding is a possibility at Cascade Creek, Cascade Lake, Mountain Lake, and Cold Creek, where "Water Ouzels" have been sighted in breeding season. An American Dipper was seen foraging in the intertidal zone of Castle Island (NWR) on June 19, 1977, a very bizarre occurrence considering the time of year and this species' aversion to marine habitats.

OLD WORLD WARBLERS AND THRUSHES
(Muscicapidae)

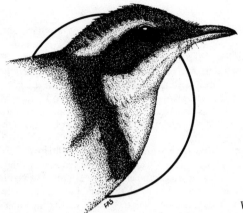

Varied Thrush

This is the largest family of passerine birds in the world with over 1,400 species included. Primarily an Old World group, it is represented in the San Juan Islands by two subfamilies, the kinglets (Sylviinae) and thrushes (Turdinae). Some of our most familiar birds are included here and they make up a large proportion of our winter bird communities. The kinglets are small, active insectivores with thin bills and drab colors, with the exception of their bright crown patches. True generalists, the thrushes are omnivorous birds with both terrestrial and arboreal habits. They have spotted breasts (in some species only when juvenile) and stout legs and feet. Both of these cosmopolitan subfamilies, especially the thrushes, have well-developed singing abilities and migrate long distances.

Golden-crowned Kinglet (*Regulus satrapa*). To the bird-watching enthusiast, a large, noisy group of kinglets is a potential gold mine. The Golden-crowned Kinglet forms the matrix of our wintering flocks of woodland birds and one can never tell what "rarities" might be discovered lurking about in its company. Flitting among the woods, the talkative aggregations are best inventoried by ear, sifting through the dominant "tsee-tsee-tsee" of the Golden-crowned Kinglets and the similar sounding Chestnut-backed Chickadees. Any unusual call notes should be zeroed in on with binoculars and identified, a process that occasionally yields a lingering warbler, rare titmouse, or Hutton's Vireo. If you don't happen to find anything particularly unusual, don't despair. The abundant Golden-crowned Kinglet, the smallest passerine in North America, should prove entertaining with its friendliness and fiery crown. Sustained "pishing" will bring it down from the upper branches and close enough to render your binoculars useless. When this fearless bird is foraging on the ground in early winter, one must be careful not to step on it! As summer approaches, the kinglet flocks break apart and many depart for Alaskan and Canadian breeding grounds. In the San Juan Islands the Golden-crowned Kinglet is a common breeder in thick coniferous forests, where it melts into anonymity.

Ruby-crowned Kinglet (*Regulus calendula*). Outnumbered 20 to one by its smaller cousin, the Ruby-crowned Kinglet is still a common migrant and winter visitor in the San Juan Islands from October through mid-April. The first fall migrants show up here in mid-September and the last individuals depart our area for northern fir forests in mid-May. When present in the islands, these birds are found lower in the canopy than the Golden-crowned Kinglet and prefer deciduous and shrubby habitats near trees. Their "zi-dit" call sounds like a little electrical spark, matching their incandescent (and usually concealed) crest.

Western (*Sialia mexicana*) and **Mountain Bluebirds** (*Sialia currucoides*). Bluebirds used to be a favorite of North Americans as their bright colors and cheerful warbling sounds could be enjoyed near most farms, orchards, and wood-lots. Unfortunately, these beautiful thrushes have completely disappeared over large portions of their former range. Victims of the invading European Starling hordes, they were quickly overwhelmed in the competition for nesting cavities. Hardest hit in the San Juan Islands was the Western Bluebird, once a common breeder and migrant and uncommon winter resident.[93] Flocks of these birds were seen migrating on the south and west sides of San Juan in fall and spring up until 1963. The last reported breeding pair was present on Lopez in 1964. Presently this species is a very rare migrant and possible summer visitor with the chances for finding it best in September, October, February, and March. The more fortunate Mountain Bluebird has fared better because its mountainous and arid nesting habitats are less coveted by the aggressive starling or by real estate developers. This thrush has never been known to breed in the San Juan Islands and its status here seems to be unchanged. Mountain Bluebirds are rare migrants and winter visitors, showing up mostly in spring from late March through mid-May and again during the fall from late September through November. A young male Mountain Bluebird spent the entire winter of 1983–84 sitting on the fences and telephone wires on the southern flank of Mt. Finlayson.[94] Both bluebird species frequent open wood-lands, agricultural fields, and prairies, especially where there is an abundance of low perches.

Townsend's Solitaire (*Myadestes townsendi*). In mid-March, a silent gray thrush begins its passage through the San Juan Islands. Sitting motionless on a storm-snagged Douglas-fir or fly-catching from a gnarled Garry Oak, the slender sil-houette of the Townsend's Solitaire may be uncommonly seen until early May. We don't see this bird again until the following winter, usually beginning in Novem-ber, when it rarely occurs in open habitats and dry slopes such as are found on Entrance Mountain and Mt. Dallas. Interestingly, Townsend's Solitaires avoid the low country on their southern migration and are extremely rare in September and October. Berry-laden Rocky Mountain Junipers, such as those found at English Camp, are magnets for solitaires, and checking these trees may provide the Christ-mas Bird Count with a gem.

The Townsend's Solitaire often perches on snags and darts out, flycatcher fashion, to snatch insects in mid-air.

Swainson's Thrush (*Catharus ustulatus*). Beneath the autumn moon, a yearly phenomenon of nature occurs with very few people ever aware of its performance. Sleeping outdoors on a lofty promontory will allow one to experience this primeval event, the southbound passage of migratory birds. Countless celestial navigators fill the night air with their muffled wing beats and anxious notes as they repeat an ancient rhythm of survival. A dominant sound in this hurried chorus is the "queep" of the Swainson's Thrush, passing overhead in tremendous numbers during September, on the way to its Mexican and South American wintering grounds. This species is also a common breeder in the San Juan Islands, and its beautiful flutelike, upward-spiraling song floats through the moist forests in spring and summer. The first Swainson's Thrushes return to our area in early May and the last lingering birds are seen rarely into October.

Hermit Thrush (*Catharus guttatus*). The San Juan Islands are one of the few places in Puget Sound where a bird watcher still has a chance to see five different species of thrushes on a winter day. One of these birds, the Hermit Thrush, is locally a fairly common bird along the west side of San Juan Island in stands of Pacific Madrone. Here it may be seen associating with flocks of Varied Thrushes in pursuit of the delicious red fruit provided by these handsome trees. The elusive and skulking Hermit Thrush quickly darts into the understory when disturbed, uttering a peculiar "chuck" note and flashing a rufous tail before disappearing. It is an uncommon winter visitor to residential shrubbery, thickets, and wet coniferous forests over most of the islands until migration begins in early spring. Common throughout the month of April, one may occasionally hear a Hermit Thrush haunting the dark woods of Mt. Constitution with its ethereal, bell-like song. The last one departs for the north country in late May, not to be seen again until the following September.

American Robin (*Turdus migratorius*). Few birds are so appreciated and well loved as the American Robin. There are good reasons for this popularity: the beauty of its caroling, the warm color of its plumage, and its ubiquity. From residential lawns in Friday Harbor to the peak of Mt. Constitution and nearly all habitats in between, the American Robin is an abundant breeding resident. As our summer birds disappear in the fall, they are replaced by fresh arrivals from the north, which masks the species' highly migratory habits. During the warmer months, watch these industrious birds scuttle across lawns and cock their heads as they visually scan for the movements of earthworms. With quick jabs of their bills they seize their wriggling prey and wing it back to the nests to stuff it down the gullets of the gaping young. Their inherent trust of humans creates an excellent opportunity to observe breeding behavior, as they readily construct their nests on or near our habitations.

Varied Thrush (*Ixoreus naevius*). The deeper forests of the San Juan Islands are home to the robin's counterpart. Residing year-round in these shady and moist habitats is the beautiful and secretive Varied Thrush. This bird is one of the most common breeding species above 1000 feet on Mt. Constitution and may be uncommonly found during the summer right down to sea level. Varied Thrushes become very numerous in winter when the nesting population is augmented with birds from outside the archipelago, forced down to lower latitudes and elevations by inclement weather. Large flocks frequent the west side of San Juan, especially where Pacific Madrone abounds, and they have been seen visiting feeding stations for small grains. Their eerie song is a well-spaced series of rapid, harmonic trills that rise or fall a half tone or more on each successive utterance.

PIPITS

(Motacillidae)

Water Pipit

These slim, sparrow-sized birds are found in treeless places like sandy shorelines, mown or plowed fields, lake and marsh edges, and grasslands. Similar to larks in many ways, pipits walk and run across the ground on their long legs, picking about for insects and seeds with their small, slender bills. Always pumping their tails up and down, they expose white outer tail feathers and call "pip-pit" when flushed. The pipits are well-camouflaged birds dressed in streaked brown plumage, often presenting difficulties in separating the various species. In the San Juan Islands such problems are minimal because only two kinds have been recorded, the **Water Pipit** (*Anthus spinoletta*) and **Red-throated Pipit** (*Anthus cervinus*).

Water Pipits are common fall migrants in many parts of the islands, perhaps reaching their greatest densities at American Camp and San Juan Valley. In some years they are abundant, and flocks of over 1000 birds have been recorded. The September and early October peak passes into a more moderate period, lasting until mid-November. Through the winter Water Pipits are rare visitors becoming fairly common again during the spring movement from mid-April through mid-May.

The Red-throated Pipit is a Eurasian and African bird, restricted to the Old World except for a fair-sized breeding colony in the northwestern corner of Alaska and a few that visit southern California nearly every winter. They are very rare migrants down the Pacific coast in the fall, with only two records from Washington State. Both those sightings occurred in the San Juan Islands at American Camp when two Red-throated Pipits were found with the usual large numbers of Water Pipits in fall migration.[95] Combing through the big flocks may pay off in the future with another one of these birds or perhaps something even more unexpected.

WAXWINGS
(Bombycillidae)

*Cedar Waxwings pass fruit to others
unable to perch near the source.*

Sleek and velvety, the fawn- and gray-colored waxwings are elegant birds with many fine ornamental touches. Waxy red droplets are present on the tips of their secondary wing feathers, giving them their familial name. Their tails end in a band of bright color, and jaunty crests cap their black-masked faces, making them look like swashbuckling bandits as they rapidly clean out the fruit in Mountain Ash and crabapple trees. Sometimes they will pass berries down a line of birds as in a bucket brigade, assuring that all members of the flock get fed even if out of reach of the food source. Waxwings have been known to gorge themselves until they are unable to fly and also to get drunk on fermented fruit. The gluttonous flocks are highly nomadic and wander far in search of food during fall and winter, often descending on ornamental plantings in towns and gardens. The waxwings nest late in the summer, having synchronized their breeding cycle with the first ripening fruits. In the interim period, they feed themselves flycatcher style, snapping up insects with their broad hooked beaks.

Both of our North American species of waxwings talk incessantly with distinctive lisping voices, a good means of identification. The **Cedar Waxwing** (*Bombycilla cedrorum*) has a high soft "ssse ssee see" call and the **Bohemian Waxwing** (*Bombycilla garrulus*) speaks with a lower, buzzy "zzrr zzrr zzrr." Cedar Waxwings are common breeders and migrants in the San Juan Islands from mid-May through October. Over the winter they are erratic and much less common visitors to the islands. The Bohemian Waxwings are very rare winter visitors from mid-November through early March, but these gypsies can pop up at any time.[96]

SHRIKES
(Laniidae)

The Northern Shrike, a predatory
songbird, stores excess food by impaling
it on thorns or barbed-wire fences.

    Investigating the storm-heaped piles of flotsam that lie strewn across the up-per beach at Eagle Cove, a Song Sparrow hops and pokes about for anything that might provide some nourishment in the blustery weather. Above the eroded bank, a solitary bird, about the size of a robin, watches from its exposed perch. Cold winter temperatures have made its usual insect prey scarce. The fidgeting sparrow spots a ripe beach-grass seed directly beneath the gray-and-black watcher. Bound-ing over, it pauses to crack the grain open with its thick bill, unaware that it is the target of a **Northern Shrike** (*Lanius excubitor*).

    With flashes of white on its wings and tail, the shrike launches straight down at the Song Sparrow, prepared to strike a crippling blow with its strongly hooked beak. In a flurry of feathers, the songster drops its seed and flees for the cover of the driftlogs, leading the shrike on a winding chase through the tangled pile. The sparrow, having dodged around a giant stump, dives beneath the network of old roots and crouches so that its brown-streaked plumage blends with the surround-ings. Tenaciously, the Northern Shrike enters the maze on foot, not prepared to give up its quarry so easily. It flushes the terrified sparrow, which makes a final effort to reach the asylum of extensive rose thickets on the bluff. Uttering squeaks of fear, the tiny bird is finally caught in the open by the rapidly flapping shrike. Reaching out with its strongly clawed feet, the predator seizes its prey from the air in a powerful grip and the pair tumble down the steep bank as one. Coming to rest in a heap, the shrike recovers its equilibrium and severs the sparrow's neck verte-brae with special toothlike structures of its upper mandible.

Assured that its victim is beyond further struggle, the shrike hauls its prize to a nearby Western Hawthorn to impale it on a sharp spine. Skewering it through the head, the "Butcher Bird" hangs its meal up and begins to pull off a strip of meat, starting at the top and working down. After filling its crop, the shrike wanders off to drink and bathe in a puddle and then goes to roost for the evening. The next day, hungry again, it returns to its larder, not forgetting for a moment where breakfast awaits.

Northern Shrikes are found in the San Juan Islands from early October through March as fairly common visitors in open country. They can be seen perch-ing on utility wires, barbed-wire fences, low branches, and even television antennas. Eating insects, small mammals, and birds, shrikes regurgitate pellets of indigestible material in a manner similar to the larger varieties of raptors. Most of the time these birds are silent, but on a clear, sunny day they sometimes burst into long and varied song composed of both discordant and musical phrases.

The **Loggerhead Shrike** (*Lanius ludovicianus*), a nearly identical species, is oc-casionally reported in western Washington during spring migration or summer. A single hypothetical record of this species exists from the San Juan Islands.[97]

STARLINGS
(Sturnidae)

Through competition for nest cavities, the European Starling has contributed to the demise of several San Juan birds, including the Lewis' Woodpecker, Purple Martin, and Western Bluebird.

Starlings are a most amazing bird! They are a "do anything" and "go any-where" bird, displaying a remarkable degree of adaptability. In fields and farm-lands they behave like blackbirds. While in town they act like House Sparrows, and overhead they swoop for insects as if they were swallows. Visiting the shoreline they forage over mud and rocks like sandpipers. The **European Starling**

(*Sturnus vulgaris*) is, unfortunately, both a direct and indirect threat to our native bird communities. By preempting nest sites and evicting birds from nesting cavities they have directly affected many species of North American birds and have severely harmed some populations. In this category we find bluebirds, swallows and martins, woodpeckers, titmice, and nearly every other cavity nester. Other birds are affected by the starling's appetite and are outcompeted for limited food resources.

These newcomers to our continent were introduced from the Old World in 1890 and 1891, when a total of 100 birds were released in New York City. It took them less than 70 years to reach the San Juan Islands and by 1962 they were abundant breeding residents.[98] Two years later, our last Western Bluebirds nested in the archipelago. Simultaneously, Lewis' Woodpeckers and Purple Martins virtually vanished from Puget Sound. European Starlings, like many other introduced species, were brought over with good intentions, but this kind of ecological meddling invariably causes more harm than good. Like the "City Pigeon" and House Sparrow, other well-meant introductions, the starling is now regarded as an unwanted avian pest by farmers, city dwellers, and naturalists.

We have only ourselves to blame for this problem as the starlings themselves, like all creatures, are simply trying to survive. Our duty is to assist those species we have undermined so severely by our ill-conceived tamperings. By providing starling-proof nest boxes for bluebirds and swallows, evicting starlings from any nesting cavity, and not providing food for starlings at feeding stations, we may succeed in minimizing the losses of our native wildlife and actually help to rebuild their numbers. Remember, unlike the protections our indigenous songbirds enjoy, there is no law protecting European Starlings, and perhaps by initiating a trapping program similar to the one used by the United States Fish and Wildlife Service for controlling Brown-headed Cowbirds in Kirtland's Warbler habitat, we can reduce the numbers of these detrimental birds and regain our original avian community.

VIREOS
(Vireonidae)

The "bespectacled"
Solitary Vireo

This is a family of nondescript foliage-gleaning birds. Vireos are small, dull-colored insect eaters with large heads and swollen bills. Their sluggish habits and larger bills help separate them from the superficially similar wood warblers. They are easy for a casual bird watcher to overlook, so listen carefully for vireos in the greenery of wooded habitats. Their songs, a series of repetitive phrases, carry well through the dense foliage. Vireos are one of the most frequent hosts of Brown-headed Cowbirds.

Solitary Vireo (*Vireo solitarius*). A common breeder and migrant in mixed and coniferous woodlands, this spectacled vireo's song sounds like it is posing an endless line of questions interspersed with its own answers. Solitary Vireos are found in the San Juan Islands from mid-April through mid-September.

Hutton's Vireo (*Vireo huttoni*). Unquestionably, one of the most difficult challenges of winter bird watching is finding a Hutton's Vireo hiding among a flock of the more common passerines. Its presence is often betrayed by a buzzy scold call resembling the sound of an alarmed Bewick's Wren. Even in February, Hutton's Vireos can be heard singing when the sun bursts out from behind the dreary clouds. Very few birds can rival the endurance of this plain little vireo. Its sustained, repetitive "zu-wee, zu-wee, zu-wee" seems to go on endlessly. When glimpsed in the cedar/alder/fir thickets that this bird favors, it is often confused with the Ruby-crowned Kinglet. Look for the more robust Hutton's Vireo's spectacles, broken eye ring, stout bill, and slow, deliberate movements. Less numerous in the San Juan Islands than on the nearby mainland, it is an uncommon breeding resident most frequently detected from mid-March through October.

Warbling Vireo (*Vireo gilvus*). This deciduous-woodland vireo is the most nondescript of the bunch. In contrast, its long, rambling song is a husky, intense warbling of jumbled notes. Sounding as if delivered through clenched teeth, its song is this bird's most distinctive feature. The Warbling Vireo is so well camouflaged in its leafy surroundings that it will sing even from the nest, apparently unconcerned with the risk of attracting predators to its defenseless brood. This common migrant and breeder may be found in the San Juan Islands from early May through mid-September.

Red-eyed Vireo (*Vireo olivaceus*). Another vireo found in deciduous habitats, this bird is probably a very rare migrant in the San Juan Islands from mid-May through mid-June and again from late August through early September. The very few Red-eyed Vireos recorded in the archipelago were likely en route to and from breeding areas on east-central Vancouver Island.[99] Diligent observation should prove this bird a more frequent migrant or visitor in the archipelago, with breeding not out of the question.

Opposite: the eight Wood Warblers that breed in the San Juan Archipelago are: left, top to bottom, Orange-crowned Warbler, Black-throated Gray Warbler, Common Yellowthroat, and Yellow-rumped Warbler; right, top to bottom, Yellow Warbler, Townsend's Warbler, Wilson's Warbler, and MacGillivray's Warbler.

WOOD WARBLERS, TANAGERS, GROSBEAKS, SPARROWS, AND BLACKBIRDS
(Emberizidae)

Much of today's classification of living organisms is based on newly developed scientific methods. Until recently, details such as the analysis of microscopic cell structures and genetic materials, or the composition of egg and blood proteins were unobservable. The formation of this "superfamily" was brought about by the application of these modern techniques. The Emberizidae is composed of several quite diverse subfamilies, all restricted to the New World and each formerly classified as full families. These include the wood warblers (Parulinae), tanagers (Thraupinae), grosbeaks (Cardinalinae), sparrows (Emberizinae), and blackbirds (Icterinae).

Wood Warblers

Bright little flashes of feathers in the greenery, wood warblers are the butterflies of the bird world. Hordes of these active insectivores pass through our islands during the spring and fall migrations, affording us the best chances to enjoy these colorful birds. Exciting moments in birding occur when weather conditions ground large numbers in migrant "traps," usually isolated patches of deciduous vegetation on peninsulas and points. At these times, the air seems to hum with their activity as they frantically glean food from the greenery to fuel them through the next leg of their journey. Often these roving bands of wood warblers are joined by other small birds stalled in migration, including flycatchers, vireos, kinglets, and chickadees.

Spring warblers are clothed in bright colors, with the males far surpassing the females in extravagance of plumage. At this time identification is not difficult, especially if one learns the distinctive song of each species. The males break into song frequently, tuning up before reaching their northern breeding grounds. All eight of our regularly occurring migrant warblers are also known to breed within the San Juan Islands. Of the great numbers of these birds passing through, only a small fraction will remain to breed here over the summer months.

After the breeding season is past, wood warblers molt into duller winter plumage, making identification a great challenge. Features such as call notes, behavior, and subtle markings like eye rings, wing bars, and tail spots are helpful clues. Many practiced birders attempt to sift out unusual warblers from the migrating masses in autumn and are occasionally rewarded with a first-class rarity.

Orange-crowned Warbler (*Vermivora celata*). This is the most abundant breeding warbler in the San Juan Islands. Its trilling song can be heard from just about any thicket or dense deciduous area, even in downtown Friday Harbor. Individuals arrive as early as late March, and most appear in April and depart in September, though stragglers linger into October and may very rarely winter. This greenish bird's orange crown is seldom seen except at close range.

Yellow Warbler (*Dendroica petechia*). This chrome yellow gem is found commonly nesting and migrating in moist shrubby thickets and riparian woodland through September. The best spots to observe this bird are in extensive sections of suitable habitat such as the swampy portions of Egg and Sportsman lakes. The clear song, "sweet sweet sweet, I'm so sweet," locates the bright males starting in late April as they begin to stake out territories. During the breeding season Yellow Warblers are heavily parasitized by the Brown-headed Cowbird—even more than other species of wood warblers. To defend against this, Yellow Warblers often construct a layer of nesting material over a clutch if a cowbird's egg is detected among its own. A seven-story nest was once found, the result of two birds' determined and conflicting attempts to reproduce. Relief from this brood parasite is sometimes found in proximity to Red-winged Blackbird colonies, as the latter is an aggressive species that does not tolerate the cowbird's presence.

Yellow-rumped Warbler (*Dendroica coronata*). The ringing song of this handsome bird, emanating from a stand of naked Garry Oaks, is a telltale sign of spring. Appearing in mid-March, the Yellow-rumped Warbler is one of the earliest of all spring migrants to arrive in our area. This hardy warbler is also the one most likely to be found overwintering this far north, as it can subsist on berries and other vegetative matter in lieu of its normal insectivorous diet. This most versatile of wood warblers is also able to obtain food in flycatcher fashion, darting from its perch to snatch insects out of the air. One Yellow-rumped Warbler was observed for several days as it exploited flying insects trapped in an eddy of wind created by a house.

Formerly, this warbler was split in two species, the "Audubon's" (western race) and the "Myrtle" (eastern race). They are now considered one species as a result of observation of interbreeding where their summer ranges overlap. Our nesting birds, always found in the presence of Douglas-firs, are the "Audubon's" subspecies. Both of these races may be found during migration and winter in the San Juan Islands, but the "Myrtle" Warbler is generally less common. During this period the loud "check" note uttered by both subspecies is a clear signal of their presence.

Black-throated Gray Warbler (*Dendroica nigrescens*). This species appears to be increasing in numbers in our area, although it was once considered to be quite uncommon in the San Juan Islands.[100] The Black-throated Gray and Townsend's Warblers overlap in the altitude of their chosen breeding habitats in the San Juan Islands; each may be found nesting from sea level to the highest peak. The Black-throated Gray Warbler prefers to breed in areas of mixed broadleaf and coniferous woodlands, whereas the Townsend's is found in purer stands of fir and pine. Though distinctly different in plumage, these two very closely related species have similar songs. The Black-throated Gray's tune is slightly more musical, full of Zs, and often rises up the scale in a series of four notes. The spring migration for both species begins in earnest after mid-April, and most fall migrants pass through during September.

Townsend's Warbler (*Dendroica townsendi*). Although normally nesting above 2000 feet throughout the rest of their Washington State breeding range, Townsend's Warblers can be found right down to sea level in the San Juan Islands. These treetop denizens of thick coniferous woods are common migrants and breeders throughout the archipelago. On the plateau of Mt. Constitution, especially in the dwarf stands of 20-feet-high Lodgepole Pine, the warblers are abundant. They are delightfully easy to observe along the trail from the stone tower to Little Summit, as they go about their business as if secure in the tallest timber. A hiker on this trail is greeted every 200 paces or so by the buzzy song of a Townsend's Warbler. Becoming familiar with this bird's metallic plucking call

Three members of a typical woodland songbird flock; clockwise from upper left, Townsend's Warbler, Red-breasted Nuthatch, and Chestnut-backed Chickadee

note at this time may aid in its detection during the winter months. Lingering longer than most other warblers in fall, an occasional individual may be found overwintering at lower elevations among flocks of more common species.

MacGillivray's Warbler (*Oporornis tolmiei*). Of all regularly occurring warblers in the San Juan Islands, the most difficult to find is the MacGillivray's Warbler. This shy frequenter of brushy thickets was reported to be a common breeder in the area as recently as 1959.[101] Unfortunately, it seems to have suffered a drastic reduction in numbers over the past 20 years. The decline may be attributed to the colonization of Brown-headed Cowbirds in the 1950s and the subsequent sharp rise in population of this detrimental species. These brood parasites prefer laying their eggs in open, low-lying nests like those of the MacGillivray's Warbler. Another possible factor is that past logging activities may have artificially provided extensive areas of habitat for MacGillivray's Warblers but that these transitional plant communities are not suitable for the species today. This locally troubled bird is now regarded as a rare breeder and uncommon migrant from late April until late September. The best time to look for it is in May and again from late August through mid-September when it is passing through the archipelago.

Common Yellowthroat (*Geothlypis trichas*). At the edge of a cattail marsh or flooded farm field, a resounding "witchity witchity witchity" may catch one's attention. This is the unmistakable song of the masked sprite of the marsh—the Common Yellowthroat. In his exuberance and desire to be seen by his several potential mates hidden in the dense vegetation, the male bird will often vault into the air to deliver his notes. Common Yellowthroats appear in their wet haunts beginning in April and gradually increase in numbers throughout this month, forming dense, localized breeding colonies by May. Like the Yellow Warbler, the Common Yellowthroat is plagued by Brown-headed Cowbird parasitization and will construct new layers of nesting materials to bury the usurper's egg. The polygamous habits of this wrenlike warbler may be observed at prime locations such as Three Meadows Marsh and the Frank Richardson Wildfowl Sanctuary. These aggregations disband in September; the last departing birds rarely linger through mid-October.

Wilson's Warbler (*Wilsonia pusilla*). These tiny, tail-jerking mites are the most energetic and active warblers, and their bright yellow color makes them easy to follow as they flit through the greenery and hover to inspect the tips of branches. In the chase for airborne insects, these warblers' aerial pursuits are frequently punctuated with audible snaps of the closing beaks. They have a loud song pitched to penetrate low, dense vegetation and may be found in any wooded habitat with a brushy understory. The Wilson's Warbler is a common breeding bird and migrant in the San Juan Islands from the latter part of April through September. In the first half of May it can be quite abundant and outnumber all other warblers on the northward drive.

Accidental and Vagrant Warblers: There are a variety of warblers considered accidental or very rare in this area. Most of these are northern nesters that usually migrate east of the Rocky Mountains but have somehow become disoriented. **Nashville Warblers** (*Vermivora ruficapilla*),[102] the most likely to be encountered, have been sighted very rarely during migration, most often in August and September. Four other species of warblers have been recorded at least once within the San Juan Islands. This list includes the **Ovenbird** (*Seiurus aurocapillus*),[103] **Tennessee Warbler** (*Vermivora peregrina*),[104] **Black-and-white Warbler** (*Mniotilta varia*),[105] and **Northern Waterthrush** (*Seiurus noveboracensis*).[106] The **Hermit Warbler** (*Dendroica occidentalis*),[107] which regularly breeds just across the Strait of Juan de Fuca on the Olympic Peninsula, has never been positively confirmed in the San Juan Islands or on Vancouver Island.

TANAGERS

Western Tanager (*Piranga ludoviciana*). With plumage reminiscent of the tropics, the Western Tanager's incandescence is a treat to behold. Despite its bright appearance, this bird is rather difficult to view as it prefers to remain high in the forest canopy. Listen for its "pit-ir-tuc" call or a hoarse, slow, robinlike song to reveal its presence. In areas with a mixture of broadleaf and coniferous trees, the Western Tanager, our only member of the subfamily Thraupinae, is a fairly common breeding bird and migrant. It graces our woodlands from early May through September.

GROSBEAKS

Black-headed Grosbeak (*Pheucticus melanocephalus*). The grosbeaks and buntings have their own subfamily, the Cardinalinae. A colorful group, they are generally quite scarce west of the Cascades, with the exception of the Black-headed Grosbeak. Much more plentiful on the mainland, it is at best a locally uncommon breeder in the San Juan Islands, owing to a deficiency of riparian habitat. This songster, sounding like a drunken robin, seeks stands of deciduous trees and especially favors willows and alders growing near bodies of water. The Eastsound area and Enchanted Forest Lane seem to provide the most hospitable environment for this lovely bird. Black-headed Grosbeaks often patronize birdbaths, feeding stations, and ornamental berry bushes in towns and gardens. Sometimes the tame juveniles, with beaks stained purple from berry feasts, allow a close approach. Present only from May through August, or, rarely, mid-September, they are one of the earliest departing summer visitors.

Lazuli Bunting (*Passerina amoena*). Perhaps a very rare summer visitor to the San Juan Islands, the Lazuli Bunting's status here is unclear.[108] Formerly more common elsewhere in western Washington and on Vancouver Island, it is now a much decreased species in the region. The continued presence of a few nesting pairs on the Saanich Peninsula of Vancouver Island suggests that this bird may be, or once was, a rare breeder in the San Juans. This thicket dweller may have met the same fate as the MacGillivray's Warbler in our area. The **Indigo Bunting** (*Passerina cyanea*), a close relative, is an accidental species in western Washington and has been seen once in the San Juan Islands.[109]

New World Sparrows and Allies

*Vesper Sparrows thrive at many San
Juan locations despite their decline in
neighboring areas.*

The evolution of this advanced subfamily is closely associated with the rise
and diversification of grassy plants. These conical-billed seed eaters heavily exploit
habitats dominated by grasses, their primary source of food. Prairie communities
and shrubby thickets abound in San Juan County, thereby providing a home to
large numbers of these birds. Small size and, in most cases, cryptic coloration allow sparrows and their allies to hide well in their chosen haunts. Some people consider them the bane of bird-watching and refer to them all as LBBs, "little brown
birds." A knowledge of their calls and songs will end most of the difficulty in locating and identifying the 16 species that may be found here. Bird-feeding stations
readily attract and support large mixed flocks of wintering sparrows, and here
their subtle plumages may be carefully studied.

Rufous-sided Towhee (*Pipilo erythrophthalmus*). Hearing a loud rustling in the
dry San Juan understory, a curious observer may try to find its source. Expecting a

deer or rabbit, he may be surprised to find a noisy pair of foraging Rufous-sided Towhees. This species vigorously scratches with both feet simultaneously and then jumps back to inspect the overturned leaves with a glaring red eye. Its catlike mewing can be heard from nearly any clump of shrubs, and it can easily be enticed into view by mimicking this call or by "pishing." The most brightly colored and largest of the New World sparrows, this bird is an abundant and familiar breeding resident in the San Juan Islands.

Chipping Sparrow (*Spizella passerina*). A bird with a declining population, apparently having serious problems in western Washington and on Vancouver Island, the Chipping Sparrow finds some refuge within the San Juan Islands. Here it remains a common breeder in open woodland habitat, although it was formerly more abundant.[110] Again the indictment may go to the Brown-headed Cowbird, as the Chipping Sparrow is one of its most frequent hosts. Although sure to be found in dry savannahs punctuated with open lichen balds, as on Mt. Dallas and Turtleback Mountain, this is our most arboreal sparrow. Its rapid, dry, unmusical trilling is heard sometimes as early as mid-March but usually not until April. By late September this bird will have vanished south for the winter.

Vesper Sparrow (*Pooecetes gramineus*). The scientific name of this species translates to "grass dwelling grass lover," leaving no mistake as to this bird's chosen home. Disappearing habitat is causing a gradual abandonment by Vesper Sparrows of former nesting areas in most of western Washington and Vancouver Island. Their clear, sweet songs still resound over the cacaphony of other grassland birds in the San Juan Islands. Dry prairies and rocky slopes lining the southern shores of these islands, from Iceberg Point to Mt. Dallas, remain the stronghold for this bird in the western half of Washington State. Smaller colonies may be found throughout the islands, as on Eagle Cliff, Kellet Bluff, and Turtleback Mountain. Look for this common sparrow with the white outer tail feathers and chestnut shoulder patches from mid-April until late September.

Savannah Sparrow (*Passerculus sandwichensis*). Far outnumbering all other kinds of birds in fields and meadows, the subtle Savannah Sparrow is an abundant breeder and migrant in the San Juan Islands. Small and demure with an insectlike call and song, this bird is the classic LBB. When disturbed, it rises with a soft "tseep" and flutters off a short distance before diving back into the concealing stalks of grass. Usually found from mid-March through the first half of October, some individuals will rarely remain throughout the winter.

Fox Sparrow (*Passerella iliaca*). A skulking, dusky-brown inhabitant of shrubs and thickets, the Fox Sparrow is one of the finest singers among this group. We are treated to this song for a brief period in autumn when it first returns to its winter home. After this, the only sound heard from it will usually be a sharp call note, reminiscent of a piece of chalk being struck against a blackboard. To tell the Fox Sparrow from the more common Song Sparrow, look for the uniformly dark back, more heavily streaked breast, and straw-colored lower mandible of the larger Fox. From mid-September until the first week of May, this bird is a common but unobtrusive winter visitor and migrant. Suspicions that this species may be a local breeder in the San Juans have been caused by the sighting of individuals in midsummer.[111] Fox Sparrows are confirmed nesters at sea level nearer the mouth of the Strait of Juan de Fuca and at Mandarte Island in the Canadian Gulf Islands.

Fox Sparrow

Song Sparrow (*Melospiza melodia*). A ubiquitous breeding resident, this is our most common year-round sparrow. Occupying virtually all terrestrial habitats, other than those heavily timbered, the sight and song of this bird is familiar to all. The Song Sparrow bears many epithets, including "silver tongue," "brush sparrow," and "everybody's darling." It can be heard emitting occasional snatches of melody even in the winter months. Interpretations of the bird's utterances vary from "pres-pres-presbyteri-eri-erian" to "maids! maids! maids! hang up your teakettle-ettle-ettle"; you decide which is most accurate.

Song Sparrow

Lincoln's Sparrow (*Melospiza lincolnii*). Probably the most overlooked bird in this group is the dainty Lincoln's Sparrow. Although it it is a fairly common migrant and rare winter visitor, its extreme reluctance to leave the shelter of heavy, tangled vegetation prevents casual observation. A determined birder should search for this sparrow in thickets at Cattle Point and American Camp during the peak of its fall migration in September, when dozens may be seen in a single day. The latter part of April and first half of May are also productive times for locating the Lincoln's Sparrow. Try "pishing" the bird into view and then check for the thinly streaked buffy breast to confirm the identification.

Golden-crowned Sparrow (*Zonotrichia atricapilla*). Alaskan gold miners called this bird "Weary Willie," after its three-note song that sounded to them like the bird was as tired as they themselves felt. Less exhausted listeners hear "three blind mice" or "oh dear me" plaintively whistled. In our area, this song is heard frequently during the peak of spring migration in mid-April through mid-May, when the Golden-crowned Sparrow is adorned with its bright yellow cap bordered in black. The fall migration reaches its height from mid-September through mid-

October, but the bird remains one of our commonest winter sparrows and can be found in any brushy location.

White-crowned Sparrow (*Zonotrichia leucophrys*). The White-crowned Sparrow is the counterpart of the closely related and larger Golden-crowned Sparrow. It is a common breeding resident but is much scarcer during the winter months. As the population of Golden-crowned Sparrows swells in autumn, the White-crowned Sparrow declines in numbers. In the spring and summer you can hear this bird singing from nearly every patch of brush, even at night under a bright moon. One strange sparrow found on San Juan Island was determined to be the hybrid offspring of White-crowned and Song Sparrow parents.[112]

Dark-eyed Junco (*Junco hyemalis*). A common trait of many ground-foraging birds is the presence of white on or near the tail. This is believed to be a distraction to attacking predators as the bird makes its escape, both by alerting neighboring members of the flock and by offering a harmless target for teeth or claws. The Dark-eyed Junco provides an excellent example of such defensive coloration with its white outer tail feathers that it scissors in and out when taking flight. This bird is abundant in winter in open habitats and remains through the summer as a common breeder in more concealed and wooded locations. Its trilling song is easily mistaken for the Chipping Sparrow's, but note the slight musical tone of the junco's and its choice of densely wooded and moist breeding habitat.

Lapland Longspur (*Calcarius lapponicus*). A bird of the high arctic, the Lapland Longspur sometimes visits our sand spits and dry fields, usually within a stone's throw of salt water. It is an uncommon migrant from mid-September through October but may rarely be seen throughout the winter and spring until the first few days of May. Individuals and small flocks are found at Cattle and Eagle points, South Beach, or Fisherman Spit and can be immediately recognized by their dry, three-syllabled rattle, "pututut," given as the birds depart in undulating flight.

Snow Bunting (*Plectrophenax nivalis*). Another tundra species, the Snow Bunting breeds farther north than any other perching bird. It prefers the same treeless habitats as Lapland Longspurs and they are occasionally seen together. Like our other arctic sparrow, the Snow Bunting is a treat to behold and its beauty and relative scarcity make sighting a flock of these birds a special moment. In flight they seem to move like a swirling cloud of wind-whipped down. Snow Buntings make sporadic appearances from mid-October through March but most encounters with these uncommon birds take place in November and December.

Rare and Casual Sparrows: The very rare **Lark Sparrow** (*Chondestes grammacus*)[113] has been recorded in spring twice now on southern San Juan Island. The desert-inhabiting **Black-throated Sparrow** (*Amphispiza bilineata*), a casual species in western Washington during migration, has been seen but once in the San Juans.[114] **White-throated Sparrows** (*Zonotrichia albicollis*)[115] are rare winter visitors from late September through mid-May; occasionally one may linger on well into June. The **American Tree Sparrow** (*Spizella arborea*)[116] is a very rare winter visitor that could be encountered from the last half of October until the first week of April. **Harris' Sparrows** (*Zonotrichia querula*) have been overlooked in the San Juan Islands. This species should be a rare winter visitor among our flocks of thicket-loving sparrows from October through mid-May.

BLACKBIRDS AND ALLIES

A Western Meadowlark sings from a fence post on a sunny winter morning.

A highly visible and abundant group of birds makes up the blackbird sub-family. Most of our species are found in close association with humans and can be seen roaming the islands in vast, noisy flocks. Colors range from wonderfully iridescent black to firey orange, and the males are usually much brighter than the females. In general, they are open-country birds and depend on grains, seeds, and insects for sustenance, which they obtain with strong, tapered beaks.

Red-winged Blackbird (*Agelaius phoeniceus*). This striking blackbird may be the most abundant species of bird in North America. During the summer it is restricted to marshy habitats where it is a semicolonial and polygamous breeder. Starting in March, its strident "conk-la-ree" can be heard as the birds begin organizing their vigorously defended territories. Chasing crows, hawks, cats, or even humans from its nesting area, the Red-winged Blackbird is a bold guardian until breeding is finished. Huge fall flocks are encountered as the birds forage in farm fields and pastures. Gradually these diminish over the winter months as weather becomes more severe.

Western Meadowlark (*Sturnella neglecta*). The Lewis and Clark expedition collected a number of birds previously unknown to ornithologists. One widespread bird that they overlooked was the Western Meadowlark, its scientific name bearing testimony to the explorers' carelessness. An enigmatic bird, it was once one of the most common nesting species of San Juan grasslands. No one seems to know why it has vanished as a breeder from our area or nearby Vancouver Island, but it was plentiful at least until 1960.[117] It still persists as a fairly common winter visitor and migrant from mid-September through mid-April. Rare summer sightings lend hope for the bird's eventual return as a nesting species. Prime sites for Western Meadowlarks are central Lopez Island, South Beach, and San Juan Valley near False Bay. Small flying flocks, resembling overgrown European Starlings with white outer tail feathers, glide over fields and occasionally whistle their bright tune.

Brewer's Blackbird (*Euphagus cyanocephalus*). This unappreciated farm resident is often found mingling with Red-winged Blackbirds and Brown-headed Cowbirds. Brewer's Blackbirds are one of the easiest birds to find in the San Juan Islands. As you drive through any cultivated area, glance up at the telephone lines strung along the roadside. Here you will see the handsome iridescent males gazing about with cold yellow eyes from among the drabber females. Livestock feeding pens and plowed fields are favorite buffets, attracting swarms of Brewer's Blackbirds year-round. As in other parts of this bird's expanding range, it has become much more abundant with the clearing of land for agricultural purposes.

Brown-headed Cowbird (*Molothrus ater*). Making no nests of their own, Brown-headed Cowbirds lay their eggs in other birds' nests, a practice known as brood parasitism. The intruding young hatch before the rightful occupants and, being larger and older, forcefully evict the host chicks when they hatch. The unsuspecting host adults continue solicitous care of the cowbird chicks even when they grow to twice their foster parents' size. Brown-headed Cowbirds have benefited immensely from human activities. Quickly exploiting newly cultivated regions, it has preyed upon communities of birds that had no previous contact with a brood parasite. In many areas, including the San Juan Islands, birds lacking a defense against the cowbird have suffered a severe decline in population. Other species, such as the Dark-eyed Junco and Song Sparrow, seem to have no trouble keeping their own population healthy while raising legions of cowbirds. As its name suggests, this scoundrel is often in the company of livestock. It also mingles with other blackbirds. Cowbirds feed on the insects disturbed by the hooves of cattle and sheep and frequently ride on the backs of these animals. Brown-headed Cowbirds first colonized the San Juans in the 1950s and were well established by 1957.[118]

Rare Blackbirds: Not often thought of as a blackbird, the **Northern Oriole** (*Icterus galbula*) is much different from its relatives. Far from black in color, this flaming bird shuns open areas to inhabit mature deciduous trees. It has recently increased its numbers and breeding activities in the Puget Trough, especially around city parks and riparian woods. The San Juan Islands don't offer much in this regard and its expansion here has been limited. It is regarded as an extremely rare potential nester from May until mid-August.[119]

More typical of the subfamily are the **Yellow-headed** (*Xanthocephalus xanthocephalus*) and **Rusty Blackbirds** (*Euphagus carolinus*). Lucky birders may be able to pick these rarities out of flocks of the more common San Juan blackbirds. The very rare Yellow-headed Blackbird is the more likely of the two to be seen and can occur at any time except in the coldest winter months.[120] Rusty Blackbirds, having never been confirmed in the San Juan Islands, require great care in their identification and usually get passed off as light-colored female Brewer's Blackbirds. Look for them in the vast hordes of fall migrants or possibly lingering into early winter.

FINCHES
(Fringillidae)

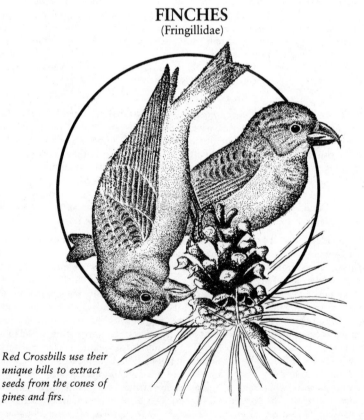

Red Crossbills use their
unique bills to extract
seeds from the cones of
pines and firs.

The thick conical bill, large jaw muscles, and strong gizzard possessed by these robust birds are testimony to their seed-eating habits. Finches move about in flocks for most of the year, often behaving erratically in their choice of seasonal homes. In some years there are irruptive invasions of these birds far south of their usual range. Listen for their distinctive calls as they fly overhead, since each kind may be identified by its unique voice. These flight notes are the best way to be alerted to the elusive presence of some of the arboreal finches.

Purple Finch (*Carpodacus purpureus*). The rich, warbling song of the Purple Finch is one of the most beautiful sounds in our moister woods. When not bubbling forth with music, as in the winter months, this bird often goes unnoticed. Whatever the season, the wine-stained male contrasts strongly with his surroundings. This common breeding resident spends more time foraging at the tops of trees and in smaller groups than does its close relative, the House Finch. Both are welcome guests at feeding stations, adding warm color to yards and gardens.

House Finch (*Carpodacus mexicanus*). A recent colonizer to the San Juan Islands and surrounding region, the House Finch arrived in this area around 1960. Before this date it had not been recorded in the archipelago.[121] Today it is a locally common breeding resident, utilizing drier and more populated areas of the islands than the Purple Finch. Telling these similar birds apart can be tricky, but the crimson color of the male House Finch is restricted to the forehead, eyebrow, and throat. The females present the greatest challenge, but the larger Purple Finch's more distinct eyebrow stripe and facial pattern helps in recognition.

Red Crossbill (*Loxia curvirostra*). "Kip-kip-kip" heralds the undulating approach of a flock of Red Crossbills. Using their crisscrossed beaks to pry seeds out of pine cones, these overlooked birds are common residents in the San Juan Islands, at times even abundant. Perhaps nowhere else in western Washington can you reliably and predictably locate such large numbers of these feathered gypsies. Normally highly sporadic in other areas, their loyalty to the islands is attributed to our abundance of cone-bearing trees, especially the Lodgepole Pine. As long as a bountiful supply of food is present, these unique birds will nest at any time of year—in the San Juans they have been seen copulating in February and feeding juveniles through the summer and well into October.

Pine Siskin (*Carduelis pinus*). The tiniest member of the finch family is the demure Pine Siskin, an abundant breeding resident, with its "zzwweeeep!" note heard in many habitats. In the San Juan Islands siskins are found nesting in moist stands of conifers and foraging and wintering in any wooded, shrubby, or weedy area. They are especially fond of alder cones and seed heads of thistle and Dandelion, which they probe with sharply pointed beaks. Amorphous clouds of Pine Siskins gather in the winter months, erratically wheeling about from one stand of alders to the next. These tight flocks chatter incessantly among themselves and flash bright yellow wing stripes whenever they take wing.

American Goldfinch (*Carduelis tristis*). Our state bird, the American Goldfinch, is well represented in the San Juan Islands. It is a specialist at harvesting the seeds of many weeds, particularly thistles, dock, and Queen Anne's Lace. Extremely dependent on these food crops, "Wild Canaries" delay their nesting period until July and August. In this way they can be assured of enough ripened seed heads, which they devour and later feed in a regurgitated form to their young. During August

American Goldfinches gather in flocks to feed on the downy seeds of Canada Thistle at Cattle Point.

and September they become very abundant and the flocks roam widely between downy patches of thistle. After this peak time, both their numbers and colors subside. Quite rare through the winter months, they return in late April, displaying once again their dashing black and yellow dress.

Evening Grosbeak (*Coccothraustes vespertinus*). Like the crossbills, these birds are usually missed unless one listens for their strident call. They are extremely gregarious and you can hear members of the flock constantly maintaining contact with a loud "peeer" or "cleeep." Evening Grosbeaks, generally uncommon, are most plentiful when migrating in May and again from late August until mid-October. A number of summer records exist in the San Juan Islands and they probably do nest here at least occasionally.[122] On southeast Vancouver Island, where they are confirmed breeders, large numbers gather each summer where there are outbreaks of Oak Looper Caterpillars. This behavior should be looked for in the San Juans. Small flocks or individuals occur sporadically over the winter when this bird is highly unpredictable. Keep an eye out for this striking finch in Bigleaf Maples and Pacific Madrones where they seek seeds and fruits. At bird feeders they show an extreme fondness for sunflower seeds, which they crack with their massive bills.

Vagrant Finches: Harsh winter weather and depleted food supplies in the mountains and to the north sometimes force four other varieties of finches down to our low elevations in the San Juan Islands—all are considered very rare and are sporadic in occurrence. The **Rosy Finch** (*Leucosticte arctoa*) is a bird of alpine meadows that is most likely recorded from October through April along shorelines similar to those preferred by Lapland Longspurs and Snow Buntings. Spring migrants have been recorded on high peaks in the San Juan Archipelago, including Mt. Erie and the subalpine tip of Mt. Constitution.[123] The **Pine Grosbeak** (*Pinicola enucleator*) is most often found wintering in habitats other than its name would suggest. Fond of fruit, tree buds, and sunflower seeds, this tame, gregarious finch irregularly wanders down from mainland peaks, usually between mid-October and mid-March.[124] Some years **White-winged Crossbills** (*Loxia leucoptera*) will irrupt from their mountain retreats and can appear in the San Juans from mid-December until late April.[125] During these invasions they may be seen with Red Crossbills visiting evaporated tide pools, as both species are very fond of salt and crushed shells. A bird of the tundra, the **Common Redpoll** (*Carduelis flammea*) is able to survive colder temperatures than any other perching bird. Its ability to store food of high caloric value in an enlarged esophagus ensures a constant supply of life-sustaining energy throughout the long and frigid winter night. Perhaps the relative mildness of the San Juan Islands is one reason why this bird is so seldom found here. When it is present, it would be found in thickets and fields from mid-November until mid-March.[126]

OLD WORLD SPARROWS
(Passeridae)

A House Sparrow roams the sidewalks of Friday Harbor.

This family is represented by only one species in our region, the **House Sparrow** (*Passer domesticus*). Introduced in 1850 to New York, this aggressive bird has exploded across the continent and lives in close association with human structures. The earliest published record in the San Juan Islands is 1948, when it was already common at the docks in Friday Harbor.[127] Today House Sparrows are a familiar sight in all of the larger towns and villages among the islands. Only recently have House Sparrows begun moving into the rural portions of the islands, usually around horse barns and paddocks. In downtown Friday Harbor they may be seen picking insects from automobile grills and scrounging for junk-food crumbs on the sidewalks. More opportunistic and adaptive urbanites would be hard to find.

Appendices

A: CHECKLIST

LEGEND:

The bar-graph system used here assumes that the observer is in the appropriate habitats of each species for at least part of the day. Some birds are localized in distribution and the graphs have been determined with the best possible area for these species in mind. To be represented with greater accuracy, adjustments were made for birds that inhabit relatively inaccessible areas, are nocturnal or secretive, or are simply more common than sightings indicate.

▬▬▬▬▬ **Common to Abundant**—species occurs in all or nearly all suitable habitat; usually found daily in large numbers.

▬▬▬▬ **Uncommon to Fairly Common**—species occurs in only some of the available habitat; sometimes goes undetected but is recorded frequently, usually in small numbers.

▬▬▬▬ **Rare to Very Uncommon**—species occurs regularly but is recorded infrequently; usually present singly or in very small numbers.

.... **Very Rare**—species is within its normal range but is not recorded every year.

- • **Isolated Record**—an individual record; shown in the case of accidental and casual species or because it falls outside of the usual dates of occurrence.
- ? **Undated Record**—a sighting that lacks a precise date.
- X **Accidental or Casual**—a species found beyond its normal range; unexpected or highly irregular in occurrence.
- H **Hypothetical**—an apparently valid record but lacks the appropriate documentation for full acceptance.
- tbe **To Be Expected**—a species that has not been recorded in the San Juan Islands but whose eventual appearance is anticipated; recorded with some degree of frequency from southeast Vancouver Island and Puget Sound.
- N **Breeder**—a species known to breed in the area; at least one nesting record exists.
- pN **Presumed Breeder**—a species believed to breed in the area but no nesting records exist.
- ?N **Possible Breeder**—a species that may breed in the area but very little evidence has been obtained to indicate this.
- iN **Introduced Breeder**—a breeding species that has been artificially established in the San Juan Islands; does not include species introduced elsewhere that have colonized this area.
- eN **Extirpated Breeder**—a species that formerly bred but is now unknown to nest in the area; nonmigratory birds in this category are no longer extant in San Juan County.

Species	Code	JAN	FEB	MAR	APR	MAY	JUN	JUL	AUG	SEP	OCT	NOV	DEC
Chilean Tinamou	eiN												
Red-throated Loon													
Pacific Loon													
Common Loon	eN												
Yellow-billed Loon													
Pied-billed Grebe	N												
Horned Grebe													
Red-necked Grebe													
Eared Grebe													
Western Grebe													
Clark's Grebe	X												
Short-tailed Albatross	X					?							
Northern Fulmar													
Sooty Shearwater													
Short-tailed Shearwater													
Fork-tailed Storm-Petrel													
Leach's Storm-Petrel	X												
Brown Pelican													
Double-crested Cormorant	N												
Brandt's Cormorant													
Pelagic Cormorant	N												
American Bittern	?N												
Great Blue Heron	eN												
Great Egret	tbe												
Cattle Egret	tbe												
Green-backed Heron	?N												
Black-crowned Night-Heron	X												
Tundra Swan													
Trumpeter Swan	N												
Mute Swan	iN												
Greater White-fronted Goose													
Snow Goose													
Emperor Goose	HX												
Brant													
Canada Goose	N												
Wood Duck	N												
Green-winged Teal	N												
American Black Duck	tbe												
Mallard	N												
Northern Pintail	?N												
Blue-winged Teal	N												
Cinnamon Teal	N												
Northern Shoveler	?N												
Gadwall	N												
Eurasian Wigeon													
American Wigeon													
Common Pochard	HX												
Canvasback													
Redhead													
Ring-necked Duck	N												
Tufted Duck	tbe												
Greater Scaup													
Lesser Scaup	?N												
King Eider	X												
Harlequin Duck													

Species	Status	JAN	FEB	MAR	APR	MAY	JUN	JUL	AUG	SEP	OCT	NOV	DEC
Oldsquaw													
Black Scoter													
Surf Scoter													
White-winged Scoter													
Common Goldeneye													
Barrow's Goldeneye													
Bufflehead													
Smew	X		•										
Hooded Merganser	N												
Common Merganser	N												
Red-breasted Merganser													
Ruddy Duck	?N												
Turkey Vulture	N												
Osprey	N												
Bald Eagle	N												
Northern Harrier	?N												
Sharp-shinned Hawk	N												
Cooper's Hawk	N												
Northern Goshawk	?N												
Swainson's Hawk								•					
Red-tailed Hawk	N												
Ferruginous Hawk	HX											?	
Rough-legged Hawk													
Golden Eagle	N												
American Kestrel	N												
Merlin	?N												
Peregrine Falcon	N												
Gyrfalcon							•. •				..		
Prairie Falcon													
Gray Partridge	eiN												
Chukar	eiN												
Ring-necked Pheasant	iN												
Blue Grouse	N												
Ruffed Grouse	eN												
Wild Turkey	iN												
Northern Bobwhite	eiN												
California Quail	iN												
Mountain Quail	eiN												
Virginia Rail	N												
Sora	N												
American Coot	N												
Sandhill Crane													
Black-bellied Plover													
Lesser Golden-Plover							•						
Semipalmated Plover													
Killdeer	N												
Black Oystercatcher	N												
Black-necked Stilt	X							•					
American Avocet	X					•	•						
Greater Yellowlegs													
Lesser Yellowlegs								•					
Solitary Sandpiper													
Willet	X	•				•							
Wandering Tattler													
Spotted Sandpiper	?N												

	Species	Status	JAN	FEB	MAR	APR	MAY	JUN	JUL	AUG	SEP	OCT	NOV	DEC
☐	Whimbrel													
☐	Marbled Godwit	tbe												
☐	Ruddy Turnstone													
☐	Black Turnstone													
☐	Surfbird													
☐	Red Knot	tbe												
☐	Sanderling													
☐	Semipalmated Sandpiper													
☐	Western Sandpiper													
☐	Least Sandpiper													
☐	Baird's Sandpiper													
☐	Pectoral Sandpiper													
☐	Sharp-tailed Sandpiper													
☐	Rock Sandpiper													
☐	Dunlin													
☐	Stilt Sandpiper	tbe												
☐	Buff-breasted Sandpiper	X												
☐	Short-billed Dowitcher													
☐	Long-billed Dowitcher													
☐	Common Snipe	N												
☐	Wilson's Phalarope													
☐	Red-necked Phalarope													
☐	Red Phalarope													
☐	Pomarine Jaeger													
☐	Parasitic Jaeger													
☐	Long-tailed Jaeger													
☐	Franklin's Gull													
☐	Little Gull													
☐	Bonaparte's Gull													
☐	Heermann's Gull													
☐	Mew Gull													
☐	Ring-billed Gull													
☐	California Gull													
☐	Herring Gull													
☐	Thayer's Gull													
☐	Western Gull													
☐	Glaucous-winged Gull	N												
☐	Glaucous Gull													
☐	Black-legged Kittiwake													
☐	Red-legged Kittiwake	HX												
☐	Sabine's Gull													
☐	Caspian Tern													
☐	Common Tern													
☐	Arctic Tern													
☐	Black Tern	X												
☐	Common Murre													
☐	Thick-billed Murre	X												
☐	Pigeon Guillemot	N												
☐	Marbled Murrelet	pN												
☐	Kittlitz's Murrelet	X												
☐	Ancient Murrelet													
☐	Cassin's Auklet													
☐	Rhinoceros Auklet													
☐	Tufted Puffin	N												
☐	Rock Dove	N												

Species	Code	JAN	FEB	MAR	APR	MAY	JUN	JUL	AUG	SEP	OCT	NOV	DEC
Band-tailed Pigeon	N												
Mourning Dove	N												
Common Barn-Owl	N												
Western Screech-Owl	N												
Great Horned Owl	N												
Snowy Owl													
Northern Hawk-Owl	HX											?	
Northern Pygmy-Owl	pN												
Burrowing Owl													
Barred Owl													
Long-eared Owl	N												
Short-eared Owl	?N												
Northern Saw-whet Owl	N												
Common Nighthawk	N												
Black Swift													
Vaux's Swift	pN												
Anna's Hummingbird	?N												
Rufous Hummingbird	N												
Belted Kingfisher	N												
Lewis' Woodpecker	epN												
Red-naped Sapsucker	X									•			
Red-breasted Sapsucker													
Downy Woodpecker	N												
Hairy Woodpecker	N												
Northern Flicker	N												
Pileated Woodpecker	N												
Olive-sided Flycatcher	N												
Western Wood-Pewee	N												
Willow Flycatcher	N												
Hammond's Flycatcher	?N												
Western Flycatcher	N												
Say's Phoebe													
Ash-throated Flycatcher	X									•			
Western Kingbird				•									
Eastern Kingbird	tbe												
Eurasian Skylark	N												
Horned Lark	eN												
Purple Martin	N												
Tree Swallow	N												
Violet-green Swallow	N												
N. Rough-winged Swallow	N												
Bank Swallow	tbe												
Cliff Swallow	N												
Barn Swallow	N												
Steller's Jay	N												
Blue Jay	X												
Clark's Nutcracker								•					
Black-billed Magpie													
American Crow	N												
Common Raven	N												
Black-capped Chickadee													
Mountain Chickadee	H												
Chestnut-backed Chickadee	N												
Bushtit	N												
Red-breasted Nuthatch	N												

		JAN	FEB	MAR	APR	MAY	JUN	JUL	AUG	SEP	OCT	NOV	DEC
Brown Creeper	N												
Rock Wren	N												
Bewick's Wren	N												
House Wren	N												
Winter Wren	N												
Marsh Wren	N												
American Dipper	?N												
Golden-crowned Kinglet	N												
Ruby-crowned Kinglet													
Western Bluebird	eN												
Mountain Bluebird													
Townsend's Solitaire													
Swainson's Thrush	N												
Hermit Thrush													
American Robin	N												
Varied Thrush	N												
Mockingbird	tbe												
Red-throated Pipit	X												
Water Pipit													
Bohemian Waxwing													
Cedar Waxwing	N												
Northern Shrike													
Loggerhead Shrike	H												
European Starling	N												
Solitary Vireo	N												
Hutton's Vireo	N												
Warbling Vireo	N												
Red-eyed Vireo													
Tennessee Warbler	X												
Orange-crowned Warbler	N												
Nashville Warbler													
Yellow Warbler	N												
Yellow-rumped Warbler	N												
Black-throated Gray Warbler	N												
Townsend's Warbler	N												
Hermit Warbler	HX					?							
Black-and-white Warbler	X												
Ovenbird	X												
Northern Waterthrush	HX							?					
MacGillivray's Warbler	N												
Common Yellowthroat	N												
Wilson's Warbler	N												
Western Tanager	N												
Black-headed Grosbeak	N												
Lazuli Bunting	?N												
Indigo Bunting	X												
Rufous-sided Towhee	N												
American Tree Sparrow													
Chipping Sparrow	N												
Vesper Sparrow	N												
Lark Sparrow	X												
Savannah Sparrow	N												
Fox Sparrow	?N												
Song Sparrow	N												
Lincoln's Sparrow													

		JAN	FEB	MAR	APR	MAY	JUN	JUL	AUG	SEP	OCT	NOV	DEC
☐ White-throated Sparrow													
☐ Golden-crowned Sparrow													
☐ White-crowned Sparrow	N												
☐ Harris Sparrow	tbe												
☐ Dark-eyed Junco	N												
☐ Lapland Longspur													
☐ Snow Bunting													
☐ Red-winged Blackbird	N												
☐ Western Meadowlark	eN												
☐ Yellow-headed Blackbird													
☐ Rusty Blackbird	tbe												
☐ Brewer's Blackbird	N												
☐ Brown-headed Cowbird	N												
☐ Northern Oriole	?N												
☐ Rosy Finch													
☐ Pine Grosbeak													
☐ Purple Finch	N												
☐ House Finch	N												
☐ Red Crossbill	N												
☐ White-winged Crossbill													
☐ Common Redpoll													
☐ Pine Siskin	N												
☐ American Goldfinch	N												
☐ Evening Grosbeak	pN												
☐ House Sparrow	N												

Additional Sightings

	JAN	FEB	MAR	APR	MAY	JUN	JUL	AUG	SEP	OCT	NOV	DEC
☐ Horned Puffin							●					
☐ Gray Jay	●											
☐ Black-throated Sparrow					●							
☐												
☐												
☐												
☐												
☐												
☐												
☐												
☐												
☐												
☐												
☐												
☐												
☐												
☐												
☐												
☐												
☐												
☐												
☐												
☐												
☐												
☐												
☐												

B: Agencies and Authors

Whale Sightings and Strandings

Washington 1-800-562-8832
British Columbia 1-800-334-8832

The Whale Museum
P.O. Box 945,
Friday Harbor WA 98250
206-378-4710

Harassment of Marine Mammals

The Whale Museum
(see above)

National Marine Fisheries Service
Law Enforcement Division
7600 Sand Point Way NE
Seattle WA 98115
206-526-6133 (Seattle)
206-676-9268 (Bellingham)

U.S. Coast Guard,
Channel 16 on VHF marine radio

Disturbance or Trespassing on National Wildlife Refuge Islands

National Marine Fisheries Service
U.S. Fish and Wildlife Service
Nisqually National Wildlife Refuge
100 Brown Farm Road
Olympia WA 98506
206-753-9467

Poaching or Harassment of Birds and Mammals

Washington State Wildlife Department
16018 Mill Creek Boulevard
Mill Creek WA 98012
206-775-1311

Poaching Hotline 1-800-562-5626
San Juan County Sheriff Department
911

Oil Spills and Hazardous Wastes

Coast Guard Pollution/Emergency
Response 206-422-1853

Coast Guard National Response Center
1-800-424-4923

San Juan Islands Oil Spill Association
206-378-5000 or 911

Additional Names and Addresses

San Juan Islands Audubon Society
Route 1, Box 1700
Lopez, WA 98261

Wolf Hollow Wildlife Rehabilitation
Centre
P.O. Box 391
Friday Harbor WA 98250
206-378-5000

Three Meadows Association
P.O. Box 1091
Friday Harbor WA 98250

Mark Lewis
P.O. Box 2424
Friday Harbor WA 98250
206-378-5767

Fred Sharpe
12724 42nd NE
Seattle WA 98125
206-365-0905

C: NOTED REFERENCES

1. **Common Loon.** Miller et al. (*Murrelet* 16:55) wrote "Undoubtedly resident in small numbers about freshwater lakes on larger islands. Breeds (D. Brown, J. Edson). Seen on Blakely Lake, summer of 1926 (R. Wolcott)." Z. McMannama assumed breeding occurred at Sportsman Lake when she reported two adults with fully feathered young on 21 July 1948 (*Audubon Field Notes* 3:249).
2. **Yellow-billed Loon.** Up to three records per winter season. The latest dates were an adult in summer plumage found 22 May 1986 at Cowlitz Bay by F. Sharpe and an immature seen by W. Harm at Spencer Spit, 11 June 1981.
3. **Clark's Grebe.** One record. T. Wahl observed two near the west end of Obstruction Pass, 9 November 1985.
4. **Short-tailed Albatross.** One specimen, no date. Collected by J. Edson near Sinclair Island around the turn of the century (*Murrelet* 16:55).
5. **Northern Fulmar.** Three records. One in Haro Strait near Sydney Island, B.C., during a Christmas Bird Count, 15 December 1973 (*American Birds* 28:499). S. Atkinson found another in Bowman Bay, 12 October 1985. A photograph of a Northern Fulmar was taken by A. Hoelzel over the Salmon Bank in October 1981.
6. **Sooty Shearwater.** Extreme dates are 7 July 1984, when K. Lowe spotted three or more from Cattle Point, and 24 November 1983, when M. Lewis observed four from Eagle Point; conditions during both of these sightings were stormy with strong westerly winds. Miller et al. reported them "common in migration in the late summer" and the largest flock, several hundred, was observed in foggy weather off the southwest side of San Juan Island, 3 September 1985 (*Murrelet* 16:55).
7. **Short-tailed Shearwater.** One record. A single individual was reported by T. Wahl near Bird Rocks (NWR) in Rosario Strait, 4 December 1977 (*AB* 32:390).
8. **Fork-tailed Storm-Petrel.** Five or six records. W. Goodge saw three with unidentified shearwaters, 9 August 1948, off Cattle Point during stormy weather (*Murrelet* 31:27). One was seen near the south shore of Orcas Island, 20 August 1958 (G. Bakus, *Avifauna of San Juan Island and Archipelago, Washington*, page 7). A single individual was observed both 15 and 16 August 1981 near Point Lawrence in northern Rosario Strait by F. Morlock and G. Walker. T. Wahl found one each in Upright Channel and San Juan Channel, 13 November 1982. A spring migrant was reported 24 March 1985 in Rosario Strait near Bird Rocks (NWR) by B. Harrington-Tweit.
9. **Leach's Storm-Petrel.** One record. A single bird was seen by F. Morlock and G. Walker near Clark and Barnes islands in Rosario Strait, 24 October 1981.
10. **Brown Pelican.** Four records. One reported by D. Linstrom at Cattle Point, 27 July 1981 (*Earthcare Northwest* 22:1:4), an anonymous sighting of two at Charles Island, 26 August 1983 (*Earthcare Northwest* 24:4:13), one in San Juan Channel seen from the ferry by K. Herrmann, October 1983 (*Trumpeter* 3:9), and one reported by W. Garfield near Iceberg Point, 28 August 1985 (*Earthcare Northwest* 26:3:5).
11. **Double-crested Cormorant.** In July 1957 "breeding at two locations in San Juans for the first time in many years" (*Audubon Field Notes* 11:426); July 1964 "none breeding on Colville Island, perhaps due to shooting by salmon fishermen" (*AFN* 18:530); July 1970 "nesting on Colville Island for first time in many years" (*AFN* 24:636); July 1974 "none nesting on Colville Island" *American Birds* (28:938).
12. **Great Blue Heron.** Miller et al. (*Murrelet* 16:56).
13. **American Bittern.** At least four records. One specimen, identified by Z. McMannama in summer 1948, was apparently shot during a fall pheasant hunting season

(*Murrelet* 31:29). B. Wood heard one "booming" in a marsh on Orcas Island during summer 1981 and K. Lowe repeatedly heard "booming" emanating from the cattails at Sportsman Lake. May–June in both 1982 and 1983. J. and K. Vedder saw one at Three Meadows Marsh, 23 July 1987.

14. **Black-crowned Night-Heron.** F. Richardson saw a single individual at least three times near Deer Harbor in the winter of 1976–77.

15. **Mute Swan.** W. Harm and B. Meyer recorded a resident pair breeding successfully at Fowler Pond from 1982–85. The pair was apparently released at the site.

16. **Mallard.** The nest was discovered 21 June 1948 (*Murrelet* 31:28).

17. **Gadwall.** C. Eaton observed a hen with a clutch of nine eggs in July 1977.

18. **Ring-necked Duck.** Three nesting records. Five drakes and a brood were observed by A. Richards at Three Meadows Marsh, 24 June 1978 (*AB* 32:1200). A pair and brood were found at the same location in late June 1985 by R. Wright. A female with a brood of 3 ducklings were located at the Frank Richardson Wildlife Sanctuary, 27 June 1987, by W. Harm. Numerous summering pairs have been recorded without broods in the last several years at Three Meadows Marsh and at least three other locations.

19. **Emperor Goose.** Hypothetical. A. Sobieralski reported what was probably an Emperor Goose in Mosquito Pass, 26 November 1984, but it was seen only briefly and was unconfirmed.

20. **Common Pochard.** Hypothetical. A bird fitting the description of a male Common Pochard was studied by M. Lewis and A. Speers at Ackley Pond, 26 September 1983. It departed before a photograph could be taken or another party of observers brought to the scene. If this duck was not an escapee from an aviary then it would be the first record of the species on this continent south of Alaska.

21. **Redhead.** Two records. One may be considered accidental due to the unusual date. M. Lewis observed a female diving for marine algae next to the busy ferry dock in Friday Harbor, 30 July 1983. Four were recorded at Hummel Lake, 19–20 December 1986, by R. Wilson and B. Myhr.

22. **King Eider.** Two records. Two females were studied by I. Burr near the Orcas ferry dock, 22 February 1967 (*Murrelet* 48:7). M. Lewis and K. Pehoushek photographed a single female off Fisherman Spit, 29 October 1986.

23. **Smew.** The first and only record in Washington State. Two drakes appeared near the Friday Harbor ferry dock, 22 February 1981 (*AB* 35:328).

24. **Turkey Vulture.** K. Lowe observed a pair nesting under an overhanging rock formation near the north tip of San Juan Island from 1982–85. Winter records include two on Mt. Dallas, 27 November 1981, by M. Lewis; three on Shaw Island, 6 February 1983, by D. Paulson; three on Lopez Island, throughout November 1983, by W. Beecher; two on Lopez Island, January-February 1984, by W. Beecher; and three on Lopez Island, 30 November–15 December 1984, by R. Wilson and three on Lopez Island, 9 December 1986, by R. Wilson.

25. **Osprey.** One winter record. An Osprey was seen 18 January 1982 at Orcas Island (*AB* 36:324).

26. **Sharp-shinned Hawk.** A nest was found by M. Lewis in a stand of dense, young conifers near sea level on the north end of Cypress Island, 7 July 1984. Summering adults have been consistently found at a few other locations in the archipelago, and these are likely breeders.

27. **Cooper's Hawk.** J. McNutt and K. Franklin located 22 active nests on San Juan Island in 1978.

28. **Northern Goshawk.** Two adults and three immatures were observed hunting in the area between False Bay and Cattle Point throughout August 1968 by J. Fackler. A single individual was recorded 7 July 1984 on Lopez Island by W. Beecher. W. English found freshly molted feathers on Mt. Dallas during a recent summer.

29. **Merlin.** An adult male was seen atop Eagle Cliff, 7 July 1984, by M. Lewis and F. Sharpe. A pair was observed being harassed by crows at Beaver Point, Saltspring Island, B.C., on 25 July 1986 by M. Lewis.

30. **Peregrine Falcon.** A pair was found nesting by J. Edson and W. Dawson on the cliffs at Point Disney in 1905 (*Murrelet* 10:1–7; *Murrelet* 16:57). A quarrying operation destroyed the eyrie sometime later and the species was lost as a breeder in the San Juan Islands for several decades. Peregrine Falcons are again nesting in San Juan County at an undisclosed location. Birds nesting in the Gulf Islands, B.C., and at Lummi Island, Whatcom County, Wash. are also likely to be seen visiting the San Juan Islands during the breeding season.

31. **Swainson's Hawk.** Four records. Two on 13 July 1968 were observed by T. Wahl (*AFN* 22:639) and one on 1 February 1975 was reported by N. Lavers (*AB* 29:732); both from Lopez Island. A light-phase adult was sighted by J. O'Connell in Beaverton Valley, April 1979. C. Chappel found one at American Camp, 6 September 1979 (*AB* 34:192).

32. **Ferruginous Hawk.** Hypothetical. An immature was present for several days in November 1970 at American Camp. It was carefully studied by several falconers (S. Layman, K. Franklin, et al.) who believed that it was a completely wild bird.

33. **Gyrfalcon.** S. Layman reports that he saw at least one on San Juan Island nearly every winter from 1970–73. K. Franklin sighted one near the south end of San Juan Island in December 1984. Some individuals may be escaped falconers' birds. The Gyrfalcon seen on Lopez Island from late May through 10 June 1981 was likely an escapee.

34. **Prairie Falcon.** A group of experienced falconers (S. Layman, K. Franklin, et al.) watched an apparently wild Prairie Falcon hazing a falconer's Goshawk at American Camp in October 1970. After it ceased harassing the manned bird it flew off and was followed for several miles by automobile. S. Layman reports that single immature female Prairie Falcons were observed in 1972 and 1973 on San Juan Island and K. Franklin reports occasional sightings after these dates. Although no exact dates were reported, all sightings have been from late September through November.

35. **California Quail.** The first reference to this species' presence in the San Juan Islands was reported by Miller et al. (*Murrelet* 16:57), who considered it a fairly comon breeding resident on San Juan and other islands.

36. **Ring-necked Pheasant.** In 1935 Miller et al. reported this species common on Orcas Island, widespread on San Juan Island with many young seen, and abundant near the Friday Harbor Marine Laboratories (*Murrelet* 16:58). G. Bakus (p. 13) also considered it a common breeder on San Juan in 1958 and 1959. Observers on San Juan, Orcas, and Lopez islands all witnessed a gradual die-out of this species in the late 1970s.

37. **Gray Partridge and Chukar.** The only reference to these species comes from L. Retfalvi (*Murrelet* 44:13). He considered Chukars to be "abundant" and Gray Partridges "not so abundant" on San Juan Island in the summer of 1962. He also thought that they had been introduced in the decade previous to his observations.

38. **Northern Bobwhite.** J. Edson collected many specimens on Orcas and other islands; he considered this species to be locally common before 1905. J. Edson and W. Dawson observed the birds at Davis Bay in June 1905 (*Murrelet* 10:1–7; *Murrelet* 16:57). R. Wolcott reported them from Shaw Island in 1926 (*Murrelet* 16:57). Apparently a decline took place before 1935 as Miller et al. (*Murrelet* 16:57) considered this species "formerly quite common."

39. **Mountain Quail.** J. Edson collected specimens from Waldron and Orcas islands and believed the species to be quite numerous by 1905 (*Murrelet* 10:1–7). Miller et al. considered Mountain Quail "scarce, if not absent" by 1935 (*Murrelet* 16:57).

40. **Ruffed Grouse.** According to J. Edson this species was "found in suitable habitat on most of the islands" early this century (*Murrelet* 16:57). However, he may have been referring to the islands close to the mainland, such as Fidalgo and Lummi, and not those within the borders of San Juan County.

41. **Chilean Tinamou.** F. Richardson and W. Beecher considered them common on

Lopez Island in 1975. P. Kennedy (1980) remarked that they were numerous there in 1978. The last reported sighting was made by J. Beecher in 1981.

42. **Sandhill Crane.** At least three records. A specimen was collected by D. Lyall on Orcas Island, June 1858 (*Murrelet* 16:58). The Washington State Department of Game has a record on file of two that flew over Cattle Point on 11 November 1979. M. Lewis and S. Atkinson independently observed two fly over the south end of San Juan Island, 18 September 1985. J. Edson saw them at Orcas Island early this century, leading Miller et al. (*Murrelet* 16:58) to list this species as a spring and fall migrant.

43. **Black-necked Stilt.** A single record from Cattle Point on 7 August 1977 by R. Warpala (*AB* 32:247).

44. **American Avocet.** Two records. S. Atkinson found one at Richardson Ponds on both 17 and 18 June 1980. M. Mallea located three at Swift Bay Ponds 26 May 1987.

45. **Rock Sandpiper.** A lone bird observed by M. Lewis at Whale Rocks, 16 September 1981, was unusually early.

46. **Red Phalarope.** Recorded twice. G. Orians saw one on 26 November 1960 near the Lopez ferry dock (G. Bakus, p. 33). Two were observed from the ferry on 27 November 1969 by D. Paulson.

47. **Willet.** Two records. J. Sproul found one at Fisherman Bay, 30 April 1978 (*AB* 32:1047). K. and J. Lowe observed three roosting with a flock of Sanderlings at Cattle Point and then flying north up San Juan Channel on 12 January 1985.

48. **Sharp-tailed Sandpiper.** Two or three records. M. Lewis observed a juvenile at Panorama March, 25–28 September 1985. A. Greenberg and F. Sharpe found a juvenile at False Bay, 1 October 1986. A juvenile, perhaps the same individual, was photographed by M. Lewis at False Bay, 6 October 1986.

49. **Buff-breasted Sandpiper.** A single record. E. Hunn found one at American Camp, 14 September 1979 (*Earthcare Northwest* 22:2:4).

50. **Pomarine Jaeger.** Three records. One in Thatcher Pass on 2 September 1978 is on file with the Washington State Department of Game. E. Hunn saw a dark immature near Cattle Point, 12 September 1980. F. Morlock reported one near Patos Island, 5 September 1981.

51. **Long-tailed Jaeger.** Three records. An immature was seen from the ferry by E. Hunn in Upright Channel, 18 October 1975 (*AB* 30:115). T. Wahl found one near the south end of San Juan Channel, 26 September 1979. Another was reported by S. Atkinson off South Beach, 16 September 1984.

52. **Thayer's Gull.** One seen by M. Lewis on 22 August 1984 at San Juan County Park was unusually early.

53. **Glaucous-winged Gull.** In July 1964 the gull "colonies showed much molestation" as did the cormorants (*AFN* 18:531). Human disturbance seemed to be causing reduced breeding success again in July 1967 (*AFN* 21:598).

54. **Glaucous-winged Gull.** Amlaner et al. (*Murrelet* 57:18–20).

55. **Black-legged Kittiwake.** A flock of 60 was reported in San Juan County, 10 May 1972, by the Washington State Department of Game. A Black-legged Kittiwake apparently overwintered in Friday Harbor; it was first seen 15 December 1973 during a Christmas Bird Count (*AB* 28:499) and again 3 January 1974 (*AB* 28:681). An immature was observed 4 December 1977 by D. Paulson. Single birds were seen on two more CBCs, 27 December 1976 and 18 December 1978 (*AB* 31:832, *AB* 32:837). B. Harrington-Tweit recorded one near Bird Rocks (NWR) in Rosario Strait, 24 March 1985.

56. **Little Gull.** Six records. One was reported by C. Eaton at Limestone Point, 25 October 1977. T. Wahl found a winter-plumaged adult near Friday Harbor in September 1979 (*AB* 34:193). A spring migrant was recorded by T. Wahl from the ferry near Orcas Island, 8 April 1984 (*AB* 38:950). M. Lewis photographed a

winter-plumaged adult in Friday Harbor, 23 September 1984. An adult was seen in Thatcher Pass, 24 June 1985, by D. Powell, T. Smythe, and D. Sevitch. A winter-plumaged adult was observed at the south entrance of Friday Harbor, 14 September 1986, by M. Lewis.

57. **Glaucous Gull.** One record. T. Wahl found an adult near Friday Harbor, 13 November 1982.

58. **Sabine's Gull.** Two records. W. Goodge saw two with shearwaters during stormy weather, 9 August 1948, off Cattle Point (*AFN* 3:30, *Murrelet* 31:28). Three were reported by A. Richards and D. Wechsler from the ferry in Rosario Strait, 15 September 1979 (*SAS Notes* 20:4:3).

59. **Red-legged Kittiwake.** Hypothetical. A kittiwake with bright red legs was observed for several minutes in good weather in Upright Channel, 1 August 1960, by J. Larsen (G. Bakus, p. 33). See also G. Alcorn, *Checklist of the Birds of the State of Washington*, p. 193.

60. **Caspian Tern.** The first San Juan record is of one adult seen by Z. McMannama at Davis Bay on 18 June 1949 (*Murrelet* 31:29).

61. **Arctic Tern.** Three records. T. Wahl observed single birds among flocks of Common Terns in Wasp Passage and central San Juan Channel, 17 August 1978. E. Hunn saw one or more from the ferry, 11 September 1981.

62. **Black Tern.** Three records. One was observed in Haro Strait near Henry Island by B. Wood, 22 August 1981. Another, in Rosario Strait, was reported by P. DeBruyn in June 1983 (*AB* 37:1020). M. Lewis saw a winter-plumaged adult in Thatcher Pass, 27 September 1986.

63. **Thick-billed Murre.** One record. T. Wahl saw the first one ever recorded in Washington State in San Juan Channel near the entrance to Friday Harbor, 6 December 1979 (*AB* 34:300).

64. **Kittlitz's Murrelet.** A single sighting; the only state record for this species. One was photographed in Friday Harbor, 2 January 1974, by D. Heinemann (*Western Birds* 7:15).

65. **Cassin's Auklet.** Three records. The Washington State Department of Game has a sighting on file of one near Williamson Rocks (NWR) and two near Bird Rocks (NWR), 21 June 1967. E. Peaslee saw two from the ferry in a flock of Rhinoceros Auklets near the entrance to Friday Harbor, 4 April 1979. A flock of 15 were carefully studied in Upright Channel by E. Seabloom on 22 March 1985.

66. **Horned Puffin.** One record. A single bird circled Williamson Rocks (NWR) and foraged in nearby tiderips in the company of several Tufted Puffins 24 July 1977 (*Western Birds* 12:56).

67. **Mourning Dove.** A common summer breeder at least until 1959 (G. Bakus, p. 18).

68. **Common Barn-owl.** The first record for the archipelago was provided by two specimens found dead on a road near an abandoned church on San Juan Island, 1 July 1947 (*Murrelet* 29:11). The first nest, containing three young, was discovered in a barn in San Juan Valley, 25 June 1960 (*Murrelet* 43:51).

69. **Northern Pygmy-owl.** S. Atkinson and F. Sharpe heard calls at two high-elevation locations on Orcas Island in March 1983.

70. **Short-eared Owl.** A pair was observed hazing a Northern Harrier at American Camp in March 1984 by M. Lewis. It was recorded at this location through 7 May 1984 by K. Lowe. R. Wright saw six or more Short-eared Owls at American Camp through 28 June 1985 and located a communal roost in a small patch of sedges growing in a slight depression of the prairies. Predators eventually took most of these individuals.

71. **Northern Saw-whet Owl.** Miller et al. (*Murrelet* 16:59) considered this species "formerly rather common at the Friday Harbor Marine Laboratories, now none detected for years," although one was heard at the Orcas ferry dock on 14 August 1935. Saw-whets were heard at the Friday Harbor Marine Laboratories through-

out the summer 1959 and an immature was seen there 4 July 1960 (G. Bakus, p. 19). One was heard "tooting" at Shark Reef, 28–31 May 1981, by E. Rockwell, and two were heard at Iceberg Point, 17 April 1984, by S. Atkinson and F. Sharpe. Two adults, presumably breeding, were seen and heard near Three Meadows Marsh from March through June 1986 by M. Lewis.

72. **Northern Hawk-Owl.** One undated hypothetical record. S. Layman carefully studied an adult flying over the hedgerows and perching atop conifers in San Juan Valley in early winter 1970.

73. **Burrowing Owl.** Two records. One seen near Turn Point by L. Retfalvi on 14 July 1962 (*Murrelet* 44:18) and another found by B. Harrington-Tweit, 24 November 1980, at an American Camp rabbit warren.

74. **Barred Owl.** One record. S. Speich heard one at the Friday Harbor Marine Laboratories, 15 December 1981 (*AB* 36:324).

75. **Long-eared Owl.** Two records. T. Angell found a single secondary feather and several breast feathers beneath an active Bald Eagle nest at McArdle Bay in September 1982. A blind juvenile being cared for at the Wolf Hollow Wildlife Rehabilitation Centre was identified by M. Lewis, 12 June 1987. The bird was found at the south end of San Juan Island in mid-May of 1987.

76. **Anna's Hummingbird.** The first sighting of this species in the archipelago was a single male on 13 November 1983 at a feeder on San Juan Island (*fide* W. Harm). W. Beecher found a dead female at his home on Lopez Island, 19 June 1986, and a live one at the same location, 23 June 1986.

77. **Lewis' Woodpecker.** Miller et al. (*Murrelet* 16:60) listed this species as an "occasional summer resident" and reported it from the Friday Harbor Marine Laboratories in September 1928. The last sighting of one was made during a Christmas Bird Count on Orcas Island, 2 January 1960 (*AFN* 14:257).

78. **Red-naped Sapsucker.** One record. M. Lewis observed an immature male at Panorama Marsh, 28 September 1985.

79. **Say's Phoebe.** Three records. M. Goodwin saw one on San Juan Island, 22 March 1975 (*AB* 29:733); F. Richardson reported one at Deer Harbor, 31 August 1979 (*AB* 34:194); and R. Wilson found one at Shoal Bay, 3 April 1986.

80. **Ash-throated Flycatcher.** The only San Juan archipelago record for this species was one at Olga, 13 September 1979, reported by B. Meyer (*SAS Notes* 20:4:3).

81. **Western Kingbird.** Three records. One was seen by P. Illg at Friday Harbor, 19 October 1975 (*Earthcare Northwest* 16:4:4); another was observed by S. Atkinson on Lopez Island, 19 March 1979; and one was reported by E. Rockwell at Spencer Spit, 15 May 1981.

82. **Eastern Kingbird.** One hypothetical record. W. Harm reported an undated sighting of this species at Summit Lake in the summer of 1979.

83. **Eurasian Skylark.** A single individual observed by J. Bruce in a field just south of Friday Harbor, 15 August 1960, was the first for the archipelago (*Condor* 63:418). The first two nests were reported by T. Wahl at American Camp, 17 May 1970 (*Condor* 73:254).

84. **Horned Lark.** W. Goodge and Z. McMannama reported this species to be frequent in the summers of 1948 and 1949 at Cattle Point and Davis Bay (*Murrelet* 31:28–29). G. Bakus (p. 22) found it to be common from Cattle Point to False Bay in summer 1960. L. Retfalvi (*Murrelet* 44:13) saw seven at Cattle Point, 3 July 1962.

85. **Gray Jay.** A single record. One was reported by K. and M. Mottola on Cady Mountain, 1 February 1975.

86. **Blue Jay.** One record. In October 1966 a Blue Jay frequented B. Weaver's bird feeder for several days at Cowlitz Bay (*fide* F. Richardson).

87. **Clark's Nutcracker.** Four records. E. Hunn saw four on Mt. Constitution, 20 October 1979. One was observed by K. and M. Mottola on Cady Mountain, 18 June

1985. M. Sacca reported one on a ridge beside Cady Mountain, 20 September 1986. Perhaps the same bird was seen by M. Sacca and M. Lewis on Cady Mountain, 21 October 1986.

88. **Black-billed Magpie.** One record. One was seen in Crow Valley, 31 October 1983 (*fide* F. Richardson).

89. **Black-capped Chickadee.** Several unconfirmed records. J. Gove reported them on Lopez Island in May 1938 (*Murrelet* 27:34) and the Washington State Department of Game has a record on file for 13 April 1973 at Point Colville. S. Atkinson reported one on Lopez Island, 31 May 1976, and six or more birds visited E. Reid's feeder at West Sound during a recent winter.

90. **Mountain Chickadee.** Hypothetical. Two were reportedly present at E. Reid's feeder in West Sound for several days in December 1980.

91. **Bushtit.** J. Gove (*Murrelet* 27:34).

92. **Rock Wren.** The first record of this species in the archipelago was for a specimen collected, 22 August 1936, on Mt. Dallas by R. Miller (*Murrelet* 31:28), W. Goodge found them "quite numerous" at this same location in summer 1948 (*Murrelet* 31:28). None were found in 1958 and 1959, but a singing bird was located 19 June and 3 July 1960 (G. Bakus, p. 24). F. Richardson saw one enter what he thought was a nesting crevice on Mt. Dallas in June 1960. Other records are: T. Wahl heard one singing on San Juan Island, 5 August 1973 (*AB* 28:97); B. Harrington-Tweit found two singing on the southwest side of San Juan, spring 1978 (*AB* 32:1048); W. and H. Hesse found one at Moran State Park, 28 May 1982 (*AB* 36:887); F. Sharpe and M. Lewis heard one singing at Eagle Cliff, 7–8 July 1984; M. Lewis saw one on the south shore of Stuart Island, 29 September 1984; and another was observed by M. Lewis on the west shore of Orcas Island, 18 September 1986.

93. **Western Bluebird.** R. Miller et al. (*Murrelet* 16:61) found them to be common in summer on the south side of Mt. Dallas in the 1930s. G. Bakus (p. 25) considered them "somewhat common" nesters in summer with flocks gathering at Deadman Bay and Mt. Finlayson. The last important records were two small flocks at Mt. Dallas, 19 October 1963 (*AFN* 19:66) and a breeding pair on Lopez Island in July 1964 (*Audubon Warblings* 5:1:6).

94. **Mountain Bluebird.** Five records. One was observed on San Juan Island, 23–26 March 1975, by T. Wahl (*AB* 29:734). Another was reported from the south end of San Juan Island in early May 1982 by R. Ricks (*Earthcare Northwest* 23:1:10). B. Wood saw one in his San Juan Island yard, 15 June 1982. R. Wright, M. Lewis, F. Sharpe, et al. observed an immature male remain December 1983 through February 1984 near Cattle Point. J. Vedder saw one at Three Meadows Marsh, 3 November 1985.

95. **Red-throated Pipit.** Only one state record for this species. E. Hunn et al. saw a bright male at American Camp, 14 September 1979 (*AB* 34:193). A. Richards reported a duller individual at the same location, 16 September 1979.

96. **Bohemian Waxwing.** A single bird in a flock of Cedar Waxwings was observed by S. Atkinson and F. Sharpe at Haida Pont, 16 June 1983, a very unusual date.

97. **Loggerhead Shrike.** One hypothetical record. L. Hays et al. reported one in open farmland on San Juan Island, 24 June 1982. The possibility that this bird was a Northern Shrike could not be positively ruled out by the description given. But, given the time of year, it is most likely that this bird was indeed a Loggerhead Shrike, as the observers reported.

98. **European Starling.** The first report of this species in the San Juan Archipelago came from R. Dickerman who saw two fledglings and an adult on San Juan Island, 26 June 1959 (G. Bakus, p. 25). L. Retfalvi observed flocks numbering several hundred individuals on San Juan Island in fall 1962 (*Murrelet* 44:13).

99. **Red-eyed Vireo.** Three records. One was reported from Cowlitz Bay, May 1984

(*fide* F. Richardson). Another was observed by F. Richardson near Deer Harbor, 7 May 1985. S. Atkinson saw an adult on the north part of San Juan Island, 16 June 1986.

100. **Black-throated Gray Warbler.** G. Bakus (p. 27) considered this species to be an uncommon breeder 1958–1960.

101. **MacGillivray's Warbler.** G. Bakus (p. 27) thought this species to be a common breeder in 1958 and 1959 and mentioned several locations where they were numerous (all below 1000 feet in elevation) including False Bay, Mt. Dallas, and the Friday Harbor Marine Laboratories. The only breeding evidence since then was a territorial pair observed in breeding habitat by M. Lewis, C. Powell, and F. Sharpe near Three Corner Lake, 20 May–20 June 1986, and a singing male reported by R. Wright to have occupied the same San Juan Island location for several consecutive summers in the early 1980s.

102. **Nashville Warbler.** Four records, only two confirmed. M. Trautman reported one on San Juan Island, 2–5 August 1958 (G. Bakus, p. 26). K. Lowe reported one on San Juan Island, 20 August 1984. R. Wright made a careful study of one on San Juan Island, 14 September 1984, as did F. Sharpe on the south slope of Mt. Dallas, 26 September 1986.

103. **Ovenbird.** The second western Washington record of this species was a singing male located by S. Atkinson and F. Sharpe at the entrance to the Friday Harbor Marine Laboratories, 17 June 1983.

104. **Tennessee Warbler.** The sixth state record for this warbler came from American Camp Headquarters, 11 September 1982, where it was studied by E. Hunn et al. (*AB* 37:217).

105. **Black-and-white Warbler.** One record. This bird was found by R. Morse at Mountain Lake, 31 May 1963.

106. **Northern Waterthrush.** One hypothetical record. W. Harm reported one at Cold Creek in July 1976.

107. **Hermit Warbler.** One hypothetical record. J. Gove reported this species on Lopez Island sometime during a visit that spanned 10–20 May 1938 (*Murrelet* 27:34).

108. **Lazuli Bunting.** One record. An adult male, found dead beneath a window at Olga on 28 June 1976, was preserved as a study specimen by F. Richardson.

109. **Indigo Bunting.** One record, the fifth for Washington State. An adult male was observed by T. Heatley et al. along Cattle Point Road, 17 July 1984 (*Earthcare Northwest* 25:11:5).

110. **Chipping Sparrow.** R. Miller et al. (*Murrelet* 16:62) considered this species abundant through 1935 as did G. Bakus (p. 30) through 1959.

111. **Fox Sparrow.** One was seen on Puffin Island by Z. McMannama, 23 July 1949 (*Murrelet* 31:29). S. Atkinson reported an immature on Lopez Hill, 15 June 1975. Eight nesting pairs were reported present through summer 1987 at Mandarte I., B.C., by University of British Columbia researchers.

112. **White-crowned × Song Sparrow.** A hybrid specimen was collected June 1959 on San Juan Island by R. Dickerman (*Auk* 78:627–632).

113. **Lark Sparrow.** Two records. A. Whiteley saw two near Griffin Bay, 22 May 1983 (*Earthcare Northwest* 23:9:11) and F. Sharpe one at Eagle Cove, 26 April 1984.

114. **Black-throated Sparrow.** One record. F. Sharpe and C. Howe located an individual at Kellett Bluff, Henry Island, 26 May 1987.

115. **White-throated Sparrow.** Three records. L. Retfalvi (*Murrelet* 44:13) saw one on Mt. Dallas, 3 May 1962. F. Richardson observed a singing male for three weeks at Tide Point, 1–21 June 1973. M. Lewis, et al. carefully studied a tan-striped adult at Fish Creek, 28 September 1986.

116. **American Tree Sparrow.** One record. A single bird was seen on the Orcas Island Christmas Bird Count, 27 December 1955 (*AFN* 10:211).

117. **Western Meadowlark.** M. Miller (*Auk* 61:396) had high counts of 12 and 10 birds breeding on a 30-acre plot on San Juan Island in the summers of 1936 and

1937. In the late 1940s W. Goodge (*Murrelet* 31:28) considered them common on Mt. Dallas and fairly common in appropriate habitat in other parts of San Juan Island. G. Bakus (p. 27) found them to be common breeders from False Bay to Cattle Point at least up until 1960.

118. **Brown-headed Cowbird.** They were considered to be "well-established and multiplying" on Lopez Island, July 1957 (*AFN* 11:426).

119. **Northern Oriole.** Two records. A pair of the Bullock's race was reported at Olga in May 1984 by B. Johnson. M. Lewis photographed an immature male of the same race on the south side of Mt. Dallas, 30 July 1986.

120. **Yellow-headed Blackbird.** Three records. Two birds were seen by J. Beecher on Lopez Island, 6 May 1980. A female was at C. Merrill's feeder on Buck Mountain, 3–4 June 1985. Two adults, reported by P. Henriksen, visited Sperry Peninsula 10 July 1987.

121. **House Finch.** The first recorded occurrence of this species in the archipelago was summer 1960 when D. Berrett and L. Binford found them "not uncommon at False Bay and the west side of the island" (G. Bakus, p. 29). They were not reported in 1958 or 1959.

122. **Evening Grosbeak.** E. Willis saw a few in July 1958 and 1959 on San Juan Island (G. Bakus, p. 28). S. Atkinson reported them on Orcas Island, 25 June 1976, and M. Egger found them in small numbers throughout July 1980 at the Friday Harbor Marine Laboratories. A pair visited C. Merrill's feeder on Buck Mountain, 26 June 1984.

123. **Rosy Finch.** Two upper-elevation records. J. Horder saw one on Mt. Constitution, 10 April 1984 (*AB* 38:952). F. Sharpe saw one on Mt. Erie, 30 May 1984 (*AB* 38:952).

124. **Pine Grosbeak.** Two confirmed records. S. Atkinson found one at Port Stanley during January–February 1973. From one to three birds were seen at Tide Point from late November–early December 1973 by F. Richardson.

125. **White-winged Crossbill.** Three records. One was seen on the Orcas Island Christmas Bird Count, 31 December 1951 (*AFN* 6:162). Two visited a birdbath at McArdle Bay, 8 January 1980, according to T. Angell. C. Chappell and M. Sacca heard them on Cady Mountain, 2–3 April 1986.

126. **Common Redpoll.** One unconfirmed report. A. Sobieralski briefly saw small flocks of finchlike birds that fit the description of this species north of Friday Harbor on both 26 November 1984 and 5 January 1985.

127. **House Sparrow.** The first published record of this species in the archipelago came from W. Goodge (*Murrelet* 31:28) who noted that they were abundant around the docks in Friday Harbor in 1948.

Bibliography

Alcorn, Gordon D. 1962. *Check List of the Birds of the State of Washington.* Dept. of Biol., Univ. of Puget Sound, Tacoma, Wash. Occas. Pap. No. 17. 156–199. Revised in 1971 as Occas. Pap. No. 43.

———1972. *Bibliography: Birds of the State of Washington.* Museum of Nat. Hist., Univ. of Puget Sound, Tacoma, Wash. Occas. Pap. No. 44.

American Ornithologists' Union. 1983. *Check-list of North American Birds.* 6th ed. Am. Ornithol. Union, Baltimore, Md.

Amlaner, C.J. et al. 1977. Increases in a Population of Nesting Glaucous-winged Gulls Disturbed by Humans. *Murrelet* 57:18–20.

Angell, T., and K.C. Balcomb III. 1982. *Marine Birds and Mammals of Puget Sound.* Univ. of Washington Press, Seattle, Wash.

Atkinson, S.R., and F.S. Sharpe. 1985. *Wild Plants of the San Juans.* The Mountaineers Books, Seattle, Wash.

Bakus, G.J. 1965. *Avifauna of San Juan Island and Archipelago, Washington.* Allan Hancock Foundation, Univ. Of California, Los Angeles.

Brandon, M.T. et al. 1983. Pre-tertiary Geology of the San Juan Islands, Washington and Southeast Vancouver Island, British Columbia. Geological Association of Canada, Victoria, B.C.

Bruce, J.A. 1961. First Record of European Skylark on San Juan Island, Washington. *Condor* 63:418.

———1962. Nesting of the Barn Owl, *Tyto alba,* on San Juan Island, Washington. *Murrelet* 43:51.

Burr, I.W. 1967. King Eider (*Somateria spectabilis*) in the San Juans. *Murrelet* 48:7.

Dawson, W.L., and J.H. Bowles, 1909. *The Birds of Washington.* 2 vols. Occidental Pub. Co., Seattle, Wash.

Dickerman, R.W. 1960. Dowitcher Notes from San Juan Island. *Murrelet* 41:15.

Edson, J.M. 1929. Afield and Afloat with Dawson. *Murrelet* 10:1–7 & 27–33.

Flahaut, M.R. 1948. Barn Owls on San Juan Island, Washington. *Murrelet* 29:11.

Goodge, W. 1950. Some Notes on the Birds of the San Juan Islands. *Murrelet* 31:27–28.

Gove, J.G., Mr. and Mrs. 1946. Birds Seen and Heard on Lopez Island, Washington. *Murrelet* 27:33–34.

Grubb, T.G. 1976. A Survey and Analysis of Bald Eagle Nesting in Western Washington. M.S. thesis, Univ. of Washington, Seattle, Wash.

Grubb, T.G., D.A. Manuwal, and C.M. Anderson. 1975. Nest Distribution and Productivity of Bald Eagle in Western Washington. *Murrelet* 56:2–6.

Hayward, J.L., and A.C. Thoreson. 1980. Dippers in Marine Habitats in Washington. *Western Birds* 11:60.

Hunn, E.S. 1982. *Birding in Seattle and King County.* Seattle Audubon Society, Seattle, Wash.

Jewett, S.G. et al. 1953. *Birds of Washington State.* Univ. of Washington Press, Seattle, Wash.

Johnston, D.W. 1961. *The Biosystematics of American Crows.* Univ. of Washington Press, Seattle, Wash.

Larrison, E.L. 1952. *Field Guide to the Birds of Puget Sound.* Seattle Audubon Society, Seattle, Wash.

Laycock, G. 1976. *Bird Watcher's Bible*. Doubleday & Co., Garden City, New York.

Lewis, M.G. 1985. San Juan Islands Seasonal Status of Birds and Wildlife Checklist. San Juan Islands Audubon Society, Friday Harbor, Wash.

Manuwal, D.A., P.W. Mattocks, Jr., and K.A. Richter. 1979. First Arctic Tern Colony in the Contiguous Western United States. *Am. Birds* 33:144–145.

Mattocks, P.W., Jr., E.S. Hunn, and T.R. Wahl. 1976. A Checklist of the Birds of Washington State, with Recent Changes Annotated. *Western Birds* 7:1–24.

McMannama, Z. 1950. Additional Notes on the Birds of the San Juan Islands. *Murrelet* 31:29–30.

Miller, M.R. 1944. A Two-Year Bird Census of San Juan Island, Washington. *Auk* 61:395–400.

Miller, R.C., E.D. Lumley, and F.S. Hall. 1935. Birds of the San Juan Islands, Washington. *Murrelet* 16:51–65.

National Audubon Society. 1947–1970. *Audubon Field Notes*. Vols. 1–24.

———1971–1985. *American Birds*. Vols. 25–39.

———1980. *The Audubon Encyclopedia of North American Birds*. Alfred A. Knopf, Inc., New York.

———1983. *The Audubon Society Master Guide to Birding*. Alfred A. Knopf, Inc., New York.

National Geographic Society. 1983. *Field Guide to the Birds of North America*. Nat. Geographic Soc., Washington, D.C.

National Oceanic and Atmospheric Administration. 1983. Strait of Juan de Fuca to Strait of Georgia. Map #18421. 31st Ed. Dept. of Commerce, Washington, D.C.

Peterson, R.T. 1961. *A Field Guide to Western Birds*. Houghton Mifflin, Boston.

Phillips, E.L. 1966. Washington Climate. Paper for Cooperative Service Extension, Washington State Univ., Pullman, Wash.

Ratti, J.T. 1981. Identification and Distribution of Clark's Grebe. *Western Birds* 12:40–46.

Retfalvi, L. 1963. Notes on the Birds of San Juan Islands, Washington. *Murrelet* 44:12–13.

Richardson, F. 1961. Breeding Biology of the Rhinoceros Auklet on Protection Island, Washington. *Condor* 63:456–473.

———1973. Shore-associated and Marine Birds of Cypress Island. Paper for Univ. of Washington, Seattle, Wash.

Robbins, C.S., B. Bruun, and H.S. Zim. 1983. *A Guide to Field Identification: Birds of North America*. 2nd ed. Golden Press, Inc., New York.

San Juan Islands Audubon Society. 1981–1985. *The Trumpeter*. Vols. 1–5.

Schoen, J.W. 1972. Mammals of the San Juan Archipelago: Distribution and Colonization of Native Land Mammals and Insularity in Three Populations of *Peromyscus maniculatus*. M.S. thesis, Univ. of Puget Sound, Tacoma, Wash.

Seattle Audubon Society. *Seattle Audubon Society Notes*. Vols. 7–21.

———*Earthcare Northwest*. Vols. 22–27.

Speich, S.M. and R.L. Pitman. 1984. River Otter Occurrence and Predation on Nesting Marine Birds in the Washington Islands Wilderness. *Murrelet* 65:25–27.

Speich, S.M., H.L. Jones, and E.M. Benedict. 1985. Review of the Natural Nesting of the Barn Swallow in North America. *Am. Midland Naturalist* 115:248–254.

Speich, S.M., S. Thompson, and G. Eddy. 1984. Inventory of Breeding Marine Birds, San Juan Islands. Unpublished paper.

Stevens, W.F. 1975. The Biology of the European rabbit (*Oryctolagus cuniculus*) on San Juan Island, Washington. M.S. thesis, Univ. of Washington, Seattle, Wash.

Sturman, W.A. 1967. Habitat Occupancy and Utilization in the Breeding Season by the Chickadees. *Parus atricapillus* and *P.rufescens*. M.S. thesis, Univ. of Washington, Seattle, Wash.

Taylor, K. 1983. *A Birder's Guide to Vancouver Island.* Self-published, Victoria, B.C.

Thorsen, A.C. 1981. Midsummer occurrence of the Horned Puffin in Rosario Strait, Washington. *Western Birds* 12:56.

Udvardy, M.D.F. 1977. *The Audubon Society Field Guide to North American Birds.* Alfred Knopf, New York.

United States Fish and Wildlife Service. 1982. *Sensitive Bird Species, Region One.* Portland, Or.

Wahl, T.R., and D.R. Paulson. 1981. *A Guide to Bird Finding in Washington.* Rev. ed. Whatcom County Museum, Bellingham, Wash.

Wahl, T.R., and H.E. Wilson. 1971. Nesting Record of European Skylark in Washington State. *Condor* 73:254.

Wahl, T.R., et al. 1981. *Marine Bird Populations of the Strait of Juan de Fuca, Strait of Georgia, and Adjacent Waters in 1978 and 1979.* U.S. Environmental Protection Agency, Washington, D.C. EPA-600/7–81–156.

Index

Page numbers in boldface type indicate illustrations.

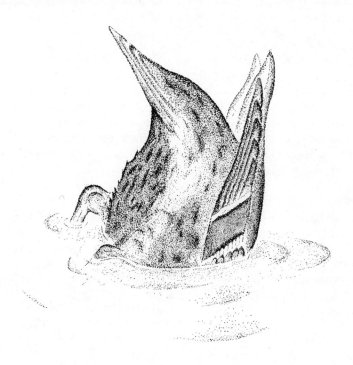

A Mallard "tips up" to forage on submerged vegetation.

James Longley

Grant W. Sharpe

About the authors:

MARK G. LEWIS lives on San Juan Island, where he is an ornithologist on the research staff of The Whale Museum. Between leading sea kayak expeditions and natural history tours over much of the continent, Lewis has prolonged completion of studies toward a degree in biology at The Evergreen State College, Olympia. His spare time is spent photographing wildlife and adding more birds to his "life list."

FRED A. SHARPE has worked as a naturalist at The Whale Museum, Friday Harbor; as a shipboard naturalist for Greenpeace, and as a glacier technician on the Blue Glacier Project, Mt. Olympus. He was ship's scientist with Intersea Research, Inc., researching humpback whales in Southeast Alaska, during summer 1987. Sharpe, who holds a degree in botany from the University of Washington, continues research on plants and birds in the northwest. He is a member of the Audubon Society and Washington Native Plant Society.